THE PHANTOM UNMASKED

THE
PHANTOM
UNMASKED

AMERICA'S FIRST SUPERHERO

KEVIN PATRICK

UNIVERSITY OF IOWA PRESS | IOWA CITY

University of Iowa Press, Iowa City 52242
Copyright © 2017 by the University of Iowa Press
www.uipress.uiowa.edu
Printed in the United States of America

Design by April Leidig

The University of Iowa Press is a member of Green Press Initiative
and is committed to preserving natural resources.

Printed on acid-free paper

Library of Congress Cataloging-in-Publication Data
Names: Patrick, Kevin, 1968–author.
Title: The Phantom unmasked : America's first superhero /
Kevin Patrick.
Description: Iowa City : University of Iowa Press, 2017. |
Includes bibliographical references and index.
Identifiers: LCCN 2017005973 | ISBN 978-1-60938-500-2 (pbk) |
ISBN 978-1-60938-501-9 (ebk)
Subjects: LCSH: Phantom (Fictitious character) | Comic books,
strips, etc.—History and criticism. | Superheroes.
Classification: LCC PN6728.P5 P38 2017 | DDC 741.5/973—dc23
LC record available at https://lccn.loc.gov/2017005973

Dedicated to the memory of my father,
Robert "Barney" Patrick

CONTENTS

ACKNOWLEDGMENTS

While I am the sole author of this book, I would like to pay tribute to just some of the people who have helped me write it, in so many ways, and across many lands.

I am indebted to Dr. Simone Murray and Dr. Andy Ruddock at Monash University (Melbourne, Australia), who oversaw my doctoral thesis upon which this book is based, and provided me with indispensable guidance and encouragement throughout my candidature.

I would like to thank my editor, Catherine Cocks, for her initial interest in my doctoral research and for her long-distance editorial oversight, which helped me refashion my thesis into an accessible book. I must also thank everyone at the University of Iowa Press who have helped turn my raw manuscript into the finished volume you now hold in your hands.

I am especially grateful to the hundreds of "phans" who took part in my online readers' survey and willingly shared their thoughts and memories about "The Ghost Who Walks." I am also thankful to the many online comic-book stores, and the creators of numerous Phantom "phan" websites, blogs, and message boards, who freely publicized my research. I hope they find this book a sufficient reward for their efforts.

I must also acknowledge the tremendous support I received from the Australian comics historian John Clements for providing me with copies of hundreds of newspaper and magazine articles concerning the Phantom, which greatly enriched my research.

I would also like to thank the editors, writers, and illustrators involved with the production of *The Phantom* comic magazine in Australia, Sweden, and India, who graciously agreed to be interviewed for my doctoral thesis. While only a handful of their comments have been included in this book, they provided me with thoughtful insights and observations, and I remain grateful to them for their time and generosity. I would like to also thank Andreas

Eriksson for introducing me to many key members of "Team Fantomen" prior to my research trip to Sweden in 2012.

I must also thank Yinan Li, who selflessly put aside her own work to help me improve my own, and ensured that I got my draft-version manuscript over the finish line.

Finally, my wife, Sophie, deserves my greatest thanks of all. Her support for me throughout my PhD candidature never wavered, and she never lost faith in my ability to complete this book, even though there were many times when I doubted myself. I may be the sole author of this book, but none of what you are about to read would have been possible without her. For these reasons, and so many more, this book is for Sophie.

THE PHANTOM UNMASKED

THE FORGOTTEN SUPERHERO

D avid Gonzalez paid just over $10,000 for an abandoned, 1930s-era house in Elbow Lake, Minnesota, not realizing that it held a treasure worth many times that amount. While renovating the property, Gonzalez discovered an old comic book among some newspapers used as insulation in a wall cavity. It was a copy of *Action Comics* no. 1, featuring the debut of Superman, dated June 1938. The back cover was accidentally torn by one of Gonzalez's relatives during an excited family tussle following its discovery, stripping an estimated $50,000 from its market value. Nonetheless, Gonzalez eventually pocketed half of the $175,000 that it fetched at auction on June 12, 2013. Stephen Fisher, auctioneer and CEO of ComicConnect.com, described Gonzalez's discovery as miraculous, given that just 100 copies from the comic's original 250,000-copy print run were known to exist (Kelsey, 2013).

Impressive as this auction result no doubt was, it would be but a fraction of the revenues generated by *Man of Steel*, the latest motion-picture adaptation of the *Superman* comic-book franchise published by DC Comics, which was released in over 4,200 cinemas across the United States on July 14, 2013, coinciding with the 75th anniversary of the character's debut in *Action Comics*. Distributed by Warner Bros. (which, like DC Comics, is a subsidiary of the Time Warner media conglomerate), *Man of Steel* took in a record-breaking $125,000,000 at the U.S. box office on its opening weekend. By December 2013, *Man of Steel* had earned over $662,000,000 in global box-office receipts, comfortably exceeding its estimated $225,000,000 production budget (Box Office Mojo, 2013).

Global exposure for *Man of Steel* would extend far beyond the foyers of multiplex cinemas. Warner Bros. Consumer Products division oversaw a massive "multi-category licensing campaign" to coincide with the film's release, which led to a new generation of Superman merchandise encompassing children's books, novelty goods, apparel, and footwear (Warner Bros., 2013). The launch of the *Man of Steel* motion picture illustrates the extent to which comic-book superheroes today underpin vast, multibillion-dollar global media franchises that span publishing, audiovisual entertainment, and licensed merchandise — even if the print medium which launched them is no longer critical to their continued profitability.

Yet how did a once unheard-of character in a ten-cent comic book become such a lucrative property for one of the world's largest media corporations? It seems difficult to link David Gonzalez's chance discovery with such a vast commercial enterprise; even his wife Deanna seemed unimpressed at the time: "I didn't think anything of it," she said. "It's just a comic book" (Brown, 2013). Stephen Fisher of ComicConnect.com, however, claimed to know precisely why Gonzalez's damaged copy of *Action Comics* no. 1 generated such intense public interest. "It's so noteworthy because [the comic] was a historic milestone," Fisher explained. "There was no such thing as a superhero or a man in costume [in 1938]" (Kelsey, 2013).

Fisher was understandably keen to emphasize the comic book's historical significance, if only to drum up media coverage for the auction itself. But he was entirely wrong in claiming that there was "no such thing" as costumed superheroes prior to the arrival of Superman. For even as American children were handing over their dimes for a copy of *Action Comics* no. 1 in 1938, many of their parents were no doubt already familiar with the exploits of another costumed hero appearing in their daily newspapers. His name was the Phantom.

Clad in a skin-tight costume, cowl, and mask, the Phantom was a mysterious crime-fighter who used his totemic Skull Ring to brand his enemies with "the sign of the skull." Dedicated to "the destruction of all forms of piracy, greed and cruelty," the Phantom was thought to be immortal and was thus known throughout the world as "The Ghost Who Walks, Man Who Cannot Die." Created by writer Lee Falk and illustrator Ray Moore, *The Phantom* comic strip debuted in *The New York Journal* on February 17, 1936. A full-color version of *The Phantom*, produced by Falk and Moore for Sunday newspapers' comic-strip supplements, premiered on May 28, 1939. The comic strip is presently written by Tony DePaul and jointly illustrated by Mike Manley (weekday episodes) and Terry Beatty (Sunday episodes). *The Phantom* is owned and licensed by King Features (a division of the Hearst Corporation) and is published in 15 different languages, and currently appears in over 500 newspapers published in 40 countries (King Features Syndicate, 2016).

The Phantom remains a historically significant comic strip which brought many of the dramatic devices commonly associated with the "hero pulp" magazines of the 1930s, such as *The Shadow* and *Doc Savage*, to the adventure-serial comic strip. *The Phantom* blended thematic and visual elements not previously seen in comic strips and thus presaged the dawn of the costumed superhero. Yet *The Phantom* has largely receded from American audiences' collective "pop culture" consciousness. Although it is one of the few Depression-era comic strips to remain in continuous production, by 2005 it was said to be appearing in just eighteen newspapers throughout the United States (Goulart, 2005). Even among comic-strip aficionados, *The Phantom* has never garnered the level of acclaim enjoyed by such contemporaneous serials as Alex Raymond's *Flash Gordon* or Hal Foster's *Prince Valiant*, and has received, at best, only passing mentions in most published histories of the American comic strip.

Despite predating the "Man of Steel," *The Phantom* was soon eclipsed in its American homeland by the unprecedented popularity of Superman, and has thus endured a troubled career as a comic-book franchise since the 1930s, and has not appeared in its own mass-market comic magazine on American newsstands since the late 1970s. Recent years have seen a string of small American comic-book publishers try their hand—without lasting success—at reviving *The Phantom*, but their modernized (and excessively violent) portrayals of the character are frequently at odds with the canonical newspaper comic-strip version. However, these latter-day *Phantom* comics are seldom seen beyond the confines of specialty comic-book retailers, and so remain largely invisible to the wider American public.

While the Phantom may be all but forgotten in his American homeland, he has consistently enjoyed greater success and popular recognition abroad. Throughout the course of the character's eighty-year history, the Phantom has appeared under many different names (and, occasionally, in different-colored costumes) in newspapers and periodicals throughout Europe, Latin America, Asia, and Oceania. Yet nowhere does the Phantom enjoy a more ardent following than in Australia, Sweden, and India, where he occupies unrivaled status as an adopted national hero in each of these countries. Singling out these three countries above all others is not as arbitrary as it might first seem. *The Phantom* comic strip has enjoyed its longest unbroken publishing history in all three nations, where it has appeared in various formats (and, in the case of India, numerous languages) since the character's debut in 1936. Moreover, the Phantom has become an entrenched part of the everyday, vernacular culture of Australia, Sweden, and India in ways that few other American comic-strip characters have achieved. The following anecdote, published in an Australian *Phantom* fan club newsletter, vividly illustrates how the legend of "The Ghost Who Walks" had reached the farthest corners of the globe:

> Doug [Callaghan] was travelling through Nepal a couple of years back, and one day was checking out a little bazaar in [Kathmandu]. Being the good Phantom fan that he is, Doug was sporting the Skull Ring (on his hard-hitting right fist, of course!) . . . Suddenly, this bloke in a turban jumps out from behind his stall with a *Phantom* comic in his hand (written in Indian [*sic*]), and starts pointing at Doug's Skull Ring and shouting "Phantom . . . Ghost Who Walks . . . Cannot Die!" This, of course, both shocked and delighted Doug, who says that [the Phantom] has quite a strong following throughout all of India [*sic*]. (*Jungle Beat*, ca. 1989: 5)

The remarkable story of *The Phantom*, whereby its relative obscurity in the United States has been offset by its phenomenal success in Australia, Sweden, and India, is the subject of this book. It is a fascinating story which provides new insights about the international production, dissemination, and consumption of popular mass media. *The Phantom Unmasked* brings a multifaceted approach to the study of global comics culture, which goes far beyond the textual analysis mode that has until now dominated most academic studies of comic books. However, in order to appreciate the significance of this approach, we must briefly consider how this controversial medium has been historically examined.

Comic strips and comic books have earned high praise and thunderous condemnation in near-equal measure from academics, journalists, and popular historians. Since the 1920s, millions of words have been written about these entwined forms of graphic narrative. Countless profiles have been written about their most celebrated practitioners, while numerous attempts have been made to divine the popular appeal of their most notable creations. Early academic interest in comics reflected a long-standing preoccupation with the potentially harmful effects of mass media on children's welfare which, according to Daniel G. McDonald (2004), underscored much of the early media effects research conducted in the United States during the first half of the twentieth century. By the early 1950s, M. Spiegelman, C. Terwilliger, and F. Fearing argued that comic strips had clearly become "an important medium of mass communication" capable of reflecting and molding "cultural patterns and beliefs" (1952: 39). The medium's cultural significance, they claimed, could be best understood through a multidimensional, analytical framework:

> A complete communication analysis of comic strips would be concerned with a study of the intent of the producers of the strips, an analysis of the content, and a study of the audiences' responses. (Spiegelman, Terwilliger, and Fearing, 1952: 39)

Yet few researchers in the United States and elsewhere — either then or now — have made any systematic effort to look beyond the medium's visual novelty to understand the industrial practices and economic imperatives which have historically governed the production, circulation, and reception of both comic strips and comic books. Consequently, our present-day understanding of this "important medium of communication" still remains, at best, underdeveloped and incomplete.

It was not until the 1970s and 1980s, which saw the emergence and consolidation of cultural studies as an academic discipline that frequently championed formerly despised media forms — such as television soap operas (Ang, 1985) and romance novels (Radway, 1991) — that new opportunities arose for the intellectual reconsideration of comics as a communication medium worthy of sustained critical attention. Yet cultural studies' enthusiastic engagement with popular media forms, such as cinema, television, and genre fiction, did not automatically extend to comic books. Given the once near-ubiquitous popularity of comic books, such an oversight seems almost inexplicable. However, this paradox becomes understandable once we consider how some of the earliest — and most influential — (British) cultural studies' practitioners were trained in literary studies, and thus regarded comics with suspicion, if not outright derision. Richard Hoggart, author of *The Uses of Literacy* — widely regarded as a seminal cultural studies text — famously dismissed comic books as "bad mass-art geared to a very low mental age" (1998: 153). Stuart Hall and Paddy Whannel's subsequent inquiry into the publishing practices and editorial conventions of British romance comics was a notable exception (1964: 167–68, 180–90), but it was an isolated example which only underscored cultural studies' persistent disregard for comics, and reflected the discipline's historic predilection for studying audiovisual media instead.

Paradoxically, the anti-comics campaigns of the 1950s formed the basis for one of the earliest, and most significant, cultural studies investigations of comic books and their audiences. Martin Barker's account of the British "crusade" against horror comics, *A Haunt of Fears* (1984), documents the extensive role played by members of Britain's Communist Party in mobilizing public opinion against American "horror" comics. However, Barker's later case study of the controversial 1970s-era British comic magazine *Action* is arguably of even greater relevance to this book (Barker, 1989: 17–61). Barker examined his subject from multiple angles: recounting the commercial publishing industry context that led to the creation of *Action*; interviewing key editorial personnel about their deliberate cultivation of the comic's aggressive image; engaging in sustained textual analysis of the magazine's comic-strip serials (paying particular attention to censored artwork); and, finally, asking the comic's former readers what they thought of *Action*. Barker thereby painted a near-complete picture which documented the production, reception, and ultimate demise of a comic book. *The Phantom Unmasked* adopts a similarly multifaceted approach, but one which gives equal weight to examining comic strips and comic books as parallel media texts, while recounting the historical circumstances surrounding their creation, investigating the industries which maintained their production, and interrogating the audiences which consumed them.

The preceding discussion of the *Man of Steel* motion picture illustrates how popular and pervasive comic-book superheroes have become in today's media-entertainment landscape. Yet this is by no means a recent phenomenon; Weston Anson claims that although character licensing did not become a major industry until the late 1970s, comic-strip characters had already become successful licensing properties by the early 1930s (1984: 4). By charting the commercial exploitation of *The Phantom* across Australia, Sweden, and India since the mid-1930s, this book will delve into the largely unexplored pre-history of modern media licensing industries.

While comic-book characters like Superman are indisputably valuable commercial entities in their own right, the print medium which launched them is no longer pivotal to their success. Yet syndicated comic strips (serialized in newspapers and periodicals), comic magazines, and other allied print-media products have remained vital to the continued financial well-being of *The Phantom* media franchise. This book will identify the persistent commercial and creative linkages between newspaper comic strips, comic magazines, and book-format publications (such as comic-strip novelizations and graphic novels), and how they have helped sustain *The Phantom*'s "brand" in Australia, Sweden, and India.

The Phantom Comic-Book Readers' Survey

Newspaper syndication agreements and comic-book circulation figures provide some bald statistical measures for gauging the popularity of *The Phantom* among Australian, Swedish, and Indian audiences. What they do not reveal is who reads *The Phantom*—and why. This book draws upon the findings of an in-depth, online survey of nearly 600 readers of *The Phantom*, making it the largest international survey of comic-book audiences ever conducted. Canvassing these readers' opinions about *The Phantom* brings a new geographic and cultural dimension to the traditionally Anglo-American focus evident in previous studies of comic-book fandom and thus enriches the existing body of audience reception literature. Given the extensive discussion of the survey results throughout this book, it is appropriate to take this opportunity to discuss in some detail the survey's design and methodology.

The survey sought to obtain a mixture of quantitative and qualitative data from a targeted sample of *Phantom* comic-book readers (aged between 18 and 65 years) from Australia, Sweden, and India. (A small number of readers living outside these three countries also completed this survey. In some cases, they identified themselves as expatriate Australian, Swedish, and Indian citizens living abroad, but in other instances, they appeared to be foreign nationals who also happened to be *Phantom* comic-book fans. Nevertheless, comments from members of these two subgroups have been occasionally cited throughout this book.) The survey canvassed a broad range of topics, such as how participants first discovered *The Phantom*, their opinions about the character's portrayal in print and audiovisual media, and the extent to which they were involved in other aspects of comic-book fan culture. This was done in order to establish whether survey participants could be broadly classified as members of a self-contained fan community solely aligned with *The Phantom*, or whether they crossed over into the broader currents of comic-book fandom in their respective countries. The survey consisted of twenty-six questions, featuring a combination of multiple choice and open-ended formats (see the appendix). Participants could complete the survey anonymously, and, aside from seeking some initial demographic data (e.g., gender, age group, nationality, etc.), no further personal or identifying information was sought, nor collected, from respondents.

A companion blog/website, *Phantom Comic Book Survey* (https://phantom comicsurvey.wordpress.com), was launched to promote the survey, and to direct readers to the online questionnaire, which was hosted by Rational Survey (http://www.rationalsurvey.com). The survey was further promoted on *Phantom* fan websites and message boards, including ChronicleChamber .com (http://chroniclechamber.com) and the now-defunct Phantom Phorum. While both of these websites were created and hosted in Australia, their message board threads suggested they attracted regular input from *Phantom* fans in Sweden, India, and the United States. Further promotional announcements were sent to English-language blogs and websites dedicated to Indian comics, including *Lost World—Indrajal Heroes* (http://dara-indrajal .blogspot.com) and *Comic World* (http://comic-guy.blogspot.com).

A similar announcement was submitted to the Swedish fan site Fantomen .org (http://fantomen.org), which was translated into Swedish and published online in March 2012. This announcement was subsequently reprinted in the "Fantomen Klubben" (Phantom Club) page featured in the Swedish edition of the *Fantomen* comic magazine (nos. 14–15, 2012). A full-page advertisement for the survey also ran in the Australian edition of *The Phantom* (no. 1638, 2012). News of the survey was also circulated to members of the Lee Falk Memorial Bengali Explorers' Club via their electronic mailing list in May 2012 (see chapter 8).

The survey was conducted exclusively online from March 18, 2012, to March 16, 2013, and received 595 completed surveys. While the survey's key findings are discussed elsewhere in this book, it is worth noting some further observations and anomalies which arose from the survey and considering their implications for future research in this field.

According to the survey website's analytics, only 28 percent of respondents completed the entire set of 26 survey questions. There are several possible explanations for this. Some respondents may have simply chosen not to answer some questions, while others may not have wished to spend an excessive amount of time completing the entire survey. (Usage reports indicate that the average survey completion time was twenty-six minutes.) Fluency in written English may have also been a contributing factor, as some of the noticeable shortfalls were evident in open-ended questions, which asked participants to provide answers written in their own words. For example, Question 13, which asked readers to nominate their favorite *Phantom* stories, received 472 responses, which accounts for nearly 80 percent of all submitted surveys. (Some Swedish respondents, however, chose to answer these open-ended questions in Swedish.)

Another statistical anomaly became apparent—nearly 3 percent of survey respondents neglected to indicate their country of residence. Whether people simply overlooked this question (it was the final question on the survey) or declined to answer it remains open to conjecture. But such omissions might have some bearing on the comparatively low response rate from Indian readers, who accounted for just 6 percent of survey respondents. This does not necessarily tally with the proliferation of English-language (or bilingual English-Hindi) websites dedicated to the 1960s-era Indian magazine *Indrajal Comics* (which featured *The Phantom*), or Indian comics generally. Nor are such low survey participation figures borne out by the comparatively higher number of Indian fans who linked to the companion Facebook page launched to promote the survey, where they accounted for over 31 percent of "followers" by January 2013. But then, it is easier to "like" a Facebook page than it is to complete an online survey. However, this apparent disparity demonstrates how readers' different levels of engagement with comic books may define their relative status as "passive" or "active" members of the wider comics fan community.

One audience segment that is noticeably absent from these survey results is readers aged eighteen years and under, who may have started reading *Phantom* comic books during their childhood or adolescence, and whom publishers no doubt hope will sustain the *Phantom* media franchise in years to come. Despite their potential demographic significance, the administrative and ethical burden associated with surveying children and adolescents under eighteen years of age (which typically requires obtaining permission from their parents and/or guardians to secure their participation) made it impractical to include younger readers in this online survey.

Comics Studies and Comics Fandom

Phantom fans from Australia, Sweden, India, and elsewhere actively supported this research project from the outset. They did so possibly out of gratitude that an academic "outsider" was taking a genuine interest in the Phantom, and were keen to share their enthusiasm for this comic-book hero with a wider audience. One survey participant said: "I enjoyed doing this survey a lot, so many thanks, and best of luck with your academic endeavor" (male respondent, 36–49 years old, Sweden, July, 5, 2012). Favorable academic scrutiny could, from the survey participants' perspective, both valorize the Phantom as a unique comic-book hero and legitimize their own cultural status as fans.

Comic-book readers have, in recent years, been the subject of increased scholarly attention, being recognized as a significant audience cohort in their own right, and as a discernible subculture within the wider constellation of media fandom. Recent studies have considered the importance of letter columns published in comic magazines, since these were one of the earliest channels of communication open to comic-book readers (Dittmer and Larsen, 2007: 735–53; Pustz, 2007: 163–84; Gordon, 2012: 120–32). Others have employed quasi-ethnographic methodologies in surveying fans' interactions within specialty comic-book stores in an effort to better understand contemporary comic-book fan culture (Tankel and Murphy, 1998: 55–68; Pustz, 1999; Botzakis, 2009: 50–59). More recently, there have been case studies of fans who aligned themselves with specific comic-book publishers (Brown, 2001), or individual comic-book characters, such as Judge Dredd (Barker and Brooks, 1998) and Batman (Burke, ed., 2013; Pearson, Uricchio and Brooker, eds., 2015). This book adopts similar strategies by considering the editorial functions of letter columns appearing in different editions of *Phantom* comic magazines, and by questioning fans themselves about their individual engagement with the Phantom in order to understand why they favor this particular comic-book hero above all others.

Phantom comic-book fans' keen endorsement of this research project may have also owed something to the public declaration of my own fan credentials when recruiting survey participants. Placing a full-page advertisement for the survey in the Australian edition of *The Phantom* comic magazine, I included a brief biographical note about my lifelong involvement in Australian comics fandom, and disclosed that the first *Phantom* story I read as a child in 1978 was "The Diamond Hunters" (Falk and Moore, 1992 [1937]: 6–54). Such an admission carries the risk of being labeled a "scholar-fan" or an "aca-fan"—an academic researcher who is also a "fan" of his chosen area of study. Occupying such a position might outwardly undermine the traditional academic stance of the objective, impartial observer. As Matt Hills points out:

> The scholar-fan must still conform to the regulative ideals of the rational academic subject, being careful not to present too much of their enthusiasm while tailoring their accounts of fan interest and investment to the forms of "confessional" (but not overly confessional) academic writing. (Hills, 2002: 11–12)

Conversely, Henry Jenkins, writing in *Textual Poachers*, drew attention to his own involvement with science fiction and television fandom. This level of personal involvement, he argued, allowed him to study popular culture from a fan's perspective, thus creating a unique opportunity to combine an understanding of relevant theoretical frameworks and critical literature with firsthand "access to the particular knowledge and traditions [of fan communities]" (Jenkins, 1992: 5).

Indeed, much of what we do know about the history of the Phantom, in all his media incarnations, can be found in the vast body of fan literature dedicated to the character, both in print and online. However, Charles Hatfield warns that "the pool of [comic] fan literature . . . [can be] of variable quality and trustworthiness" (2006: 368). Hatfield's reservations arise partly from fan literature's disproportionate emphasis on the superhero genre. This lopsided focus, he argues, "[vacuums] out history in such a way as to reinforce . . . the misconception of comic books as contiguous with superheroes" (2006: 368). Hatfield may well be right in sounding this cautionary note. But comic-book fans have nonetheless performed much of the heavy lifting of discovery, documentation, and research which, in any other field of inquiry, would have been the preserve of academics. This is especially true of the Phantom, where it has fallen to an informal, international network of fans — most of whom live outside the United States — to piece together the historical and bibliographical narratives surrounding this character and his creators. Given the relative dearth of comics studies literature from Australia, Sweden, and India, any meaningful account of the *Phantom* media franchise must draw upon this unofficial body of knowledge, albeit with a degree of critical caution.

Overview

The Phantom is a fascinating text in its own right, and one that can provide the basis for a truly holistic case study which can draw historical connections between the aesthetic, commercial, and cultural dimensions of both comic strips and comic magazines. This book maps the singular — and often unpredictable — journey that *The Phantom* undertook on its way towards achieving international acclaim in Australia, Sweden, and India, a journey that only emphasizes the complexities which attended the global transmission of American popular culture throughout the twentieth century and which remain no less evident in the present millennium.

Central to the Phantom's enduring appeal is the character's quasi-mythical origin story, his fantastic Afro-Asian milieu, and the diverse ensemble cast who lend both mystery and realism to his adventures. Chapter 1 recounts the dynastic legend behind the Phantom before mapping the boundaries of his fictional world and introducing some of the key supporting characters who have shared in his adventures over several decades. It looks at how the author, Lee Falk, drew on a range of historical, literary, and popular culture sources in creating *The Phantom* and considers the series' contribution to the development of the adventure-serial comic strip throughout the 1930s. This chapter begins delving into the reasons behind the Phantom's enduring popularity by considering the survey responses given by Australian, Swedish, and Indian readers, with specific reference to their assessment of the character's intrinsic appeal, his embodiment of "traditional" ideals, and the exotic allure of his jungle realm.

The Phantom is but one member of the stable of popular comic-strip characters owned and licensed by King Features, which is responsible for syndicating opinion columns, puzzles, comic strips, and other "non-news" content to newspapers, magazines, and websites across the United States and throughout the world. Chapter 2 reveals the important role that King Features Syndicate (as it was originally called) played in making comic strips an integral, and hugely popular, part of American newspapers in the opening decades of the twentieth century. It will examine how King Features successfully exploited comic strips' popularity as a means of boosting circulation figures and generating advertising revenues for its newspaper clients. This chapter will document the beginnings of the licensed merchandise industry which grew up around comic-strip characters during the 1920s and 1930s, and examine the Phantom's earliest forays into allied print media formats. It will illustrate the character's troubled transition into America's nascent comic-book industry in the 1940s, and ask why the Phantom—acknowledged as the forerunner of the costumed superhero—failed to enjoy the same level of success attained by the likes of Superman, Batman, and Captain America in this dynamic new medium.

The Phantom debuted just as King Features Syndicate was accelerating its international expansion, which was being driven in part by the success of its comic-strip features in foreign markets. Chapter 3 recounts the vital role played by foreign media entrepreneurs, such as David Yaffa (Australia) and Cornelius Bull (Sweden), who—as King Features' overseas representatives—helped foster local acceptance of American comic strips by making them palatable to local publishers and audiences alike, often by concealing their American provenance. This chapter looks at how their efforts in selling *The Phantom* to women's magazines (rather than newspapers) in Australia, Sweden, and India helped secure national exposure for the series and cemented the character's appeal as a "family favorite" with readers in these three countries for decades to come.

Prior to World War II, countries such as Australia, Sweden, and India had little or no tradition of publishing comic magazines for juvenile audiences. Popular, homegrown comic-strip characters were largely confined to newspapers, and the perceived dearth of local writers and artists familiar with the comic-book format meant that domestic publishers resorted to using cheaply syndicated American comic strips to fill the pages of the earliest comic magazines published in these countries during the 1930s and 1940s. Chapter 4 looks at the raft of political, economic, and cultural factors which governed the dissemination of American comic books in Australia, Sweden, and India before, during, and after the war. It will examine the growing outcry against "American-style" comic books which gathered force in these three countries during the 1950s, and consider how—and why—the Phantom was able to circumvent some of the worst criticisms leveled against American comics. This chapter will also demonstrate how the popularity of *The Phantom* helped galvanize domestic comic-book production in Australia, Sweden, and India during the immediate postwar era.

But even as "The Ghost Who Walks" was enjoying considerable success abroad, tumultuous changes affecting America's newspaper industry throughout the 1960s and 1970s would ultimately have a direct bearing on the international production of *The Phantom* comic-book franchise. Chapter 5 discusses how competition from television, together with rising newsprint costs, prompted many newspapers to reduce the space devoted to comic-strip sections—a cost-saving measure which had deleterious effects on adventure-serial comic strips, including *The Phantom*. In response to these changes, the Swedish publisher Semic Press began commissioning locally drawn Phantom stories that were better suited to its domestic market, a strategy which saw Sweden emerge as a major production node in the international *Phantom* comic-book franchise throughout the 1970s and 1980s. While the Swedish version of *The Phantom* (published as *Fantomen*) proved popular in neighboring Scandinavian countries, this chapter shows how its subsequent syndication to the Australian and Indian markets frequently met resistance from local publishers (and their readers), who objected—on commercial and aesthetic grounds—to the sometimes-radical Swedish reinterpretation of the character.

Just as the Phantom has been historically overshadowed by other comic-book superheroes, he has also failed to secure lasting success for King Features as a multimedia property, starring in a series of mostly ill-fated television shows, feature films, and animated cartoons. Chapter 6 juxtaposes the relative failure of these officially sanctioned media adaptations with a diverse range of unauthorized interpretations of *The Phantom* which have circulated in Australia, Sweden, and India since the 1960s. This chapter demonstrates how these frequently subversive portrayals of the Phantom, spanning underground films, TV parodies, and avant-garde artwork, are testimony to the character's enduring appeal. It will also show that the appropriation of the Phantom by government agencies for use in public education programs—

particularly in Australia—is a tacit acknowledgment of how the Phantom has captured the imagination of foreign audiences in ways that more recognizably "American" superheroes (such as Superman) have otherwise failed to match. That the Phantom has been enormously popular among Australian, Swedish, and Indian audiences for decades is beyond doubt; but why does "The Ghost Who Walks" loom so large in the public imagination of three such different and distinctive cultures? Chapter 7 delves further into the finding of the international survey of Phantom "phans"—as they often refer to themselves—in order to understand why so many Australian, Swedish, and Indian readers identify with this comic-book hero. This chapter will look at how the political economy of newspaper and magazine publishing in these three countries has influenced readers' exposure to—and perceptions of— *The Phantom* comic. It will examine the correlations between Phantom "phans" and mainstream comic fandom in Australia, Sweden, and India, and will ask how (and why) "phans" have historically set themselves apart from other comic-book fan communities.

For some people, of course, their enjoyment of the Phantom simply stems from reading his latest exploits in their chosen newspaper or comic book. Yet this has not discouraged various Australian, Swedish, and Indian companies from actively cultivating audiences' loyalty to *The Phantom* "brand." Chapter 8 looks at the different editorial strategies which international publishers have used to encourage readers to identify with *The Phantom*, and how the construction of fan identity has often been explicitly tied to the consumption of licensed *Phantom* merchandise. This chapter addresses the symbiotic, and occasionally antagonistic, relationship between *The Phantom* franchise's licensed corporate gatekeepers and their audiences. It will also gauge the impact of digital media on the formation, conduct, and geographic reach of Australian, Swedish, and Indian fan clusters, and will look at the informal rivalry between international "phan" communities.

Eighty years after the character's debut in the United States, the Phantom faces an uncertain future. While the character has undergone significant changes since the death of his creator, Lee Falk, in 1999, comic-strip heroes like the Phantom no longer command younger readers' attention as they once did. The concluding chapter of this book reflects on the remarkable longevity of *The Phantom* comic-book franchise and asks how it can survive in today's rapidly changing media environment.

This book is, on one level, entirely about the Phantom—but it is also about a good deal more than the creative vicissitudes of an American comic-strip character. Charting the commercial passage of *The Phantom* across Australia, Sweden, and India since the mid-1930s provides fresh insights into how the interlocking structures of globalized media industries guide the international production and dissemination of popular culture. Yet although media organizations, aided by teams of writers and illustrators, actively shape the form and direction of *The Phantom* "brand" (in all its permutations), they are by no means the sole participants in this process. As Marcel Duchamp once remarked:

> The creative act is not performed by the artist alone; the spectator brings the work in contact with the external world by deciphering and interpreting its inner qualifications and thus adds his contribution to the creative act. (Sanouillet and Peterson, eds., 1989: 140)

Duchamp's observation remains no less pertinent when we consider how audiences worldwide receive and "consume" the products of (American) mass media, and the circumstances in which they do so. By canvassing Australian, Swedish, and Indian readers' opinions about the Phantom, this book reasserts the vital role that audiences continue to play in sustaining "The Ghost Who Walks" and the unique visual medium which helped endear him to generations of readers worldwide. In doing so, *The Phantom Unmasked* champions a new investigative approach which can only deepen our present understanding of global comics culture.

CHAPTER ONE

THE GHOST WHO WALKS

O n a bright winter's day, the *S.S. Trotter* steamed into New York Harbor, carrying a valuable cargo of ambergris in its hull, which had been retrieved at great risk from the South Seas by Diana Palmer, a beautiful socialite and adventurous young explorer. The ship is boarded by Fats Horgan, a pugnacious gangster, accompanied by over two dozen heavily armed thugs, and a complement of vicious pirates from the Orient. Taking Diana and her crew prisoners, Horgan demands to know the whereabouts of the ambergris, a rare substance used to manufacture fragrances. Diana taunts Horgan, demanding to know why he brought so many gunmen to overpower her unarmed crew; momentarily flustered, Horgan tells her that this "extra protection" is intended for someone else. "Sometimes I think he ain't a man, but a ghost," he raves. "But here's one job he won't snatch under my nose!" Unbeknownst to Horgan, a mysterious figure emerges from the cold depths of the harbor, using a rope to haul himself aboard the *S.S. Trotter*. Moments later, as Horgan threatens to toss Diana overboard, the interior lights across the entire ship go out, plunging Diana's locked cabin into darkness. "I don't like this," cries Horgan. "Lights don't just go out!" But before he can order his men to investigate further, the door to Diana's cabin swings open, revealing a sinister masked man, clad in grey, holding a pistol in his right hand. "Right, Horgan. Lights don't just go out," he says in a low voice. "Don't move. I'm aiming at that fat tummy of yours."

Thus ended the first week of the new comic-strip serial titled *The Phantom*, which debuted in *The New York Journal* on February 17, 1936. In the space of just six daily episodes, author Lee Falk (1911–1999) introduced the key elements that helped define his mysterious new hero for decades to come. The Phantom is unveiled as a ghostly figure, whose very name can terrify even ruthless gangsters like Fats Horgan. Diana Palmer is portrayed as a feisty, courageous, and beautiful heroine, who would embark on a tempestuous love affair with the Phantom that would take her to the farthest reaches of the world and change her life forever. Falk here depicts the Phantom as a modern-day hero, capable of matching wits with rapacious gangsters, but Horgan's turbaned pirates will soon stand revealed as the emissaries of a sinister organization which has terrorized the high seas for centuries. With each successive episode, Falk would gradually weave an intricate legend around the Phantom that set him apart from other contemporaneous heroes of popular fiction. In doing so, Falk created a mythical figure whose exploits tapped into an ancient, heroic folklore of the kind which transcended the barriers of geography and language. The Phantom thus became a universal, rather than uniquely American, hero.

If we hope to understand how the Phantom became an internationally acclaimed figure, we must consider the inherent appeal of his heroic persona, and the dramatic accouterments used to embellish the legend surrounding the character. To help us do this, we will hear from Australian, Swedish, and Indian readers themselves, as they share their own thoughts about the Phantom and his world throughout this chapter. The series' success also owes a great deal to the Phantom's exotic jungle realm, which further enhanced the character's mysterious aura and proved especially popular with international audiences. Yet as we will see, the Phantom's status as the benevolent (white) ruler of this fictional Afro-Asian landscape invited criticism from both academic commentators and avowed fans, who were troubled by the series' underlying racial politics. These concerns were gradually alleviated, if not entirely put to rest, by Falk's inclusion of an ethnically diverse ensemble cast of supporting characters, which better reflected the series' modern-day African setting.

Although the Phantom was arguably the first costumed crime-fighter of his kind to be seen in newspapers, he was by no means the first action-adventure hero to appear in "the funny pages." Nor was Lee Falk's mysterious masked hero entirely without precedent elsewhere in other forms of American mass media. We will therefore see how the advent of adventure-serial comic strips and pulp-fiction magazines in the 1920s and 1930s infused the creation of the Phantom in ways that would eventually set him apart from the costumed superheroes that would follow in his wake.

The Story of the Phantom

It would be nearly eight months after she first encountered the Phantom aboard the *S.S. Trotter* that Diana Palmer would, along with newspaper readers, finally learn the truth behind the legend of "The Ghost Who Walks." Having rescued her once again from the mysterious pirates who followed her return voyage to the South Seas, the Phantom shares the story of his life with Diana for the first time. "It's a strange story," he admits. "Sometimes I find it hard to believe it, myself" (Falk and Moore, 2010 [1936]: 112). The Phantom, we discover, is the twenty-first descendant of an English nobleman, Sir Christopher Standish, whose father was killed by pirates known as the Singh Brotherhood in 1525. Swearing an oath on the skull of his father's murderer, Sir Christopher declared vengeance "against all piracy, greed and cruelty," and pledged that "as long as my descendants walk the Earth, the eldest male of my family shall carry out my work" (Falk and Moore, 2010 [1936]: 115). Generation after generation, the eldest son had taken on the mantle of the Phantom at his father's deathbed. The Phantom explains to Diana that, upon returning from his studies at Oxford, he swore the sacred "Skull Oath" and assumed his role shortly after his own father was killed by the Singh Brotherhood in the Bay of Bengal. "I took his place at once—and the Singh thought that The Phantom had again returned from the dead!" (Falk and Moore, 2010 [1936]: 115). This unbroken succession, kept secret for centuries, led many to believe that the Phantom was immortal, thus creating the legend of "The Ghost Who Walks–Man Who Cannot Die."

Lee Falk, in collaboration with his first illustrator, Ray Moore (1905–1984), steadily crafted the image of the Phantom throughout the 1930s and 1940s as a mysterious, elusive figure who strikes without warning. The Phantom came to be known by the dreaded "Sign of the Skull," etched onto the totemic Skull Ring worn on his right hand. Whenever he felled an opponent with his powerhouse punch, the Phantom left his indelible skull symbol on his jaw, a grim reminder of their violent encounter. Sometimes the mere sight of the "skull mark" was enough to intimidate criminals; in the 1943 story line "Bent Beak Broder," the Phantom torments a gang of escaped convicts by leaving an impression from his Skull Ring wherever they go—on their clothes, their getaway vehicles—and eventually drives their terrified ringleader into the arms of the police (Falk and McCoy, 2008 [1943]: 209–47). Falk later gave the

Phantom a matching Good Mark ring, which was worn on his left hand, and was thus symbolically closer to his heart. The Phantom bestowed the Good Mark upon those who saved his life, or otherwise came to his aid in times of danger. Stamped gently onto their wrist, the Good Mark—represented by four crossed swords—granted its recipient "the protection of The Phantom for life" (Falk and McCoy, 1994c [1958]: 3).

Falk introduced a dramatic device, known as "Old Jungle Sayings," which he used in narrative captions to reinforce the Phantom's near-mythical qualities. "When The Phantom moves, he shames the lightning," used in the 1946–47 story "Mister Hog," was the first of many "Old Jungle Sayings" that Falk would coin for the series over the next fifty years (Falk and McCoy, 1992a [1946–47]: 141). Falk did, on occasion, invoke the "Old Jungle Saying" which claimed that whosoever removed the Phantom's mask against his will and gazed upon his face would die. Such was the fate met by the leader of the Toad Men, a modern-day pirate gang, who was shot dead in a gun battle moments after unmasking the Phantom (Falk and McCoy, 1997 [1952–53]: 143–44).

The Phantom wasn't averse to taking a human life, if left with no other choice; at the climax of "The Diamond Hunters," the Phantom shot and killed the criminal nicknamed "Smiley," who was about to ambush him with a hunting rifle (Falk and Moore, 1992 [1937]: 50). Falk subsequently minimized such lethal gunplay, preferring to let the Phantom shoot his opponents' guns out of their hands. Nevertheless, the Phantom drew the line when it came to using violence against women; when confronted by the villainous Sala, member of the all-female crew of air pirates known as the Sky Band, the Phantom confesses: "This is the tightest spot I've ever been in. You're all women here—and I couldn't slug a woman if I wanted to" (Falk and Moore, 1996 [1936–37]: 51).

The Phantom was an undeniably violent and vengeful figure, but he was also a compassionate hero, always prepared to come to the aid of those who needed his help the most. In one adventure, the Phantom briefly became a professional boxer known as "The Masked Marvel" in order to use his prize money to rebuild a children's hospital destroyed in a fire (Falk and McCoy, 1991 [1948–49]: 149–80). This story was frequently brought up by readers as one of their favorite *Phantom* stories. As one Australian reader put it:

"The Masked Marvel" [is] my favorite story of all time, [it's] corny [and] sentimental, but epitomizes [the Phantom's] devotion to the under-privileged and his willingness to sacrifice everything to help others . . . I love the corny innocence of some of these [stories]. (Male respondent, 36–49 years old, Australia, July 2, 2012)

The Phantom cut a striking figure, clad in a grey costume, his face concealed by a cowl and eye-mask, sporting black leather gauntlets and boots, with a pair of automatic pistols slung from his belt. There were also times when the Phantom traveled incognito, wearing his costume underneath an overcoat, scarf, and trousers, while concealing his unmasked face beneath a broad-brimmed hat and dark glasses. It was not uncommon for the Phantom to remain in his civilian disguise, particularly during his adventures abroad, where his costume might draw unwelcome attention from criminals and authorities alike. However, it wasn't until several years after the character's debut that Lee Falk granted the Phantom an alias—"Mr. Walker" (for "The Ghost Who Walks")—for everyday use (Falk and McCoy, 2008 [1943]: 213). The Phantom's constant companion was Devil, his fiercely loyal mountain wolf, who became a ferocious beast whenever danger threatened his master. They were later joined by Hero, a giant white stallion given to the Phantom by the Maharajah of Nimpore as a reward for rescuing his daughter (Falk and McCoy, 1998 [1944–45]: 33–93). Just as Devil would only accept food from the Phantom, Hero would only let himself be ridden by his new owner. Galloping through the jungle astride his mighty white horse, with a giant wolf racing alongside him, the Phantom looked every inch the storybook hero of a bygone era.

It is perhaps the totality of Lee Falk's vision of the character, built up over several decades, which has helped make *The Phantom* so popular among international audiences. As one reader argued, it was the cumulative effect of all these different facets of the Phantom which made him so appealing, so memorable:

I love the costume; the visual quality of the character is wonderful. The fact that he leaves Skull Marks on those he punches is also a wonderful idea . . . The skull motif . . . is something that appeals to me. I also really love the idea of the legacy that The Phantom mantle is passed from father to son. It's a brilliant piece of storytelling. (Male respondent, 18–35 years old, Australia, March 19, 2012)

The Phantom's World

The Phantom's identity and purpose are inextricably linked to his jungle realm. He presides over his ancestral home from within the Skull Cave, which contains more than just his throne, adorned with skull motifs; it also contains a library of handwritten chronicles documenting all his forefathers' exploits, the crypts of his twenty ancestors, and fabulous treasure rooms containing priceless antiquities, gold, and jewels acquired from pirates and criminals over several centuries. This secret lair is found in the Deep Woods, an inaccessible stretch of jungle nestled in the African nation of Bangalla. The Phantom receives counsel from his childhood friend, Guran, chieftain of the Bandar pygmies, who use their deadly poison arrows to zealously guard the secret of the Phantom dynasty from outsiders.

The Phantom's African homeland is steeped in fantasy, evoking images of lost worlds and forgotten civilizations of the sort popularized by such writers as Sir Arthur Conan Doyle, Jules Verne, and Edgar Rice Burroughs. Yet neither the Phantom nor his creator, Lee Falk, were entirely able to prevent real-world politics from pressing up against the imagined borders of the Deep Woods. As an adventure comic-strip serial, *The Phantom* stands as a remarkable document, one that has continually—although not always deliberately—touched upon the intellectually and emotionally charged issues of colonialism and racial identity for over eighty years. For these reasons alone, it is worth documenting how the character of the Phantom himself, and the politics of his dynastic mission, has changed in response to the broader cultural and political shifts which occurred throughout the United States and elsewhere, particularly in the decades following World War II.

The Phantom was initially portrayed as a godlike figure who used elaborate stagecraft to reinforce the belief that he was a supernatural being, who could appear out of thin air, and thus terrify his "native subjects" into obeying his own brand of jungle law. To this end, the Phantom was sometimes aided by tribal elders who benefited from his rule. Paying his annual visit to a remote village, the Phantom is greeted by Nobo, the resident witch doctor who guides him through a secret passage that will allow the Phantom to ascend unseen from beneath the earth, and miraculously appear on his throne before the gathered tribe. When he asks Nobo why they must persist with this "mumbo-jumbo," the witch doctor explains: "It impresses my people—and makes it easier for me to handle them—in your name" (Falk and Moore, 1989 [1937–38]: 12). The Phantom's very presence was deemed essential to the preservation of peace and order in an otherwise lawless jungle. When Diana Palmer asked Guran if the Phantom would ever leave the jungle, he declared that this would be impossible: "We would be helpless! Without The Phantom's peace, there would be wars—killing. He is our protector" (Falk and Moore, 1992 [1937]: 52). The troubling racial politics of *The Phantom* did not go unnoticed by contemporary critics; Lawrence Kessel's content analysis of American newspaper comic strips criticized *The Phantom* (among others) for propagating "hatred and distrust for foreign people" and for its frequent depiction of "negroes" (*sic*) as "ignorant, superstitious colored people"—stereotypes that Kessel claimed were conveyed more "in the way they were drawn than by what was said" (1943: 350).

Lee Falk, who always maintained that African Americans loved the Phantom "because he has always seen black people as equal human beings" (quoted in Resnais, 2011: 78) nonetheless took steps to soften the Phantom's image. In "The Childhood of the Phantom," Falk depicted the young Kit Walker being reprimanded by his father (the twentieth Phantom) for ordering his Bandar tribe playmates to grovel at his feet, and declaring that Kit must learn "how to treat [his] fellow-men" (Falk and McCoy, 1994a [1944–45]: 53). Falk even went so far as to revise the origin of the Phantom's ancestral dynasty, by recasting the first Phantom (Sir Christopher Standish) as a freedom fighter who liberated the Bandar pygmy tribe from slavery (Falk and Barry, 1993a [1975]: 56–69). In this task, Falk was greatly assisted by his artistic collaborators, such as Wilson McCoy (1902–1961), who softened the overtly racist caricatures favored by his predecessor, Ray Moore, albeit within the limitations of his "cartoony" illustration style. Seymour ("Sy") Barry (b. 1928), who took over as illustrator on *The Phantom* comic strip in 1961 and remained with the series until 1994, made a conscious effort to draw realistic portrayals of the numerous African characters who began assuming more prominent roles in the series during the 1960s, such as Dr. Lamanda Luaga, a physician who subsequently became the democratically elected premier of Bengali (later "Bangalla") (Falk and Barry, 1995 [1962–63]: 6–56).

Despite these narrative and cosmetic changes, Richard F. Patteson nonetheless contends that *The Phantom* remains a modern-day continuation of nineteenth-century imperialist romances, which expressed the need for "white civilization" to establish "European authority over native peoples" (1978: 115). Julian C. Chambliss and William L. Svitavsky further suggest that many of the adventure heroes appearing in popular American fiction from the 1910s through the 1930s "personify and reassert the racial and civil superiority of the United States" distilled by the frontier ethos which grew alongside America's westward expansion (2008: 2). They therefore argue that characters such as Tarzan—who Lee Falk acknowledged was an early influence on his creation of *The Phantom* (Madison, 1996: 48)—"successfully reimagined the frontier crucible in an exotic [jungle] locale" by reiterating contemporary American notions of Anglo-Saxon racial superiority (Chambliss and Svitavsky, 2008: 8).

The belief that the African jungle was a lawless frontier which could only be tamed by white civilization was reinforced by the introduction of the Jungle Patrol in *The Phantom* comic strip in 1951 (Falk and McCoy, 1994b [1951–52]: 244–74). This elite paramilitary force was charged with policing the dense wilderness which bordered the Deep Woods and six neighboring countries, and thus became an extension of the Phantom's power throughout the jungle. The Jungle Patrol—clearly modeled on the French Foreign Legion—was frequently called upon to put down tribal uprisings, and was originally staffed entirely by white personnel. However, Falk gradually admitted African patrolmen to their ranks and appointed an African officer, Colonel Worobu, as its titular leader, who remained answerable to the Phantom, who acted as the organization's Secret Commander (Falk and Barry, 1998 [1970]: 169–90). Despite these cosmetic changes, Fredrik Strömberg nevertheless maintains that the strip's basic premise—wherein "a white man in the jungle protects simple savages by spreading law and order"—was entirely acceptable to American audiences of the 1930s, but now remains problematic in today's postcolonial environment (2003: 81). This aspect of the comic strip became especially troublesome for some readers as they looked back on the Phantom they'd once enjoyed in their youth from a more critically informed, adult perspective:

Well, he is very different and has evolved greatly since I started to read the comic. Since The Phantom is male-oriented, as [he] also has a legacy from being a white heterosexual male in an African country, I am not very proud of the fact that I like The Phantom. It is very difficult for me, as a modern, well-educated woman, to even read these kinds of comics. (Female respondent, 18–35 years old, Sweden, June 17, 2012)

The racial themes that underscored *The Phantom* continued to draw criticism in the United States and abroad—especially in Sweden—and would, as we will see in chapter 5, eventually lead to a dramatic reconceptualization of the character and his milieu.

The series' sexual politics were, by comparison, marginally more progressive and were frequently conveyed through the turbulent romance between the Phantom and Diana Palmer, who was introduced as a New York socialite embarking on a dangerous "treasure hunt" to fund her late father's Hospital for Crippled Children (Falk and Moore, 2010 [1936]: 60–62). Throughout the 1940s and 1950s Diana was portrayed as an intrepid explorer, pilot, and professional swimmer whose exploits took her around the world. Diana's thirst for adventure would occasionally challenge the patriarchal lineage of the Phantom dynasty, especially after she heard an account from the Phantom Chronicles about Julie, the twin sister of the eighteenth Phantom, who briefly donned her brother's uniform and posed as the Phantom while he was recovering from wounds (Falk and McCoy, 1999a [1952]: 6–19). Diana tries on Julie's costume in the Phantom's absence and ventures into the Deep Woods, only to run afoul of bank robbers hiding in the jungle. Despite aiding the Phantom in their capture, Diana renounces any future intention of becoming the next female Phantom, declaring instead that "from now on, I'll just be a female!" (Falk and McCoy, 1992b [1952–53]: 50).

Diana's professional role was redefined and expanded throughout the 1960s and 1970s, commencing as a nurse attached to United Nations medical missions to Africa and culminating in her reassignment as a human rights officer for the UN (Falk and Barry, 1993b [1962]: 92–128; 1992a [1977]: 196–213). Her strong, assertive personality, combined with her glamorous beauty, made Diana Palmer especially popular with women and thus broadened the demographic appeal of *The Phantom*. As one Swedish reader observed:

I like Diana and her "independent" life and how [the Phantom] doesn't
have a problem with strong women, even though they're always [being]
rescued by him, of course. (Female respondent, 18–35 years old, July 11,
2012)

Diana's career ambitions initially placed her at odds with the Phantom's dynastic obligations; although she accepts his marriage proposal, Diana initially
balks at his insistence that she give up her job with the human rights commission to live with him in the Deep Woods. "But dear," she explains, "when
we're married I needn't quit my job . . . this is 1977" (Falk and Barry, 1986a
[1977]: 40). Nonetheless, they eventually wed and Diana (in accordance with
Phantom tradition) relocates to the Skull Cave, where she later gives birth
to twins, a boy (Kit) and a girl (Heloise) (Falk and Barry, 1986b [1978–79]:
72–99). Her dilemma over whether to choose a career instead of marriage
was subsequently resolved when she resumed her role as a human rights
investigator for the UN at its regional office in Bangalla's capital, Mawitaan.
    While Lee Falk used such stories to reflect changing attitudes about
"traditional" gender roles throughout the 1960s and 1970s, he sometimes
struggled to balance his stories' more fantastic elements with the real-world
politics of postcolonial Africa during this same period. Early episodes of *The
Phantom* were explicitly situated within the colonial milieu of prewar Asia.
The Phantom's jungle lair was originally located on the island of Luntok,
"a British protectorate off the coast of Sumatra," in the Dutch East Indies
(now Indonesia) (Falk and Moore, 2010 [1936]: 65, 87–90). In "The Prisoner
of the Himalayas," Scotland Yard detectives beseech the Phantom to travel
to Barogar—"the most dangerous spot in India"—to investigate the dis-
appearance of its reigning Maharajah, as an important "matter of Empire!"
The Phantom agrees, acknowledging that "anything that happens in Barogar
endangers my jungle people"—thus suggesting that his "home" has shifted
to the Indian subcontinent (Falk and Moore, 2000 [1938]: 56). The series'
Asian locale is reiterated in the wartime sequence "The Inexorables," when
Japanese forces invade Bengali (as the Phantom's homeland was now known),
prompting Allied military commanders to declare that "our supply lines to
the Orient will be cut in half" if the invasion succeeds (Falk, Moore, and
McCoy, 1993 [1942–43]: 12).
    These geographic distinctions became blurrier throughout the 1940s and

1950s, with stories alternating between ostensibly African jungles and mysterious highland kingdoms, presided over by Raj-era monarchs or cruel Arab despots. The confusing topography of the Phantom's world actually worked to the series' commercial advantage because it allowed international audiences to appropriate his imaginary homeland as their own:

> [The comic's] location neutrality cut the boundaries very easily for an Indian kid growing up in the 80s, [when] exposure to American pop culture was really limited and most of the superheroes like Superman, Batman [and] Spider-Man relied heavily on [this], while [the] Phantom being a culturally and location-wise neutral hero always worked well for us . . . and the universe created by Lee Falk was . . . balanced and well defined. (Male respondent, 18–35 years old, India, November 22, 2012)

The first explicit reference to Bengali's African location came in 1962 (Falk, Lignante, and Barry, 1992 [1962]: 194), before the country's name was changed to Bangalla in 1972 (Falk and Barry, 1987 [1972]: 14); similarly, the nation's capital was changed from Morristown to Mawitaan (Falk and Barry, 1988 [1972–73]: 2). The switch from European to Afrocentric place names in *The Phantom* mirrored similar transformations occurring throughout sub-Saharan Africa. Despite inserting these specific references to Africa, Lee Falk always maintained that the Phantom inhabited an imaginary continent:

> I felt the Phantom isn't actually in Africa. He is, yet he isn't. It's his own continent, really. It's Afrasian where he is . . . This is a jungle that looks very much like Africa, but a thousand miles inland there are mountain princes [who looked] very Asian, Indian or Arab . . . who still live like [they're in] the 15th century in their castles. (Quoted in Murray, 2005: 43)

Falk only occasionally alluded to the political upheavals and revolutionary wars that marred Africa throughout the 1960s and 1970s. General Bababu, one of the few recurring villains to appear in *The Phantom*, was continually plotting to overthrow President Luaga of Bangalla, and, under Falk's guidance, came to personify the political instability of postcolonial Africa. But even at his worst, General Bababu was portrayed as a vain, cowardly, and near-comical figure, rather than a truly villainous despot (Falk and Barry, 1995 [1962–63]: 6–56). This approach, according to artist Sy Barry, simply reflected the unique tenor of *The Phantom* comic strip:

It is a fantasy strip which takes place in the present day. It's done in a somewhat light vein and yet done somewhat surrealistically. You've got realistic characters who feel pain, who have the same emotions as everyone else has. But it's done with a little bit of fantasy and escape element. (Quoted in Strell, 1981: 59)

Falk's more fantastic story lines were not always greeted with approval by diehard *Phantom* readers (see chapter 5), but his undeniably successful blend of fantasy and "realism" lent the series a lighter tone that was frequently absent from other American adventure-serial comic strips. This approach was, according to Jay Kennedy (1956–2007), King Features Syndicate's comics editor, key to securing wider syndication, even for ostensibly "realistic" adventure serials like *The Phantom*. "Strips that make readers feel better in the end do better," he argued. "If someone was senselessly shot and killed, it wouldn't work" (quoted in Astor, 1995: 39).

Heroes of the Great Depression

The Ghost Who Walks may be steeped in the world of ancient lore and legend, but the medium that brought his exploits to the attention of American public was the modern publishing phenomenon of the comic strip. When *The Phantom* made its debut in 1936, it did so at a time when a new style of comic strip—the adventure serial—began captivating newspaper audiences. This new genre challenged the comic strip's long-standing reputation as a vehicle for comedy, which became entrenched when so many of its earliest, most famous exponents—such as *The Yellow Kid* (1895) and *The Katzenjammer Kids* (1897)—relied on physical slapstick and joke-telling for their subject matter. It is worth noting that American cartoonists had already begun experimenting with sequential narratives—that is, telling stories instead of jokes—well before World War I. Some, such as Charles W. Kahles's *Hairbreadth Harry* (1906) and Harry Hershfield's *Desperate Desmond* (1910), lampooned movies serials' cliff-hanger plots (Harvey, 1994: 11). Other cartoonists, such as Frank King—creator of *Gasoline Alley* (1918)—gradually abandoned the original humorous premise of their work in favor of episodic drama (Perry and Aldridge, 1971: 131).

Roy Crane's *Washington Tubbs II* (1924) is widely regarded as a pivotal series which demonstrated the medium's capacity for dramatic adventure. Discarding the strip's original grocery store setting, Crane cast his juvenile hero, "Wash Tubbs," on to the high seas, where he crossed paths with a mysterious soldier of fortune, Captain Easy. Robert C. Harvey argues that Crane "set the pace for adventure strips in the thirties" and inspired a generation of cartoonists who strove to equal Crane's work as they, too, "further refined the adventure comic strip" (1994: 71, 91). But Crane's successors abandoned his preference for exaggerated, cartoon-styled artwork in favor of more realistic forms of dramatic illustration. They were led by Hal Foster's comic-strip adaptation of *Tarzan of the Apes* (1929), which was soon followed by Noel Sickles's daring aviator, *Scorchy Smith* (1930), Eddie Sullivan and Charlie Schmidt's police drama, *Radio Patrol* (1933), and Fred Martinek and Leon Beroth's maritime hero, *Don Winslow of the Navy* (1934).

This new cohort of illustrators (as distinct from "cartoonists") rendered their subjects in a realistic fashion, thereby heightening the suspense by making their protagonists—and the dangers they faced—seem real (Harvey, 1998: 2). Yet as William H. Young observes, the adventure comic strip also freely borrowed from other media forms and mirrored a similar vogue for heightened visual realism evident in motion pictures, magazine illustration, and advertising art throughout the 1930s (1969: 406). It was in this increasingly crowded field that *The Phantom* made its debut, at a time when the "action-adventure" category accounted for approximately 25 percent of comic strips on offer from America's three major press feature syndicates—United Features, Chicago Tribune, and King Features Syndicate (Barcus, 1961: 176).

The Phantom comic strip was therefore not an isolated media sensation, but rather part of a larger generational and aesthetic shift towards dramatic realism evident in other forms of contemporaneous mass culture. But this does not adequately explain why comic strips of this kind became so popular with American audiences throughout the 1930s. Some have argued that the advent of the adventure-serial comic strip fulfilled the suppressed emotional urges of Depression-era audiences. William H. Young suggests that the three principal jungle-themed adventure strips of the 1930s—*Tarzan of the Apes*, *Jungle Jim*, and *The Phantom*—each championed the idea of "one man imposing order on a chaotic land," while their shared jungle settings embodied "a rejection of modern technological civilization in favor of a primitivism that accentuates individual worth" (1969: 411).

This desire for escape from mundane reality, made possible by comic strips, was already identified as a key reason for their popularity long before the onset of the Great Depression, nor was this need for escapist entertainment confined to adults. Harvey C. Lehman and Paul A. Witty conducted a survey of 5,000 children living in Missouri throughout 1923–24 in order to gauge their response to the "Sunday funnies" comic-strip supplements featured in their local newspapers. Lehman and Witty concluded that the popularity of comic strips was largely due to their depiction of "unhampered human activity through which the reader vicariously satisfies his thwarted and restrained desires" (1927: 10). Comic strips, they claimed, allowed children to "identify . . . with the most intrepid adventurer, or the most resolute law-defying criminal" (1927: 210–11). That Lehman and Witty could, by the late 1920s, already identify in humorous comic strips many of the archetypal characters (e.g., "adventurers" and "criminals") and dramatic scenarios more commonly associated with adventure-serial comic strips suggests that the shift towards the adventure-serial format did not necessarily represent a seismic break with the medium's "comical" traditions.

Nevertheless, the Phantom represented a new breed of comic-strip action heroes who resonated with American children coming of age during the Great Depression. Confronted by the failed legacy of Prohibition and the ongoing economic wreckage of the 1930s, Michael C. Tucker claims this generational cohort rejected the "self-righteous moral instruction" that underscored the children's literature of the sort once enjoyed by their parents (2004: n.p.). Spurning the old-fashioned, plucky boy heroes who adhered to the edicts of family, church, and state, American children—and male adolescents, especially—turned instead to "individualist heroes" who had no loyalties other than to their friends and their own ideals, who craved wealth by any means other than hard work, and who were "ready, even eager, to employ violence" to achieve their goals (Tucker, 2004: n.p.). The Phantom was not driven by the kind of mercenary self-interest pursued by soldiers of fortune like Captain Easy, but his unique moral code (dedicated to fighting piracy) and recourse to violence aligned him with this new breed of "individualist heroes."

There was another tributary of popular American mass culture which gave rise to a new type of action hero, which not only had a direct bearing on the creation of *The Phantom*, but also presaged the dawn of the costumed superhero. These new action heroes were to be found in the "pulp fiction" magazines of the 1930s, which were crammed with densely typeset novellas and short stories, frequently punctuated by lurid illustrations. Pulp magazines bore all the superficial hallmarks of twentieth-century modernity, capitalizing on readers' interest in contemporary social and technological phenomena, such as science fiction (*Amazing Stories*, 1926), Prohibition-era racketeers (*Gangster Stories*, 1929), and aerial combat (*Wings*, 1928). Despite their up-dated packaging, pulp magazines were carrying on an American publishing tradition specializing in cheap, formulaic fiction pioneered by the "dime novels" of the nineteenth century, of which Edward S. Ellis's western adventure, *Seth Jones* (1860), is considered a defining example (Bold, 1996: 23).

These in turn gave way to story magazines such as *The Argosy* (1882), which soon reached a circulation of 500,000, making it the first successful all-fiction magazine of its kind (Tebbel and Zuckerman, 1991: 174). Publisher Frank Munsey hoped to duplicate his success with *The Argosy* by launching a companion title, *The All-Story*, in 1905. But even Munsey could not have foreseen the astonishing reception which greeted the October 1912 edition of his newest magazine. That issue began serializing Edgar Rice Burroughs's second novel, *Tarzan of the Apes*, which, according to Lee Server, "drew new audiences to the pulps, and influenced a generation of pop-fiction scribes" (1993: 23). Among them was the young Lee Falk, who later acknowledged that *The Phantom* was an amalgam of Tarzan and Rudyard Kipling's *The Jungle Book* (1894) (Madison, 1996: 48).

The subsequent debut of *The Shadow* in 1931 instigated a new genre of popular fiction magazines, collectively known as the "hero pulps," which would further shape the evolution of the costumed superhero. *The Shadow* was an accidental success; in 1930, Street & Smith Publishers sponsored *The Detective Story Hour*, a radio show presided over by a mysterious narrator known as the Shadow. The program was intended to be a promotional vehicle for *Detective Story Magazine*, but listeners besieged the publisher with requests for "the magazine with that Shadow guy" (Server, 1993: 91–92). Fred Blackwell, editor of *Detective Story Magazine*, was urged to quickly produce a new title featuring the Shadow (Server, 1993: 92). He enlisted the help of author Walter B. Gibson, who (under the pseudonym "Maxwell Grant") penned his debut adventure, "The Living Shadow," and would guide the character's dark fortunes for nearly two decades afterwards. As Gibson later remarked:

> The emergence of The Shadow . . . represented a phase in the cyclic evolution of mass fiction. Viewed in retrospect, the trend it set seemed inevitable, but at the time no one expected it. (1979: 1)

The Shadow's swirling black cape and broad-brimmed hat marked a visual shift away from the pedestrian, plainclothes detectives of the dime-novel era and edged closer to the distinctive costumes that would become the uniform of the comic-book superhero.

The success of *The Shadow* did not go unnoticed by rival publishers who, in following Street & Smith's "hero pulp" formula, laid down the defining parameters of the superhero genre. Ironically, one of the most blatant imitators, *The Phantom Detective* (1932), proved to be the most enduring, outlasting even *The Shadow*. More significant, however, are claims that the Phantom Detective was the unacknowledged template for both the Phantom and Batman. As Will Murray points out, the character was always referred to in text as "The Phantom" by the series' various authors—only rarely (and erroneously) was he ever called "The Phantom Detective" (1997: 49). The character's alter ego, Richard Curtis Van Loan, was a bored Park Avenue playboy who waged war on crime—just as the Gotham City millionaire Bruce Wayne was the daytime alter ego of Batman, first seen in *Detective Comics* in 1939. There are further similarities between *The Phantom* and its pulp magazine counterparts. The Phantom's distinctive Skull Ring, for example, was not without precedent. Popular Magazines' bloodthirsty avenger, *The Spider* (1933), stamped his victims' corpses with a spider-shaped seal (Server, 1993: 99). *Operator 5* (1934), star of an apocalyptic espionage series, wore a "death's head ring" concealing an explosive charge (Hutchison, 2007: 81).

If Lee Falk had stuck to his original plans for *The Phantom*, there is every chance that his hero would have gone unnoticed amidst the jumble of masked vigilantes crowding America's newsstands during the 1930s. Falk had intended that Jimmy Wells, an idle Manhattan playboy (briefly seen in "The Singh Brotherhood"), would be the Phantom. Had he done so, Falk would have inadvertently adopted a similar device used by Frank L. Packard for his antihero, Jimmie Dale. First appearing in *People's Magazine* (March 1914), wealthy Jimmie Dale was a "gentleman cracksman" (safecracker) who left a diamond-shaped paper seal as his calling card—and thus became known throughout the underworld as "The Gray Seal" (Vineyard, 2009: n.p.). Then, as Falk later recalled, "in the midst of the first story, I suddenly got the other idea [and] moved The Phantom into the jungle and decided to keep him there" (quoted in Tollin, 1988: 44). Murray, however, suggests that Standard Magazines, publisher of *The Phantom Detective*, was closely observing Lee Falk's unfurling story to see if the society bachelor Jimmy Wells would stand revealed as the Phantom—and thus sue King Features Syndicate for breach of copyright (Murray, 1997: 52–53). Gerard Jones argues that Falk abandoned his original plan to use Jimmy Wells as the Phantom's alter ego, claiming that an unspecified "copyright dispute" prompted Falk to transfer the strip's setting to "the jungles of India" (2004: 123–24).

Falk always maintained that, although he was aware of *The Shadow* and *The Phantom Detective*, he never read them, preferring instead science fiction and fantasy magazines, such as *Amazing Stories* and *Weird Tales* (Murray, 2005: 44). The influence of pulp magazines, Falk claimed, was most evident in his first comic strip, *Mandrake the Magician*, which made great use of "serious" science fiction concepts (quoted in Gerosa, 2011: 118). But *The Phantom* bore all the melodramatic hallmarks of pulp-fiction magazines; Falk's opening story line, "The Singh Brotherhood," was dripping with exotic locales, lost treasures, Oriental villains, and fearsome jungle tribes that could have been torn from the pages of *Adventure*, *Frontier Stories*, *Jungle Stories*, and other pulp mastheads of that era. Ray Moore's moody, atmospheric artwork would not have been out of place in such magazines, either, and only accentuated the series' pulp-era roots. All of these comparisons indicate that, in its use of leitmotifs found elsewhere in popular American mass culture, *The Phantom* comic strip was—superficially at least—influenced by the "hero pulps" of the 1930s. Such comparisons are necessary in order to understand how the dramatic conventions of pulp-fiction magazines were adapted to meet the visual demands of the adventure-serial comic strip—and amplified almost beyond recognition in the exploits of comic-book superheroes.

CHAPTER TWO

THE SYNDICATED SUPERHERO

When asked how he came to create the Phantom, Lee Falk invoked the "hero stories" he read as a child, and claimed he drew inspiration from "Greek, Roman and Nordic myths" as he forged his newest comic-strip character (quoted in Tollin, 1988: 44, 48). The Phantom was unquestionably Falk's brainchild, but his hero's debut in *The New York Journal* was only made possible through the collective efforts of a vast media enterprise. The newspaper itself was owned by the controversial press magnate William Randolph Hearst (1863–1951), proprietor of one of the largest newspaper chains in the United States. Each episode of *The Phantom* bore the copyright notice of the King Features Syndicate, also owned by Hearst, which would eventually eclipse the financial worth of his newspaper mastheads (Nasaw, 2002: 593). *The Phantom*, therefore, was much more than a comic strip; it was the product of a specific organizational demand for a marketable commodity that could be sold to an optimal number of media outlets. By understanding the commercial imperatives that shaped the development of comic strips throughout the 1930s, it will become apparent how companies such as King Features Syndicate had, by the mid-twentieth century, come to exert a profound influence on the development of mass-market print culture in the United States.

The debut of *The Phantom* also coincided with the birth of the comic book, an American publishing phenomenon that would be radically transformed by the emergence of the costumed superhero genre prior to World War II. King Features Syndicate should have been able to exploit *The Phantom* to its commercial advantage in a new medium that was, in its earliest stages of development, vitally dependent on newspaper feature syndicates for its editorial content. Yet as we will see, the relative commercial failure of *The*

Phantom as an American comic-book franchise was as much due to King Features' inability to recognize the unique demands of comic magazines and their juvenile readers, as it was to the character's problematic status as a bona fide superhero. The company's decision to strike licensing deals with publishers who were themselves industry outsiders, unschooled in the dynamics of comic-book storytelling and marketing, prevented King Features from fully exploiting the superhero boom of the early 1940s, along with the subsequent postwar vogue for jungle-adventure comics.

It can be argued that the evolving commercial structures and editorial practices of America's nascent comic-book industry militated against the popular acceptance of the Phantom as the first true comic-book superhero. While "The Ghost Who Walks" has rarely received this accolade from his American compatriots, international fans have been quick to bestow such honors on the Phantom, whom they claim is the true forefather of Superman and all the costumed crime-fighters that followed in his wake. Nevertheless, charting the Phantom's troubled transition from newspapers to comic magazines allows us to better understand the dynamics of America's comic-book culture during its formative years. Doing so also emphasizes the characteristics which distinguished the Phantom from other comic-book heroes, in ways that made him palatable to foreign audiences. Just as importantly, recounting the development of the American media industries that helped launch *The Phantom* provides us with the basis for understanding how "The Ghost Who Walks" eventually came to be an internationally acclaimed comic-strip character.

Feature Syndicates and the Birth of "the Funnies"

The production of a comic strip—like that of motion pictures or recorded music—symbolizes an uneasy alliance between art and commerce. While individual writers and illustrators may be publicly identified as the sole authors of a particular comic strip, they are by no means entirely autonomous. Instead, they must produce their work in accordance with the editorial, institutional, and economic demands of the feature syndicates that ensure their work appears before the widest possible audience. If, as has been suggested, "the history of the comic strip is the history of its method of distribution" (Couperie and Horn, 1968: 135, 137), then we must understand both the history and the mechanics of the newspaper feature syndication business and how it has influenced the creative and commercial life of comic strips like *The Phantom*.

Newspaper syndicates, as they were originally known, first emerged in the United States towards the end of the American Civil War (1861–65). They initially sold sheets of newsprint with national news stories printed on one side to small-town newspapers, whose editors then printed their own local news and advertisements on the blank sides of each sheet they purchased from the syndicate (Tornoe, 2011). Newspaper syndicates gradually spread their operations to metropolitan newspaper markets throughout the 1870s and 1880s. Many of these newer syndicates, like those established by newspaper editor Charles A. Dana and independent entrepreneur Samuel McClure, initially sold stories by British and American authors (such as Rudyard Kipling and Henry James) to the magazine supplements of Sunday newspapers (Berchtold, 1935: 34–35; Watson, 1936: 44–46; Gordon, 1998a: 39). Whereas wire news services such as Reuters dealt with the instantaneous transmission of topical news stories, feature syndicates (as they were now called) gradually specialized in commissioning and selling many of the "non-news" items typically found in most newspapers and magazines today, ranging from crossword puzzles and horoscopes to serialized fiction and advice columns.

The impetus behind the formation of feature syndicates was (and still remains) largely economic. The syndication model of distribution allows companies to amortize the high front-end costs associated with commissioning editorial content by selling the material across their pool of institutional subscribers. Another key difference between news agencies and feature syndicates should be noted here. Whereas the former aimed to sell their services to as many clients as possible, the latter sought to extract higher revenues from their portfolio of editorial products by offering exclusive access (at increased rates) to newspapers operating in a specific geographic market or "circulation territory"—a business model that was pioneered by the Kellogg Newspaper Company in 1905 (Watson, 1936: 51–52).

Comic strips had, by the late nineteenth century, introduced a dynamic visual element to the composition of American newspapers and would eventually become "the backbone of the syndicate business" (MacDougall, 1942: 76). The American comic strip came of age during the circulation wars which engulfed New York City's newspaper industry during the 1890s, with Joseph Pulitzer's *New York World* and Hearst's *New York Morning Journal* as the key combatants. Determined to outdo Pulitzer's innovative use of illustrated news stories and full-page cartoons, Hearst produced the first full-color, eight-page comic strip supplement for the *Journal* in October 1896. The centerpiece was Richard F. Outcault's *The Yellow Kid*, long considered to be the first modern comic strip, which Hearst had poached (along with its creator) from Pulitzer's *New York World*, where it had begun as a weekly, full-page cartoon known as *Hogan's Alley* (Inge, 1990: 137–38). Hearst's gamble paid off, with the comic's popularity establishing the *Journal* as America's largest-selling newspaper, achieving a circulation of 1,500,000 by 1907 (Hagedorn, 1995: 31–32).

Hearst had, by this time, made his first forays into news and feature syndication, commencing with the Hearst News Syndicate (1895), followed by the International News Service (1906) and King Features Syndicate (1915). Hearst, perhaps more so than any of his competitors, recognized the commercial potential of this new entertainment medium and used comic strips to spearhead the expansion of his newspaper interests. By 1900 Hearst began publishing comic strips originally produced for the New York City market across his stable of newspapers, commencing with the *San Francisco Examiner*. By 1908 Hearst's Sunday color comic-strip supplements were appearing in more than 80 newspapers across 50 American cities (Nasaw, 2002: 233–34). Hearst's syndication strategy had, according to Ian Gordon, "opened a national market for comic strips" (1995: 54–55).

Hearst retained a lifelong interest in the comic strips appearing under his newspaper mastheads. Only after selling his first comic strip, *Mandrake the Magician* (1934), to King Features Syndicate did Lee Falk learn that strips carried by the company were personally approved by "the Chief," as Hearst was known to his senior executives. "In the first years that I was with King Features," Falk later recalled, "I would get little notes from Hearst . . . telling me what he liked and didn't like" (quoted in Elman, 2011: 234). Yet Hearst never lost sight of the comic strip's primary value as an economic asset; in 1916 King Features Syndicate put its cartoonists on full-time salaries and acquired copyright ownership of their work, so that, should any of their headline artists be poached by a rival syndicate, another staff artist could simply take their place on a particular comic strip (Lee, 1937: 592).

Comic strips eventually became lucrative sources of advertising revenue for feature syndicates and their newspaper clients. Hearst inadvertently laid the foundations for this business model when his publishing subsidiary, the International Magazine Company, purchased the humor periodical *Puck* in 1917. Unable to reverse the declining sales of this once-venerated cartoon magazine, Hearst closed it down in 1918 but retained its distinctive masthead, which he used to promote his Sunday newspapers' comic-strip supplements under the uniform banner *Puck–The Comic Weekly* (Marschall, 1999: 866). Hearst leveraged his subsidiary companies' printing and distribution networks to further the growth of his newest comic-strip supplement. The Hearst-owned Newspaper Feature Syndicate, a commercial forerunner of King Features Syndicate, established centralized color printing at several of its affiliated newspapers' printing plants, which would deliver completed comic-strip sections to other newspapers which lacked access to four-color printing technology (Koenigsberg, 1941: 398). Hearst's allied media businesses now encompassed all facets of newspaper publishing, printing, and distribution, making his empire a forerunner of today's vertically integrated media conglomerates.

In 1931 the Hearst executive Hawley Turner convinced national consumer brands to place comic-strip formatted advertisements in *Puck*; these advertisements were complemented by point-of-sale displays in retail outlets highlighting the featured product's promotion in *Puck* (Stewart, 2010).[1] By 1934 *Puck* had secured nearly $2,000,000 in advertising revenues, which accounted for almost 25 percent of the estimated $9,000,000 accrued by Sunday newspapers nationwide that opened their comic-strip sections to advertisements (Berchtold, 1935: 36). *Puck*'s market penetration was undeniable; by 1936 its circulation had grown to 5,500,000 copies (Spiegelman, Terwilliger, and Fearing, 1952: 40).

So popular had newspaper comic strips become that they they seemed capable of withstanding the economic calamity of the Great Depression. While many newspapers throughout the United States scaled back their use of syndicated content as a cost-cutting measure, few dared to reduce their range of comic strips, which remained among their most popular features. In 1932 George Gallup published results from his newspaper readership survey, which showed that comic strips were consistently read by more people than the front-page news story, and that comic strips were marginally more popular among women than with men (Gallup, 1932: 23). Little wonder, then, that even during the worst depths of the Great Depression, America's top syndicated cartoonists reportedly earned weekly salaries between $1,000 and $1,600 (Mott, 2000: 694). Feature syndicates did more than just weather the economic storm of the 1930s; by the early 1940s, it was said that the industry, comprised of 250 separate companies, garnered between $15,000,000 and $40,000,000 in gross annual sales (MacDougall, 1942: 76). By the end of World War II, King Features Syndicate was widely regarded as the industry leader, providing editorial content which reached 52,000,000 American households (Tebbel and Zuckerman, 1991: 155). Within a few years of Hearst's death in 1951, it was reported that King Features Syndicate supplied content to an estimated 5,000 clients (*Newspaper News*, 1955: 19). It was by now clear to anyone who cared to look that "the funnies" had become a very serious business.

Comic Strips and American Mass Culture

The editorial influence of feature syndicates on the aesthetic development of the comic strip grew more pronounced during the opening decades of the twentieth century. Early American comic strips, such as *The Yellow Kid*, were set in the crowded tenements of New York City and featured characters which reflected the chaotic immigrant polyglot of the 1890s. Yet as comic strips began circulating in small-town and rural newspapers throughout the country, their multiracial, working-class, urban milieu gave way to characters and settings which spoke "much less to the fringes of American society and more to 'middle America'" (Sabin, 1993: 17). This tonal shift was most visible with the advent of domestic situation-comedy strips, such as George McManus's *Bringing Up Father* (1913) and Sidney Smith's *The Gumps* (1917), which dealt with that "most bourgeois of all institutions, the family" (Couperie and Horn, 1968: 45).

The feature syndicates' business model helped make the comic strip an integral part of American public life; the cultural critic Gilbert Seldes remarked that the syndication of comic strips "enabled America to think nationally" (1957: 195). Comic strips helped shape a new form of visual print culture; Sunday newspapers' colorful comic-strip supplements in particular were enjoyed by mixed-age audiences in living rooms across the country, "thereby inviting individuals to enjoy the entertainment of the reading experience together" (Royer, Nettels, and Aspray, 2011: 280). Yet precisely because they began reaching a nationwide audience, comic strips became subject to ever more editorial and commercial edicts, as Gilbert Seldes noted:

> [The comic strip] cannot be too local, since it is syndicated throughout the country; it must avoid political and social questions because the same strip appears in papers of divergent editorial opinions; there is no room for acute racial caricature, although no group is immune from its mockery. (Seldes, 1957: 194)

This level of racial and ethnic sensitivity did not, however, automatically extend to the depiction of Africans, or African Americans, with many comic strips adhering to long-standing "Sambo" or "minstrel" stereotypes popularized by illustrated humor journals throughout the nineteenth century. This remained the case for many decades; a 1950 survey of American Sunday newspaper comic-strip lift-outs (including *Puck — The Comic Weekly*) found no examples of comic strips ostensibly about "American negroes" (*sic*), noting instead that only a handful of (non-American) "negroes" (*sic*) appeared "as natives in two strips with jungle settings" (Spiegelman, Terwilliger and Fearing, 1952: 49)—an indirect reference to *The Phantom*.

The growing homogenization of syndicated comic strips was a by-product of broader structural changes that had been steadily transforming America's newspaper industry since the late 1880s. The expansion of newspaper chains, increased concentration of newspaper ownership, and the growing influence of press associations and newspaper syndicates "contributed to the standardization of newspaper content . . . and increasingly departmentalized reportage" (Badaracco, 1997: 180–81, 185). Not everyone was perturbed by these developments. Curtis D. MacDougall maintained that although the quality of syndicated material had improved immeasurably throughout the 1920s and 1930s, it did not supplant the local news coverage or features that typically gave newspapers their unique identity. Syndication, he added, proved especially beneficial for comic strips: "One shudders to think what the comic page of the average small-town paper would be like if it were drawn entirely by local cartoonists" (MacDougall, 1942: 80–81).

The parallel expansion and consolidation of the newspaper publishing and feature syndication industries throughout the 1930s proved beneficial for *The Phantom* comic strip. The character's growing popularity led King Features

Syndicate to commission Lee Falk and Ray Moore to produce a full-color version of *The Phantom*, intended for inclusion in Sunday newspapers, which debuted on May 28, 1939. But the transition to this new format was not without problems. Falk had always referred to the Phantom wearing a grey costume in the daily version, but when the first Sunday episodes of *The Phantom* comic strip were being prepared for publication, a printer's error meant the character was given a purple-colored costume instead. "I was not present when the suit was colored," Falk later said (quoted in Ennart, 2011: 177). Nevertheless, as Falk observed, the more expansive format of the weekly color episodes of *The Phantom* offered different dramatic and visual possibilities:

> The difference between the daily adventures and Sunday adventures is that the latter are more imaginative. The format and color influence the story. In black and white [daily strips], one can have characters discuss things, while on big, colored pages, they need to act. (Quoted in Resnais, 2011: 77–78)

The Sunday color version of *The Phantom* comic strip served several purposes: it was a new product which could be sold directly to newspapers; it offered a drawcard for additional advertising revenue; and it provided further opportunities to build the character's profile as a commercial licensing "brand." *The Phantom* could now reach a vast national audience through the pages of *Puck* and attain the level of public recognition and exposure necessary for it to become a lucrative licensing property. King Features Syndicate knew firsthand just how fast this market was growing; by the mid-1930s, Popeye (the star of E. C. Segar's *Thimble Theater* comic strip) had become the company's most successful brand-name character, licensed to publishers, toy manufacturers, and food companies (*DSN Retailing Today*, 2004: 48). The Phantom did not generate the same level of licensing merchandise as Popeye, and his likeness appeared on just a few crudely manufactured items, including a wooden figure and a ceramic mug, during the early 1940s (Hake, 1993: 125). He did, however, gain a foothold in newer forms of mass-market, juvenile literature.

In 1932 the Whitman Publishing Company unveiled a new range of illustrated children's novels known as Big Little Books. These chunky, pocket-sized books contained over 300 pages per volume and sold for just ten cents, making them remarkably good "value-for-money" reading in Depression-era

America. Big Little Books were illustrated novels featuring popular characters drawn from other media, such as radio serials and motion pictures, with text printed on the left-hand page and an accompanying illustration on the right-hand page.

Adventure-serial comic strips provided ready-made content for Big Little Books, and Whitman negotiated book-publishing licenses with the country's major feature syndicates. The company's first title was *The Adventures of Dick Tracy* (1932), based on Chester Gould's police detective hero, launched by the Chicago Tribune Syndicate the year before. Whitman's editorial staff rewrote the comic-strip story lines to suit the Big Little Books' condensed prose format, while the accompanying illustrations were taken directly from the comic strips, after their narrative captions and speech balloons had been removed (Molson, 1984: 19). *The Phantom* (1936) marked the character's self-titled debut in Big Little Books, which was published before the comic strip's opening story line, "The Singh Brotherhood," had even reached its conclusion in newspapers by November 1936 (Griffin and Griffin, ca. 1999). It was the first of six *Phantom* novels — all adapted from the comic strip — released under Whitman's Big Little Book imprint over the next eleven years.

By uncoupling the integration of text and image that was the medium's defining characteristic, Big Little Books represented something of a backward step in the evolution of the comic strip. Yet by reinstating an equal balance between words and pictures, Big Little Books repackaged comic strips as suitable reading matter comparable to "real" children's books of the kind that would normally earn parental approval. These pocket-sized novels also allowed children to enjoy self-contained stories about their favorite comic-strip characters without laboriously following their exploits through each day's newspaper. Certainly, the Whitman Publishing Company could be in no doubt about their popularity; Big Little Books were reportedly selling 1,000,000 copies per month by the late 1930s (Molson, 1984: 147–48).

The Phantom's placement in Big Little Books arguably changed the public perception of the character in subtle, unforeseen ways. The comic strip's film noir atmosphere, redolent with slinky femme fatales and sadistic villains, and punctuated by scenes of explosive violence, was understandably toned down for Big Little Books' juvenile audience. The Phantom was originally conceived for an adult newspaper readership, but Whitman's editorial strategies diluted the character's sinister aura by making him "safe" for children.

Their success in doing so was borne out by the company's decision to release *The Son of The Phantom* (Robertson, 1944), a hardback novelization of Lee Falk's 1944–45 comic-strip story line "The Childhood of The Phantom." The company correctly sensed that the book's account of "the jungle childhood of the present-day Phantom" would resonate with young readers — such was the demand that the book was reprinted twice more between 1944 and 1946 (Griffin and Griffin, ca. 1999). *The Phantom*, it seemed, was well-suited to the Big Little Book format, which, as one author later observed, seemed certain to form "an enduring relationship [with young readers] had not comic books come along" (Stedman, 1977: 213).

The Comic-Book Explosion

Feature syndicates played an important role in the development of America's comic-book industry throughout the 1930s by supplying the editorial content that was vital to ensuring this new medium's success. But their involvement, much like the birth of the comic book itself, came about almost by accident, which led many feature syndicates to underestimate the creative and commercial potential of this new publishing phenomenon.

The invention of the modern comic magazine was driven by economic urgency. The Eastern Color Printing Company of New York printed comic-strip sections for several eastern seaboard newspapers, but it needed new business to keep its presses running at full capacity. Sales manager Harry Wildenberg reportedly came up with the idea of collating folded-down color comic-strip supplements into a 7" × 9" magazine, which could be sold to businesses as promotional giveaways. Securing reprint rights for comic strips owned by the McNaught, Public Ledger, and Bell feature syndicates, Wildenberg showed the prototype magazine, titled *Funnies on Parade*, to Proctor & Gamble, which placed an order for 1,000,000 copies in 1933. Eastern Color Printing subsequently struck a deal with the Dell Publishing Company to produce *Famous Funnies* (1934), a 64-page compilation of newspaper comic strips, which became the first monthly American comic book to be sold (rather than given away) via newsstands for a ten-cent cover price (Beerbohm and Olson, 2007: 383). If feature syndicates harbored any doubts about readers' willingness to pay a dime for magazines stuffed with old comic strips, they were cast aside once they took note of *Famous Funnies'* sales, which approached 1,000,000 copies by late 1934, with profit margins estimated to be around $30,000 per issue (Beerbohm and Olson, 2007: 383). Dell Publishing, which had subsequently sold its stake in *Famous Funnies* back to Eastern Color Printing, now partnered with the McClure Syndicate to launch *Popular Comics* (1936), while former Eastern Color Printing employee Lev Gleason was appointed editor of *Tip Top Comics* (1936), published by the United Features Syndicate.

William Randolph Hearst was no stranger to this emerging field, having previously issued hardcover compilations of comic strips featured in the *New York Journal*, including *The Katzenjammer Kids* (1902) and *Happy Hooligan* (1902). In the mid-1930s, King Features Syndicate formed a partnership with the David McKay Company, a Philadelphia book publisher already known for its range of licensed *Mickey Mouse* comic-strip albums. McKay launched *King Comics* (1936) and *Ace Comics* (1937), which were comprised entirely of King Features' comic strips, including *Flash Gordon*, *Krazy Kat*, and Lee Falk's first comic-strip series, *Mandrake the Magician*. McKay released the Feature Book series in 1937, which offered complete (or near-complete) collections of comic-strip stories dedicated to a single character, commencing with *Popeye and the Jeep*. The two-part serialization of the first *Phantom* adventure, "The Singh Brotherhood," in the Feature Book editions no. 20 (1938) and no. 22 (1939) is regarded by some as the first American comic book devoted to an individual "superhero." But neither King Features Syndicate nor the David McKay Company recognized the commercial opportunity before them, and failed to exploit this idea further by promoting *The Phantom* as an exciting comic book to younger readers eager for this new type of magazine.

Comic-book publishing was, at this stage, largely a matter of pouring old wine into new bottles; as Raymond W. Stedman notes, "little effort was made to adapt the borrowed [comic strips] to their new environment and there was almost no new material" (1977: 204). The almost guaranteed success of these early comic books meant there was little incentive to exercise any degree of editorial care; recalling his tenure as a young editor on *Popular Comics*, Sheldon Mayer bluntly stated "it was a schlock operation . . . we bought the material for practically nothing and slapped it together" (quoted in Wright, 2001: 4). Readers, initially at least, did not seem to mind; by 1942 *Ace Comics* had attained a monthly circulation of 280,000, while *King Comics* drew close with 256,000 readers—and both had outstripped their pioneering rival, *Famous Funnies*, which had dropped back to 180,000 (Gilbert, 2002: 72–73).

Newspaper feature syndicates held a virtual stranglehold on the supply of editorial content for America's nascent comic-book industry, which allowed them to raise their publication licensing fees from an average $5–10 per page to nearly $100 per page by the early 1940s (Gilbert, 2002: 65). Smaller publishers, keen to enter this booming market, but lacking the capital required to pay such exorbitant fees, began commissioning original stories and artwork prepared exclusively for comic magazines—typically for rock-bottom pay rates. The first of these "all-original" comics was *New Fun* (1935), printed in black and white, which offered a pulp magazine-infused selection of cowboy, aviator-adventure, and science fiction comics. The Comic Magazine Company pioneered the first single-themed comic books, *Detective Picture Stories* (1936) and *Western Picture Stories* (1937); their deliberate avoidance of the word "comic" was designed to distinguish their exciting, dramatic contents from humorous anthologies like *Funnies on Parade*. But as Ted White points out, many of these early "original" comic books still slavishly copied the regimented layout of newspaper comic strips adopted by other comic magazine reprints (1997: 22). Ironically, the turning point for America's prewar comic-book industry would come from a costumed hero previously rejected by newspaper syndicates as too fantastic, even for "the funnies"—but Superman, as it turned out, was tailor-made for comic books.

In the Shadow of Superman

Clad in a skin-tight purple costume, his face concealed by an eye-mask and cowl, and sporting a death's head symbol on his gun-belt, the Phantom was the visual prototype for the modern superhero. Despite the fact that the Phantom predated the debut of Superman in *Action Comics* no. 1 (June 1938), the character's contribution to the superhero genre has been routinely overlooked in most academic and popular surveys of comic strips and comic magazines. Nor, for that matter, has the Phantom been embraced as a superhero—at least not within the United States, the birthplace of the genre. The character's peripheral status as a "superhero," and his marginal success during the formative years of America's comic-book industry, can be attributed to an unforeseen mixture of aesthetic, editorial, and demographic factors.

From the outset, the Phantom defied straightforward categorization; by 1938 King Features Syndicate was promoting him as a "mysterious adventurer" and "strange personage" who brings "a thrilling novelty in strips" (Scandinavian Chapter, 2011: 35). While this is an indirect reference to the Phantom's distinctive costume, he is not yet described as a "superhero." This is entirely understandable, as Superman had only just made his debut in *Action Comics*, and the word "superhero" had not yet made its way into everyday use. But the company's promotional rhetoric remained unchanged long after the costumed superhero had become an established comic-book genre. By 1967, King Features' *Blue Book* sales catalog continued to refer to the Phantom as a "jungle crusader" rather than a "superhero" (King Features Syndicate, 1967: 14).

Even though he looked very much like a superhero, the Phantom possessed none of the extraordinary powers or abilities commonly associated with such characters. Like the pulp-magazine heroes who preceded him, the Phantom was undeniably powerful and used his physical strength and athleticism to overcome his enemies. Yet he could not match the extraterrestrial abilities of Superman, who could not only fly, but also possessed super-strength and was impervious to physical harm. Even the Phantom's ability to return from the dead as "The Ghost Who Walks" was an elaborate fiction designed to intimidate evildoers. It was for these reasons that the comics historian Coulton Waugh argued that, because he is mortal and can be killed, the Phantom could not be regarded as "a superman in the wild, modern meaning of the word" (1974: 260).

The Phantom may struggle to receive "official" recognition as America's first superhero, but to his international fans, there is little doubt about his rightful historical status. One reader went to great lengths to enumerate the Phantom's contributions to the superhero genre, but chose instead to draw connections between "The Ghost Who Walks" and one of Superman's earliest successors—Batman:[2]

The Phantom was the first traditional superhero. Forget Batman. The Phantom was first to become who he was due to the death of his parents, the first to wear tights with a cowl . . . The first to have a sidekick (Devil), first to have a secret identity, and first to have a cave as his hideout. And [he] was originally to be a rich playboy by day and become a hero by night (Jimmy Wells). (Female respondent, 18–35 years old, Australia, March 23, 2012)

Some fans, however, suggest that the Phantom represents an important transitional figure in the evolution of the superhero genre, as much steeped in the traditions of pulp-fiction magazines as he was in the formative development of comic books. One reader described the Phantom's adventures as "straightforward pulp action plots" (male respondent, 18–35 years old, Australia, April 27, 2012). Another reader drew connections and distinctions between the Phantom and Batman which further highlighted the Phantom's pulp-era lineage:

> Comparing him to a close competitor, Batman, the two are really quite distinct. The Phantom's characterization hasn't really changed much over time . . . For better or worse the Phantom is an old-fashioned kind of superhero, more of a pulp hero, in fact . . . [He] can come off as a two-dimensional invincible hero who's often incredibly lucky. . . . A character like Batman has moved with the times, in fact [he has] frequently done so with occasionally regrettable results. (Male respondent, 18–35 years old, Australia, August 26, 2012)

The Phantom, according to Peter Coogan, came closest to challenging Superman's status as America's first recognizable "superhero" precisely because his distinctive costume, dual identity, and superior strength and agility embodied so many definitional aspects of the superhero. Yet other elements of the Phantom's persona, historical background, and his exotic jungle milieu bore all the hallmarks of his pulp-fiction antecedents. For these reasons, Coogan maintains that the Phantom did not represent a significant break from the dramatic conventions ascribed to the Shadow, the Spider, and other "mystery men" commonly found in pulp-fiction magazines (2006: 14). Superman, by contrast, was the first truly omnipotent hero, the likes of which had never been seen before in pulp magazines, newspaper comic strips, or comic books. Furthermore, Coogan argues that Superman's near-instant commercial success led to a torrent of costumed superheroes flooding America's fledgling comic-book industry, thus initiating a cycle of "imitation and repetition" which signaled the emergence of an entirely new genre (2006: 175). The

Phantom, by contrast, did not excite the same level of popular adulation or commercial emulation.

Superman had an almost incalculable impact on the comic-book medium, but no one was entirely sure what they had on their hands with this strange new hero. Even publisher Jack Liebowitz, who chose Superman's image to grace the cover of *Action Comics*' debut issue, kept the new magazine's print run pegged at a cautious 250,000 copies (Daniels, 2003: 22). It was not until after the company conducted informal newsstand surveys, which disclosed that children were demanding "the comic with Superman in it," that National Periodical Publications (aka DC Comics) reinstated Superman on the cover of *Action Comics*' seventh issue, by which time it was selling 500,000 copies per month (Daniels, 2003: 22; Jones, 2004: 141). Superman's meteoric success invited fierce competition; by 1940 it was estimated that 80 percent of the 109 comic magazines published in the United Sates featured superhero characters (Gabilliet, 2010: 20).

But why did comic-book superheroes resonate with America's youth? Some of their success can be attributed to historical timing; appearing prior to the Japanese attack on Pearl Harbor in December 1941, comic-book superheroes soon became willing propagandists for America's war effort, exhorting readers to buy war bond savings stamps, while battling hordes of German and Japanese soldiers. Early studies of America's emerging comic-book culture argued that superheroes were modern-day expressions of the "phantasies of omnipotence" which were a recurring theme in ancient mythology, and simply embodied the "greater magic needed in modern folklore" to confront "the greater dangers which assail society and the individual" (Bender and Lourie, 1941: 546).

The intrinsic visual appeal of comic books seems now almost tailor-made for superheroes. However, the visual storytelling possibilities of this new medium were not immediately recognized by its earliest practitioners, who simply imitated the "uniform grids of equal-sized panels," which, according to Robert C. Harvey, characterized the layout of Sunday newspapers' comic-strip sections (1996: 29). They therefore ignored the comic-book's "spacious page format" which would otherwise give artists the freedom to vary the height and width of panels for greater visual and dramatic emphasis (Harvey, 1996: 29). It took the arrival of Superman, and the legions of superheroes that followed him, to show how comic books could tell stories in new and exciting ways. Some critics, however, were far from convinced that comic books represented an advance in visual storytelling:

> The composition of the [comic-book] page is often altered from the usual "panels" into a hodgepodge of blotched lines and clashing colors in order to catch the eye of the casual reader and to carry the action of the story forward as rapidly as possible. A motion picture camera technique is introduced into the "panels," crowding together "close-ups," "long shots" . . . and other compositional arrangements to keep the reader from falling asleep between murders. (Vigus, 1942: 168)

Yet it was the frenetic pace and chaotic artwork found in most comic books which excited young readers the most. Their fast and furious action was not, as Josette Frank, observed, "true to life," but it was "life as young readers would live it," if only to escape the "humdrum of their daily routine [where] 'nothing ever happens'" (1944: 220).

If the superhero genre enhanced the popularity of comic books by expanding the medium's narrative parameters, it also challenged the economic conventions of America's magazine publishing industry. Typically speaking, most magazines were reliant on revenues derived from a combination of paid advertisements, readers' subscriptions, and over-the-counter sales. By 1947 comic books had the largest aggregate sales of any group of periodicals in America (89,000,000 copies) and accounted for over 23 percent of total aggregate circulations of all periodicals in America by 1949—yet they received less than one percent of total advertising receipts accrued by the magazine publishing industry (Reed, 1997: 196–97). While advertising agencies were understandably keen to exploit this huge youth market, press reports suggested that advertisers were reluctant to deal with an industry that was still prey to "fly-by-night . . . operators," where advertising rates had not yet stabilized, and where undercutting on advertised page rates was apparently rife (Gilbert, 2002: 68–69). As a result, most comic-book advertising was confined to mail-order products and services, such as novelty gadgets and home-study courses (Malter, 1952: 507).

Yet for some publishers, the true economic value of comic books lay not in the number of pages sold to advertisers, but in the commodity value of the comic-book characters themselves. National Periodical Publications was among the first to recognize this potential when it formed a subsidiary company, Superman Inc., in 1940 to license Superman's trademarked image which, by the end of the decade, was being used to endorse breakfast cereals, children's clothing, board games, and toys (Daniels, 2003: 72–75). Superman was now "not so much a character who helped sell comic books as a product that comic books sold" (Gordon, 1998a: 133–34).

The Phantom should have flourished amidst the explosive growth of America's comic-book industry during the late 1930s and early 1940s. Even though he defied easy categorization as a "genuine" superhero, the Phantom's ties to the earlier school of pulp magazine "mystery men" need not have been an automatic barrier to success in the comic-book field. Street & Smith Publications, for example, launched popular comic-book versions of its leading pulp-magazine heroes, *Shadow Comics* (1940–49) and *Doc Savage Comics* (1940–43), which placed them among America's biggest-selling comic-book publishers by 1942 (Gilbert, 2002: 72–73). Yet the Phantom's commercial gatekeepers consistently failed to exploit his potential at a time when the superhero craze was at its peak. This failure must stem from King Features Syndicate's decision to award its comic-book publishing license to the David McKay Company, a firm best known for publishing poetry, educational textbooks, and children's literature. Even as the comic-book industry evolved and expanded throughout the 1940s, McKay published its key titles—*Ace Comics* and *King Comics*—on the same "schlock operation" principles that characterized the industry's formative years.

The Phantom fared poorly during its initial transition from newspapers to comic magazines. Oblivious to the surging demand for superhero comics, McKay did not use the Phantom's image on the covers of either *King Comics* or *Ace Comics* for the duration of the war. Nor did the company exploit the timeliness of Lee Falk's story line, "The Inexorables" (concerning the Japanese invasion of the Phantom's jungle domain), even as rival publishers regularly depicted their top-selling superheroes in combat with Japanese troops. Little thought was given to reformatting newspaper comic strips for the comic-book page; the original panel sequence from daily newspaper episodes of *The Phantom* was rearranged, or some panels were deleted altogether, in order to condense the story line into monthly, four-page installments.

At a time when comics such as *Superman* and *Captain Marvel* were boasting circulations in excess of 1,000,000 readers, how do we account for McKay's ongoing indifference to the Phantom's commercial potential as a headline "su-perhero" drawcard? It could be argued that the relative success of *Ace Comics* and *King Comics* was not dependent on adventure heroes like the Phantom for their undeniably robust sales figures. It is also possible that McKay had neither the desire nor the resources to become a dedicated comic-book pub-lisher. As the industry pioneer M. C. Gaines was already pointing out by 1942, comic-book editors were now faced with the dilemma of "developing constantly new episodes around already established characters" (1942: 20), which typically required several months for a team of writers, illustrators, and editorial assistants to produce (1942: 24). Since McKay primarily remained a book publisher throughout the war, focusing its efforts on simply repack-aging ready-made comic-strip artwork into magazines allowed the company to allocate minimal resources to sustain these otherwise profitable ancillary products.

Twilight of the Superheroes

Superheroes had an undeniable economic and cultural impact on America's comic-book industry during the first half of the 1940s, but it would be mis-leading to suggest that they entirely displaced other types of comic maga-zines. For even as superhero titles proliferated, several wartime publishers were experimenting with new genres that would eventually supplant them. These encompassed teenage humor (*Archie Comics*, 1942), literary adaptations (*Classic Comics*, 1941), and horror (*Spook Comics*, 1946). The end of the war ushered in dramatic changes for the industry, which would be most keenly felt by the costumed crusaders that had fostered its birth and exponential growth. Peacetime robbed most superheroes of their dramatic purpose; while some survived (most notably Superman, Batman, and Wonder Woman), scores of formerly top-selling superhero comics had been canceled by 1948–49 (Gou-lart, 1986: 241). Such turbulent times should have favored the Phantom, who had long been overshadowed by larger-than-life superheroes. Yet even the removal of the Phantom's chief rivals would not necessarily guarantee him a secure footing in America's postwar comic-book industry.

While the output of some publishers, such as Dell Publications and DC Comics, remained overwhelmingly geared towards children and adolescents, other, smaller companies began courting adult readers. Lev Gleason Publications ran teaser advertisements for its violent new gangster comic, *Crime Does Not Pay* (1942), which played both ends of the market by urging kids to "show it to dad, he'll love it!" (Goulart, 1986: 231). Prize Publications declared that its new title, *Young Romance* (1947), was intended "for the more adult readers of comics." This latter genre—of which *Young Romance* was the first example—was instrumental in broadening the appeal of comics beyond its traditionally male-dominated readership. By 1950, industry sources claimed that women aged between 17 and 25 years were reading more comic books than men, due largely to the popularity of romance comics (Robbins, 1999: 54).

The origins of "jungle hero" comic books date back to the late 1930s, but they assumed greater prominence following World War II, as more salacious examples of the genre began competing with "girlie magazines" for the attention of older male readers, including returned servicemen. The earliest jungle-hero comics were modeled after Tarzan and, like Edgar Rice Burroughs's creation, had their roots in pulp-fiction magazines. Publisher Martin Goodman converted his pulp character, *Ka-Zar* (1936), into a supporting feature for *Marvel Comics* (1939). Similarly, Fiction House transferred Ki-Gor, the undisputed star of its *Jungle Stories* magazine, to *Jungle Comics* (1940), where he was inexplicably renamed Kaänga (Hutchinson, 2007: 193–200). This genre proved immediately popular with American schoolchildren, who frequently nominated *Jungle Comics* as one of their favorite titles throughout the 1940s and 1950s (Witty, 1941: 102; Witty and Moore, 1945: 305; and Friedson, 1954: 80, 82, 88). Sensing a shift in the market, McKay made belated efforts to reposition the Phantom as a jungle hero by finally featuring him on the cover of *Ace Comics* (nos. 143–51, 1949) before quitting the comic-book field in 1949.

Yet even as superheroes steadily lost ground to their more primeval rivals, the Phantom was once again eclipsed by a comic-book character that left an indelible mark on the "jungle-hero" genre. Sheena, Queen of the Jungle, made her American debut in *Jumbo Comics* in 1938 and became the first successful female hero in American comic books, predating Wonder Woman's debut in *All-Star Comics* in 1941.[3] What distinguished Sheena from other "vine-swingers" was her flowing blond hair and her implausibly brief leopard-skin costume, designed to show off her voluptuous figure. In her own way, Sheena had a galvanizing effect on the postwar comic-book market. Her continued success in *Jumbo Comics*, along with her own self-titled magazine (launched in 1942), sparked a minor stampede of imitators such as Rulah, Jungle Goddess (*Zoot Comics* no. 7, 1947), *Zegra, Jungle Empress* (1948), and *Lorna the Jungle Girl* (1953).

To survive in this intensely competitive market, publishers released new titles that frequently commingled scenes of violent bloodshed, torture, gore, and sexual titillation which were particularly evident in the crime, horror, and jungle-hero genres (Vollmer, 2002: 70–85). Even Harvey Publications, which had purchased the comic-book rights to *The Phantom* in the early 1950s, billed the character's exploits as "Weird Jungle Fantasy" and used cover illustrations to promote the Phantom's appearances in *Harvey Comics Hits* that were entirely in keeping with the company's visceral range of horror comics, such as *Chamber of Chills* (1951–54) and *Witches Tales* (1951–54).

Such violent excess was, according to Stephen Becker, a by-product of America's experience of World War II, where the "constant repetition of [brutality]" in all forms of mass media—including comic books—had debased society's "capacity for horror" (1959: 242–43). It was also a reflection of the different organizational structures and public obligations that governed the newspaper industry and comic-book publishers:

> After the war, a distinction became obvious. The newspaper comic strip was part of a daily publication deemed essential to almost all American families. As such, it had to maintain the standards of propriety and taste raised by the newspaper itself. The comic book, on the other hand, was an independent publication, available to anyone for (usually) a dime, and responsible to no one for the quality of its contents. (Becker, 1959: 242)

The combination of relentless and violent action, images of scantily clad women, and the overt racism common to virtually all "jungle comics" did not go unremarked by the industry's critics, whose voices were growing steadily louder. John R. Cavanagh alleged that the comics' frequent depiction of "chained females and sexually suggestive situations" could harm the psychological development of otherwise well-adjusted, "normal adolescents" (1949: 34–35); Geoffrey Wagner's acerbic study of American popular culture, *Parade of Pleasure*, denounced Sheena, Queen of the Jungle, as an "Aryan mistress" who makes "the local natives . . . bow in terror before her" (1955: 98); and Fredric Wertham, author of the influential anti-comics tract *Seduction of the Innocent* (1954), accused jungle comics of cultivating "race hatred" by depicting "Negroes" (*sic*) as "primitives, savages and ape men" (1954: 101, 103).

These sensational publishing tactics, deployed to expand the market for a medium historically associated with children, brought unwelcome scrutiny to bear on America's comic-book industry. With retailers facing boycotts organized by citizens' committees protesting against objectionable comic books, magazine wholesalers began refusing to distribute growing numbers of titles that could be deemed offensive to community standards (Twomey, 1955: 621–29; Friedman, 2003: 201–27). With horror comics already being singled out in the televised U.S. Senate Subcommittee on Juvenile Delinquency hearings in April 1954, the industry's largest publishers formed the Comics Magazine Association of America (CMAA) in October 1954 and devised a stringent self-regulatory censorship policy (the "Comics Code") that was designed to stamp out the worst excesses of sexual and violent imagery commonly associated with (but not necessarily confined to) "jungle hero" comics (Nyberg, 1998: Wright, 2001: 86–108; and Hajdu, 2008).

While *The Phantom* newspaper comic strip had previously attracted criticism for its pejorative racial themes and imagery (Kessel, 1943: 35), it appears to have escaped notice throughout the anti-comics campaigns of the early 1950s. This seems odd, insofar as *The Phantom* dealt with many of the dramatic staples—such as warring tribes, scheming witch doctors, and greedy poachers—that were common to virtually all "jungle hero" comics. But perhaps the key difference between them was their respective levels of editorial freedom; whereas "jungle hero" comics had (prior to the advent of the Comics Code) greater scope to depict violent and sexually provocative stories and images, newspaper comic strips like *The Phantom* were subject to greater editorial scrutiny by newspaper syndicates, which ensured their content would not offend newspaper clients and their readers—in a sense, they had already been vetted prior to their comic-book serialization. Nevertheless, Harvey Publications, as a founding CMAA member, was subsequently forced to use far milder cover illustrations when it issued a further series of eight *Phantom* comics as part of its *Harvey Hits* title during 1957–61.

The Phantom could overcome the greatest physical obstacles and vanquish the deadliest foes imaginable, but his existence beyond the boundaries of the newspaper comic-strip page was beset by commercial misfortune throughout the 1930s and 1940s. Bad luck and poor timing dogged the Phantom's earliest forays into new print media formats, as the once-popular Big Little Book series in which he starred was overtaken by the rocketing sales of comic magazines, spurred on by the arrival of Superman. Although the Phantom did not readily conform to the tenets of the comic-book superhero genre, his relative failure as a comic-book franchise stemmed in part from King Features Syndicate's ill-advised partnerships with firms that did not understand the dynamics of comic-book publishing. Even when the commercial tides ran in King Features' favor, the company's licensed publishing partners moved too late in promoting the Phantom at the peak of the "jungle hero" comics craze following World War II. By cataloging and analyzing these commercial missteps, we have seen how the origins and development of America's comic-book industry—together with King Features' engagement with that industry—had adversely affected the Phantom's performance as a comic-book franchise. Having done so, we can now follow the Phantom's path to Australia, Sweden, and India, and begin to understand how "The Ghost Who Walks" came to enjoy popular acclaim in these three countries, the likes of which he has rarely known in the United States.

CHAPTER THREE

THE PHANTOM ABROAD

As a boy growing up in the Australian bush during the 1930s, Stuart Wood anxiously awaited the latest edition of the *Australian Woman's Mirror*, delivered each week to his childhood home by horse and cart. His mother may have enjoyed the magazine's short stories, recipes, and sewing patterns, but Stuart always turned instead to the latest installment of *The Phantom* comic strip. "I followed his adventures like a dedicated fan," he later recalled. As the origins of the Phantom unfolded over successive weeks in the *Woman's Mirror*, Stuart vividly remembered the Phantom living on an island called "Banda." "A sketch of the island showed a volcanic mountain . . . partially surrounded by a 'necklace' of smaller, low-lying islands," he said. "I always remembered Banda . . . fond memories from my boyhood" (Wood, 1987: 15).

Less than a decade later, Stuart was a nineteen-year-old serving as a wireless air gunner with the Royal Australian Air Force, flying missions against Japanese forces aboard a B-25 bomber patrolling the islands to the northwest of Australia's coastline. In August 1944 his squadron was sent to intercept a Japanese convoy, their flight path taking them over the Banda Islands, 500 miles north of Darwin. After successfully completing their mission, Stuart radioed his navigator and said, "Hey! Take us to the Banda Islands — I want to see The Phantom!" (Wood, 1987: 15). Thirty minutes later, he looked down from the top gun turret and saw the Banda Islands rising up from the sea:

> And do you know, there was this volcanic-looking island sticking up from the sea to about 1200 feet, and surrounding it a crescent-shaped group of small islands — for all the world a replica of what I had seen in that magazine, as a boy. (Wood, 1987: 15)

The passage of time had perhaps clouded Stuart's memory, as he confused the Bandar pygmy tribe with the Phantom's original home on the island of Luntok, off the coast of Sumatra (see chapter 1). But his recollections are nonetheless fascinating because they illustrate how comic strips had become a popular form of visual entertainment for a generation of readers growing up in the pre-television era. Furthermore, they demonstrate the international reach of American mass media which, by the mid-1930s, could already stir the imagination of a young boy growing up in the outback of Australia.

But how was *The Phantom* able to reach such far-flung readers so soon after its American debut? To find out, we must now chart the international circulation of *The Phantom* comic strip to the three countries where it has achieved its greatest success and longevity—Australia, Sweden, and India. This outward focus makes it possible to understand how the relative success and failure of American mass media abroad could be determined by the institutional structures and commercial demands of foreign markets. Such an understanding is vital in order to gauge to what extent these factors influenced the public reception of *The Phantom* in all three countries.

The international odyssey of *The Phantom* does, however, begin in the United States. Therefore, we must first identify the commercial imperatives that drove the foreign expansion of American media interests—particularly those controlled by William Randolph Hearst—during the earliest decades of the twentieth century. We can then see how foreign newspaper syndicates and magazine publishers helped disseminate American comic strips from the 1930s onwards. Particular attention will be paid to how women's magazines, rather than newspapers, played a crucial role in promoting *The Phantom* throughout Australia, Sweden, and India and helped make this "fantastic" hero acceptable to mainstream audiences. This is an especially important phase in the international publishing history of *The Phantom*; nearly 24 percent of readers from Australia, Sweden, and India surveyed for this book claimed they first met "The Ghost Who Walks" in the pages of newspapers or magazines, rather than comic books. (By contrast, only 4.6 percent of survey participants indicated they first saw the Phantom in audiovisual media, such as motion pictures or animated cartoons.) Such findings underscore the important role that print media have played in sustaining *The Phantom* comics franchise in overseas markets.

Some critics contend that the international syndication of *The Phantom* comic strip raises deeper concerns about the shifting balance of Western geopolitical influence, and the seductive appeal of American mass media. Makarand Paranjape argues that *The Phantom* represented a fusion of the British imperial adventure story and the "American comic-book fantasies of the superhero," which produced a "composite myth that combines the older declining imperialism of the British with the newer, incipient imperialism of the US" (2008: 12). The Phantom, conceived as an "undying white patriarch," allowed the West, according to Paranjape, to reinvent "new playing fields to enact its dramas of domination" (2008: 12). Paranjape here invokes the specter of American cultural imperialism, which has been historically framed as the unbridled, one-way flow of American mass media throughout the world. Plotting the often complex—and occasionally unexpected—paths *The Phantom* took to reach audiences in Australia, Sweden, and India allows us to question the stark polarities which so often characterized the cultural imperialism thesis.

Exporting American Laughter

The groundwork for the international expansion of American mass media was being prepared in the aftermath of World War I. The United States emerged from its brief and belated involvement in that conflict untouched by the physical ravages of war and poised to undergo a remarkable phase of unprecedented economic growth. The period from 1920 to 1929 was characterized by relatively low unemployment, increased wages for industrial workers, and stable consumer prices. These fortuitous conditions saw the United States' gross national product climb from $73.3 billion in 1920 to $104.4 billion by 1929, as the quantity of manufacturing output leapt by 50 percent during this same period (McCoy, 1973: 116). The United States also underwent significant demographic change, recording more urban dwellers than rural dwellers for the first time in the 1920 census (Gordon, 2004: 300). As cities and suburbs fanned outwards across America, their residents would become the bedrock of the new consumer-driven economy.

America's mass media were no less affected by these industrial and economic trends throughout the 1920s. The growth of urban population centers,

made possible by the expansion of mass transportation networks and the rise
of the automobile, provided new markets for durable consumer goods, which
were now available to more households through the provision of cheap credit
(Gordon, 2004: 296–309). The electrification of America's cities, suburbs,
and rural towns also ushered in new forms of mechanical entertainment,
from the public forum of motion-picture cinemas to the domestic enjoyment
of the phonograph and radio in the home. Thus American popular culture
flourished "as it developed facile means of communicating" with this "great
body of consumers for entertainment" (Handlin, 1966: 364).

William Randolph Hearst's sprawling media empire, in its own way, came
to resemble the "super corporations" (such as Standard Oil and General Mo-
tors) which exploited new advances in mass production, distribution, and
marketing to hold down their costs, expand their market share, and ultimately
"move toward controlling their sectors of the economy" (McCoy, 1973: 121).
Hearst's graphic, sensational newspapers were, according to Oscar Handlin,
"firmly planted in every city, briskly fighting off local emulators" (1966: 344).
In fact, Moses Koenigsberg (1879–1945), the founding director of King Features Syndicate, cheerfully recalled how he used the veiled threat of Hearst
setting up a rival newspaper in their hometown to persuade newspaper pro-
prietors to subscribe to the company's syndicated features (1941: 343–44).

American media organizations would ultimately use the financial collat-
eral, mass-production methods, and technical expertise they accrued through
their domestic business activities to propel their entry into foreign markets.
The key to their international success, according to William Read, stemmed
from their recognition that the United States was "not so much a single national market as a complex of submarkets" (1976: 9). Newspaper and magazine
publishers, for example, built up their national circulations by selling advertisers access to specific geographic and demographic markets. They developed localized editorial strategies that appealed to distinct audiences, which
were in turn supported by regional sales representation and production facilities, along with flexible, nationwide distribution networks. The knowledge
and expertise gained through servicing multiple regional markets throughout
the United States could, according to Read, be successfully applied to international markets (1976: 10).

Hearst's media organization would, over time, embark on a successful program of overseas expansion, relying on a multipronged approach that included the outright acquisition of foreign media assets, launching international editions of its American publications (tailored to regional tastes), and the global syndication of content produced by its subsidiary companies, including Hearst International News and King Features Syndicate. But the company's earliest forays into foreign markets were far from encouraging. Hearst purchased the British *Weekly Budget* in 1910 and converted it into the first British Sunday newspaper to be published in the American-styled format, with individually titled sections and supplements. Unable to find a local printer capable of producing four-color broadsheets required for the comics section, Hearst had the comics supplement specially printed in the United States and shipped directly to Britain (Gifford, 1984: 110). But according to Moses Koenigsberg, the *Weekly Budget* was nothing more than an "amusing plaything" for Hearst, who allowed it to rack up losses of \$250,000 before ceasing publication altogether (Koenigsberg, 1941: 352–53). This seemed in keeping with Hearst's oddly cavalier attitude towards his media assets; according to Piers Brendon, "life for Hearst was simply a huge spectacular and newspapers were its program" (1982: 133).

King Features Syndicate initially seemed slow to pursue international sales for its growing portfolio of comic-strip features. The company did not form an international sales division until 1928, at which time King Features' comic strips reportedly appeared in just eight overseas newspapers (*Reading Eagle*, 1974: 44). Leading this new division was John A. Brogan (1893–1974), who had served as an assistant sales manager with the firm since 1923, and under whose guidance the company's international expansion would begin in earnest. Domestic economic pressures may also have forced King Features to broaden its horizons; not only was it facing growing competition from rival syndicates, but the range of domestic media outlets for its products was shrinking. The total number of daily newspapers published in the United States began steadily to contract, from 2,600 titles in 1909 to 1,854 titles in 1947, even as nationwide newspaper circulations continued to climb during this same period (*Yale Law Journal*, 1952: 949). But expanding overseas required King Features Syndicate to collaborate with international business partners who could help it make American comic strips—such as *The Phantom*—household names in foreign lands.

Marketing Modernity:
Selling American Comic Strips Abroad

That news stories could be packaged as a profitable commodity was by no means a novel concept when King Features Syndicate decided to venture abroad. International news bureaus, such as Associated Press (est. 1846) and Reuters (est. 1851), were already well known to newspaper publishers worldwide, who relied on their services to secure international news stories they could not otherwise obtain through their own resources. However, few newspaper publishers outside the United States seemed to recognize that trading in "non-news" features, such as crossword puzzles, horoscopes, or comic strips, could form a profitable adjunct to their core publishing business. This void was often filled by independent companies which, in partnership with American firms like King Features Syndicate, introduced the features syndication business model to their domestic markets.

In Australia, that opportunity fell to David Yaffa (1893–1947), who created the Yaffa Syndicate in 1921 as an Australian outlet for international news photographs, which he sold personally through his contacts in Sydney's newspaper industry before branching interstate. Yaffa secured local syndication rights for several leading American magazines, including *Time, Fortune*, and *The New Yorker*. In 1928 Yaffa launched *Newspaper News*, a trade journal for Australia's newspaper and magazine publishing industries (*The Mail*, 1947: 4). It was around this time that Yaffa Syndicate became the Australian representative for King Features Syndicate.

David Yaffa had, by this time, cultivated strong personal ties with the Australian publishing magnate Frank Packer (1906–1974) and his Sydney Newspapers Ltd. (later Consolidated Press) group. Yaffa successfully placed several of King Features' comic strips, including *Bringing Up Father* and *Tim Tyler's Luck*, with Packer's flagship Sydney newspaper, the *Daily Telegraph*, in the mid-1930s.[1] Yaffa Syndicate expanded its operations throughout Australia and New Zealand, but not everyone was impressed by its owner's business acumen; the Australian Journalists' Association openly mocked Yaffa in the pages of its satirical newspaper, *Syndicated Weakly* (1936), arguing that his company's cheaply imported American comics were squeezing Australian cartoonists out of the market (Ryan, 1979: 39). Yaffa's close association with Packer also drew fire from the Printing Industries Employees' Union of Australia, which threatened industrial action after learning that Packer (together with Yaffa) was developing a 16-page color comic supplement to be printed in the United States for inclusion in the new *Sunday Telegraph* newspaper, due to be launched in November 1939. The threatened strike was narrowly averted, and the comic-strip lift-out (titled *Charlie Chuckles*) was eventually printed in Australia by Yaffa's own company, Rotary Color Print (Griffen-Foley, 1999: 81–86).

Bulls Press (Bulls Presstjänst AB) occupied a similarly pivotal role within Sweden's newspaper industry and throughout the Nordic region. The company was founded by a Norwegian shipowner, Cornelius Bull (1878–1931), who visited the United States on a business trip in the late 1920s and was reportedly impressed by how American newspaper columnists and comic strips appeared in so many newspapers sold throughout the country. After consulting several newspaper publishers about the feature syndication business, Bull approached both King Features Syndicate and the Ledger Syndicate and offered to represent them in Norway, Sweden, Denmark, and Finland (Bulls Press, 1994: 4–5).

Returning to Norway in 1929, he established Bulls Press as the first feature syndicate offering editorial copy, comic strips, and prefabricated advertisement layouts and illustrations to newspapers throughout Scandinavia, and he opened the company's first Stockholm office later that year. Following Bull's premature death from heart disease in 1931, Bjarne Steinsvik (1899–1968), one of Bull's closest associates, was appointed president of the company, a position he held for nearly four decades (Bulls Press, 1994: 4–5). The company encouraged the Stockholm newspaper *Aftonbladet* (est. 1830) to develop a daily, full-page comic-strip section modeled on the American newspaper format. Launched on May 28, 1934, and featuring several of King Features' series (including E. C. Segar's *Popeye* and Russ Westover's *Tillie the Toiler*), the comic-strip section was the first of its kind to appear in Swedish newspapers (*Newsweek*, 1934: 23; Bulls Press, 2004: n.p.; Gustafsson and Rydén, 2010: 205).

King Features Syndicates' expansion into India took a different path. With no domestic equivalent of the Yaffa Syndicate or Bulls Press evidently in existence,[2] King Features instead dealt directly with Bennett, Coleman & Co., which owned *The Times of India* (est. 1861), the country's largest-selling English-language newspaper. King Features' comic strips began appearing in the weekend edition *Sunday Times of India*, commencing with *Felix the Cat* in 1948. At first, Bennett, Coleman & Co. seemed content to secure comic strips from competing feature syndicates, as *Felix the Cat* shared space with a comic-strip adaptation of Robert Louis Stevenson's novel *Treasure Island* furnished by United International Features (U.S.), in the *Sunday Times*' children's section. Ultimately, Bennett, Coleman did not seek to act as King Features' local agent or regional sales representative. Instead, Bennett, Coleman opted to use its relationship with King Features to its own advantage, using the company's roster of comic-strip characters to expand and diversify its postwar publishing activities.

King Features Syndicate no doubt benefited from its timely entry into the Australian, Swedish, and Indian markets by staying ahead of its American competitors and securing the support of international business partners, who (with the exception of Bennett, Coleman & Co.) aggressively promoted the company's editorial products to local media outlets. But there were other, less tangible factors which might explain why King Features Syndicate was able to secure a dominant place within these three countries.

American comic strips, as they evolved throughout the 1920s and 1930s, were at once both familiar and exotic to foreign audiences. In some respects, they bore a superficial resemblance to the humorous cartoons that had long been staple features of local magazines and newspapers since the late nineteenth and early twentieth centuries, such as *The Bulletin* (Australia, 1880–2008) and *Allt för Alla* (*Everything for Everybody*, Sweden, est. 1912). Yet most of the cartoons appearing in these magazines usually relied on typeset captions or dialogue placed beneath a single illustration to convey its comedic message. The celebrated Swedish comic strip *91:an* (*no. 91*), about an oafish army conscript, is a case in point. Created in 1932 by Rudolf Peterson (1896–1970) for *Allt för Alla*, *91:an* was originally drawn as a series of pictures accompanied by rhyming captions, which gave it the appearance of a children's story book (Strömberg, 2010: 34). By contrast, American comic strips integrated text and image within a series of illustrated panels, which were used to tell brief, self-contained humorous episodes. So commonplace has this technique become that it is perhaps difficult for present-day audiences to appreciate the impact of this visual storytelling innovation. These comic strips were, in their own way, as excitingly modern as other American entertainments of their era, such as motion-picture "talkies" and jazz music.

American comic strips better captured the everyday social mores of urban life as it was experienced by newspaper audiences living in metropolitan centers, in ways that local cartoonists (or their editors) were sometimes slow to recognize or exploit. In Australia, for example, comical situations involving stereotypical outback characters, such as itinerant workers ("swaggies") and aboriginal farmhands, formed the basis for many cartoons published in such journals as *Melbourne Punch* (1855–1925) and *Aussie* (1920–32) well into the 1920s (Lindesay, 1983: 11–17, 95–101).

Such rustic themes seemed increasingly parochial when compared with imported American comic strips. A key example from this period was *Bringing Up Father* (1913), created by George McManus (1884–1954), which starred Maggie and Jiggs, two penniless immigrants who unexpectedly became members of the nouveau riche class. McManus's artwork embodied streamlined, Art Deco elegance, which lent the series a sophisticated patina that belied the characters' vaudeville antics. While the violent and stormy relationship between Maggie and Jiggs puzzled some readers—Danish audiences found the idea of a wife abusing her husband baffling, but amusing (*Newsweek*, 1934: 23)—*Bringing Up Father* was, prior to World War II, King Features Syndicate's most widely read comic strip, appearing in over 600 newspapers worldwide (Koenigsberg, 1941: 448).

The strip's success was not lost on foreign cartoonists and publishers; during the 1930s *Saptahik Hindustan*, a Hindi weekly based in Delhi, introduced a comic strip that gave vent to "the problems that nag . . . middle-class families in their day-to-day life" (Joshi, 1986: 213). The Swedish cartoonist Rune Moberg (1912–1999) acknowledged that *Bringing Up Father* influenced his creation of the comic-strip version of *Lilla Fridolf* (*Little Fridolf*) in 1955, starring the rotund, henpecked husband who had originally appeared as a character in a radio play (Strömberg, 2010: 35). The popularity of *Bringing Up Father* reflected the commercial and aesthetic inroads made by American comic strips abroad throughout the 1930s. Its success allowed King Features Syndicate to emphasize the universality of (American) humor as a key selling point when promoting its comic strips to international clients.[3]

Newspapers themselves were becoming a more visual medium, as advances in printing technology allowed them to reproduce halftone photographs and illustrations with greater clarity, while new typeface designs and simpler, clearer page layouts further transformed their overall appearance.

Comic strips, therefore, became an integral part of the new emphasis on graphically oriented newspaper packaging and design. Nor was this trend confined solely to the "popular" press; in Australia, for example, K. S. Inglis claims that as the twentieth century progressed, both broadsheets and tabloids alike subscribed to the "law of increasing brightness," whereby "the headlines have grown higher . . . the display advertisements more seductive . . . [and] the photographs larger and more vivid" (1962: 152).

Syndicated American comic strips also promised financial benefits for international newspaper clients. The growing emphasis on domestic comedy scenarios in American strips, with a recurring cast of characters, was designed to make reading "the funnies" a habit-forming experience for American newspaper buyers; foreign newspapers clearly hoped this ritual could be encouraged locally. Indeed, overseas newspaper staff had long taken a keen interest in American industry developments; Swedish journalists and editors who visited the United States during the late nineteenth century brought back with them news of the editorial innovations then being unfurled by Pulitzer and Hearst in New York City (Gustafsson and Rydén, 2010: 135–36). In Australia, David Yaffa's trade journal, *Newspaper News*, kept the local industry abreast of the latest trends in American newspaper publishing. American comic strips were also cheap and in plentiful supply; by the early 1930s, feature syndicates could already draw upon dozens of series, which had several years' worth of backdated daily and Sunday newspaper episodes that could be supplied to foreign clients at a fraction of their original production cost. Sometimes overseas newspapers had little choice but to use syndicated American content, especially in markets where local writers and illustrators were as yet unschooled in the techniques and traditions of modern American comic-strip storytelling. Conversely, overseas publishers would sometimes emulate American comic strips in their efforts to produce equivalent domestic series. In 1920, the Australian newspaper *Smith's Weekly* acquired samples of the American comic strip *The Gumps* to provide its staff cartoonist Stan Cross (1888–1977) with the template for developing an equivalent Australian domestic comedy strip, titled *You & Me* (Ryan, 1979: 18).

It was in this context that overseas intermediaries, such as the Yaffa Syndicate and Bulls Press, played a crucial role in brokering the international acceptance of American comic strips. They typically possessed greater local knowledge of domestic media markets and could readily identify and cultivate strategic industry contacts on behalf of their American business partners. There were also practical advantages in using overseas representatives: they could sell new features, collect licensing revenues, and arrange the distribution of syndicated content to local clients more cheaply and efficiently than American syndicates could ever hope to from afar. Local syndicates were also necessary to translate and otherwise modify American comic strips in ways that made them more palatable to international audiences. In the case of *Bringing Up Father*, Jiggs's fondness for corned beef and steamed cabbage was replaced by rice and fish for Chinese readers, and became *boeuf miroton* for the benefit of French audiences (McManus and La Cossitt, 1952: 66). Even English-language markets occasionally requested changes to American idioms and expressions; in Australia, *Flash Gordon* was renamed *Speed Gordon* (Couperie and Horn, 1968: 137),[4] while references to American dollars and cents were replaced with the then-equivalent Australian currency units of pounds, shillings, and pence (Holden, 1962: 159).

Daily newspapers were not the only print media outlets to embrace the American comic strip. The "periodical press," comprising weekly and monthly magazines, was equally keen to exploit this new medium's potential in attracting readers and boosting circulation figures—which, as with newspapers, were essential requirements for securing advertising revenue. But as will become clear, women's magazines—rather than newspapers—would become largely responsible for introducing *The Phantom* to a generation of readers in Australia, India, and Sweden.

Women's Magazines—For All the Family

"Periodical magazines" first appeared in the eighteenth century and initially catered to the "cultural interests of the gentry," but their readership gradually evolved into a "mass market of high commercial value and enormous breadth of coverage by the early twentieth century" (McQuail, 2005: 31). Despite the proliferation of specialized titles catering to niche markets, Denis McQuail maintains that the "periodical magazine still belongs largely to the domestic and personal sphere" (2005: 31)—an indirect reference to the women's-interest magazines which have long dominated this publishing category. Yet neither the volume nor the popularity of women's magazines, already evident by the mid-twentieth century, could automatically ensure that they received serious consideration from media observers. Frank S. Greenop's *History of Magazine Publishing in Australia* (1947) is perhaps indicative of contemporaneous attitudes towards women's magazines, which he dismissed as "insignificant . . . journals designed to cater for the never-jaded palates of fashion and film-minded females" (1947: 256). Such chauvinistic disregard ignores the fact that, prior to the arrival of television, many women's magazines were, in practice, consumed as general interest publications by entire households.

The initial placement of *The Phantom* comic strip in women's magazines — in Australia and Sweden, at least — owed something to the growing popularity of Lee Falk's first comic-strip serial, *Mandrake the Magician* (1934). The success of the latter strip helped demonstrate that American-style adventure serials could find an appreciative audience among magazine readers and established Falk's profile as a "brand name" author in overseas markets.

The Phantom made its antipodean debut in *The Australian Woman's Mirror* on September 1, 1936, its front cover inviting readers to "Meet The Phantom!" on page 49. The weekly magazine commenced with the inaugural *Phantom* adventure, "The Singh Brotherhood" (which had yet to reach its conclusion in American newspapers), and compiled five daily newspaper installments into a single, full-page "episode." From the outset, the *Woman's Mirror* marketed *The Phantom* as an adult feature, billing it as an "exciting picture serial" (instead of a "cartoon" or "comic strip") and situating it away from the magazine's children's supplement (*Australian Woman's Mirror*, 1936: 49). The *Woman's Mirror* took deliberate steps to portray *The Phantom* as an Australian, rather than American, comic strip. Aside from replacing American spellings and slang expressions with their "correct" Australian equivalents, the strip's weekly text synopsis referred to Diana Palmer as a "young Sydney girl," while the opening setting was changed from New York Harbor to somewhere "off Sydney Heads" (Falk and Moore, 1938: 5, 9).

When the *Woman's Mirror* purchased the local magazine rights to *The Phantom*, it did so in response to the commercial threat posed by a rival magazine. Launched in 1924 by the proprietor of *The Bulletin*, Henry Kenneth Prior (1893–1967), the *Woman's Mirror* was a modestly priced family magazine that was pitched squarely at Australian housewives, who were awarded prizes for contributing recipes and practical household tips to the magazine. These were published alongside book reviews, short stories, and feature articles emphasizing "the domestic sciences" (Lindesay, 1983: 103). Despite its drab appearance, the *Woman's Mirror* garnered a sizable following and, within a year of its debut, boasted the highest circulation of any weekly periodical in Australia (Rolfe, 1979: 290).

But its comfortable dominance of the women's magazine market was seriously challenged in June 1933, when Frank Packer launched *The Australian Women's Weekly*. Originally conceived by its founding editor George Warnecke (1894–1981) as a newspaper for women, the *Women's Weekly* was an innovative blend of topical news stories and "traditional" women's features, such as society pages, fashion supplements, and a gardening section. Selling for just two pence (one penny less than its rivals, including the *Woman's Mirror*), the *Women's Weekly* was an immediate success and sold over 121,000 copies of its debut issue—well ahead of the pre-launch estimates of 50,000 copies (Griffen-Foley, 1999: 25, 27–28).

But the *Weekly*'s success also invited competition from rival publishers; even though the magazine's circulation had already climbed to over 157,000 by 1934 (Rolfe, 1979: 300), both Packer and Warnecke were reportedly concerned about Associated Newspapers' plans to relaunch its ailing *Woman's Budget* as the upmarket *Woman* magazine in December of that year (Griffen-Foley, 1999: 40). In anticipation, new editorial features were planned for the *Women's Weekly*, including its first comic strip, Lee Falk's *Mandrake the Magician*. Warnecke, however, had grave reservations about this newest addition to the magazine:

I felt at first that *Mandrake* wasn't homely enough for our readers and too American . . . But we were urgently in need of an adult strip and *Mandrake* was the best then available. (Quoted in O'Brien, 1982: 55)

Reassured by David Yaffa that the series was gaining popularity in the United States (where it had debuted in June 1934), Packer agreed to pay the Yaffa Syndicate A£5.00 for each weekly installment of *Mandrake the Magician*, which debuted in December 1934 and would become one of the magazine's most-read features for decades to come (O'Brien, 1982: 55). Thus, the combination of their artificially low unit cost, along with the perceived dearth of a suitable local equivalent, gave imported American comic strips a competitive advantage in Australia, as elsewhere.

The Australian Woman's Mirror was therefore understandably keen to purchase the magazine serial rights to Falk's newest comic strip—*The Phantom*

— from the Yaffa Syndicate, in the hopes of fending off its biggest rival. Nevertheless, the success of *Mandrake the Magician* fed mounting public concerns over the corrosive influence of American culture within Australian society. The Cultural Defence Committee, founded by the Fellowship of Australian Writers, launched a blistering attack on the moral effects of imported American comic strips. Its 1935 pamphlet, *Mental Rubbish from Overseas*, condemned *Mandrake the Magician* in particular as an outrage not only to "common sense and science, but also common morality and intellectual decency" (Cultural Defence Committee, 1935: 5). Such comic strips were, according to the committee, the product of a debauched society where belief in witchcraft and demonology, brought to America by superstitious European immigrants, "found new stimulus from contact with Aframerican negro [*sic*] ideas of voodoo" (1935: 5). This chorus of disapproval, briefly silenced for the duration of World War II, would eventually grow louder in Australia, Sweden, and India in the postwar era.

The debut of *The Phantom* in Sweden's *Vecko-Revyn* (*Weekly Review*) magazine arose out of equally dramatic changes that were sweeping the publishing landscape. The Bonnier group (Bonnier AB), Sweden's oldest and largest media business, traced its origins back to Denmark in 1804, when Gerhard Bonnier (born Gutkint Hirschel, 1788–1862) opened a bookshop, to which he later added a lending library and publishing business in Copenhagen. It was under the direction of his son Albert Bonnier (1820–1900) that the foundations for the company's future growth were first laid (Larson, Lindgren, and Nyberg, 2008: 78). Moving to Stockholm in 1837, he established his own publishing company, Albert Bonniers Förlag, which specialized in subjects ignored by other publishers, such as child-rearing books and popular ballad collections (Gedin, 1977: 75). Greater economic prosperity in Sweden fostered the growth of a middle-class reading public during the mid- to late nineteenth century, prompting Bonnier to launch *Europeiska följetongen* (*European Serial Novel*), which published translated works by notable European authors (Gedin, 1977: 75–76). The company also purchased an initial block of shares in *Dagens Nyheter* (*Today's News*, est. 1864), one of Sweden's largest daily newspapers, and eventually became its principal owner in the 1920s (Larson, Lindgren, and Nyberg, 2008: 79).

Yet it was the explosive growth of the "popular weekly press" during the

1920s which posed both the greatest threat to, and opportunity for, the Bonnier group. Catering to general family readerships and niche audiences alike, this new generation of popular magazines emphasized colorful illustrations and eye-catching photographs. The largest and most successful of the "popular press" publishers was Åhlén & Åkerlund, whose titles included *Husmodern* (*The Housewife*), *Radiolyssnaren* (*The Radio Listener*), and *Film-Journalen* (*The Film Journal*). The company's now-sole owner, Erik Åkerlund (1877–1940), sold the firm to Bonnier in 1929, which maintained Åhlén & Åkerlund as a subsidiary firm. With this acquisition, the Bonnier group "had taken a decisive step towards becoming a modern-style media conglomerate" (Gustafsson and Rydén, 2010: 195).

Nonetheless, the purchase of Åhlén & Åkerlund was greeted with some trepidation within Bonnier family circles; not only did the purchase represent a significant financial gamble for the company, but it also highlighted the commercial threat that these new magazines posed to Bonnier's traditional publishing interests. Karl-Otto Bonnier (1856–1941), son of Albert Bonnier, expressed the dilemma in these terms:

> We felt though, more and more . . . how the huge sales of weekly magazines encroached on the sales of books . . . we had the feeling that the future belonged to the weekly press—insofar as the masses and their reading was concerned—rather than to books. (Quoted in Gedin, 1977: 79)

Bonnier's acquisition of Åhlén & Åkerlund was therefore both a defensive as well as an opportunistic maneuver, which allowed the company to stave off further losses to the popular weekly press by, in turn, becoming Sweden's dominant magazine publisher.

One of the first titles to be launched under Bonnier's newly incorporated magazine division was *Vecko-Revyn* in 1935. Conceived as a more youthful, vibrant counterpart to the literary *Vecko-Journalen* (*Weekly Journal*, est. 1914), *Vecko-Revyn* was an avowedly "modern" women's magazine which placed great emphasis on glamorous photography and lively coverage of fashion and entertainment news (Gustafsson and Rydén, 2010: 195, 206). While it was never as explicit as the *Woman's Mirror* in its attempts to promote *The Phantom* as an "adult" serial, *Vecko-Revyn* nonetheless took deliberate steps to ensure that its newest feature would appeal to its female readership. The first full-page installment of *Fantomen* (*The Phantom*) appeared in *Vecko-Revyn* on May 26, 1940; printed in red and green duotones, it reprinted (albeit in edited form) the first three daily episodes of the 1938 story line "Adventure in Algiers" (Falk and Moore, 1989a [1938]: 89–98). It helpfully began with a four-panel prelude, "The Story of The Phantom," which explained the character's origins and ancestral legacy. The story then proceeded with Diana Palmer's excited response to the Phantom's impending arrival, which provoked a stern rebuke from her Aunt Lily, who forbade Diana from marrying this "mysterious person [who] is obviously a fortune hunter" (Falk and Moore, 1989b [1938]: 89). With this first weekly episode, *Vecko-Revyn* was able to foreground the romantic drama that lay at the heart of *Fantomen*, confident that it would resonate with its readership.

The debut of *Fantomen* in 1940 coincided with the magazine's surging popularity throughout World War II; by 1945 *Vecko-Revyn* had an estimated circulation of 216,000 readers, placing it comfortably ahead of older, established "family" magazines such as *Hemmets Veckotiding* (*The Home Weekly Magazine*) and *Allas Veckotiding* (*Everyone's Weekly Magazine*), both published by the rival firm Allhem (Sandlund, 2001: 364). *Vecko-Revyn's* success would continue unabated throughout the decade, with weekly sales surpassing 400,000 copies by the early 1950s (Gustafsson and Rydén, 2010: 256). Leaving aside the intrinsic appeal of the strip itself, it seems safe to suggest that *Fantomen* achieved the level of public recognition that it did because of its prominent placement in Sweden's most popular women's magazine.[5]

The Phantom came considerably later to India and took a somewhat different route to reach this vast new market. When the opening episode of *The Phantom* story titled "The Rope People" (Falk and McCoy, 1998b [1951]: 128–49) first appeared in *The Illustrated Weekly of India* on February 24, 1952, both the magazine and its publisher had undergone significant changes in the few short years since India had gained independence from Great Britain. For over a century, Bennett, Coleman & Co. was the British-owned publisher of *The Times of India*, the largest-selling English-language newspaper in the country. It had grown out of *The Bombay Times and Journal of Commerce*, a twice-weekly publication launched by a consortium of British firms and individual investors in 1838 (Barns, 1940: 228–29; Pande, 2011: n.p.). *The Bombay Times* was subsequently amalgamated with two other English-language newspapers in 1859 and was eventually relaunched as *The Times of India* in September 1861 (Barns, 1940: 270; Natarajan, 1962: 83, 116).

When Thomas Bennett was appointed editor of *The Times of India* in 1892, the company was restructured and renamed Bennett, Coleman & Co.[6] and undertook a program of modernization and expansion, including the construction of new editorial offices and the installation of new printing presses (Natarajan, 1962: 170). The newspaper's illustrated weekly supplement—first published in January 1880—was redesigned and relaunched as *The Times of India Illustrated Weekly* in 1901 (Barns, 1940: 307). By the 1920s, *The Illustrated Weekly of India* (as it was now called) had become India's "main popular organ of non-political journalism," which catered to the growing (middle-class) public's interest in science, technology, and commerce (Natarajan, 1962: 190). This lucrative demographic proved particularly receptive to Western-style media formats.

Bennett, Coleman & Co. remained in British hands until 1946, when it was purchased by Ramkrishna Dalmia (1893–1978), a colorful and eccentric Calcutta (Kolkata) stock market speculator and industrialist who used to consult astrologers prior to making major investment decisions (Sahni, 1974: 195). Dalmia subsequently sold the firm to his son-in-law, Sahu Shanto Prasad Jain, in 1948, whose family still retains control of The Times of India Group, as it is now known (Pande, 2011: n.p.). By 1947, when India gained independence from Great Britain, the *Illustrated Weekly* had become the nation's most popular magazine, with weekly sales of 50,000 copies outstripping those of its nearest rival, the *Orient Illustrated Weekly*, which had estimated sales of 30,000 copies (Taussig, 1947: 31). By now, the magazine was increasingly modeled after Western photojournalism magazines such as *Life* (U.S.) and *Picture Post* (U.K.), and it billed itself as "Asia's Finest Picture Magazine." Western-style comics and cartoons were steadily becoming a regular (if not integral) feature of India's English-language "periodical press" (Malhan, 1980: 19). This was certainly true of the *Illustrated Weekly*, which now devoted a single, full-color page to American comic strips. *The Illustrated Weekly*, however, clearly regarded *The Phantom* (and comic strips generally) as essentially children's fare and promoted its comic-strip page in tandem with its children's supplement, "The Young Folk's League." This was in contrast to Sweden and Australia, where *Vecko-Revyn* and *The Australian Woman's Mirror* both promoted *The Phantom* as an "adult" comic-strip serial.

The Phantom: Romantic Hero for the Middle Class

Of course, knowing how and when *The Phantom* comic strip came to be published in these foreign magazines is one thing; understanding *why* these publications chose *The Phantom* is an altogether more speculative matter. Yet it is one worth exploring further, if only to understand how the Phantom's lengthy affiliation with these magazines helped secure readers' lifelong devotion to "The Ghost Who Walks" throughout Australia, Sweden, and India.

In aesthetic terms, comic strips complemented the visual appeal of such magazines as *Vecko-Revyn* and the *Illustrated Weekly*, which made eye-catching photography and colorful illustrations a cornerstone of their editorial appeal. Conversely, the addition of *The Phantom* introduced a much-needed, dynamic visual component to the somewhat drab *Woman's Mirror*, which now faced serious competition from the colorful and stylish *Women's Weekly*. Adventure-serial comic strips also became increasingly sophisticated graphic narratives throughout the 1930s and 1940s and mirrored the visual excitement common to many Hollywood movies of that era, which were also extensively documented in these magazines.

Mention should also be made of the Phantom's role as a romantic hero. Many of Lee Falk's earliest story lines (ca. 1936–40) dwelt on the "cliff-hanger" love affair between the Phantom and Diana Palmer. A mysterious, masked lover, the Phantom would frequently appear out of the shadows and seize Diana in a passionate embrace before departing once again on a perilous mission. They were frequently separated (or threatened) by nefarious villains, or (just as effectively) by Diana's interfering Aunt Lily, who plotted to find a wealthy bachelor for her niece, usually with disastrous results. Competing with the Phantom for Diana's affections were two dashing army officers, Captain Melville Horton and Lieutenant Byron. The tempestuous relationship between the Phantom, Diana, and her uniformed suitors made *The Phantom* a perfect companion piece to the romantic fiction serials that were already popular staples in such magazines as the *Woman's Mirror*.

These factors go some way towards explaining why *The Phantom* was deemed appropriate for women's magazines and their readers; but how did its inclusion in such publications ultimately aid the commercial success of *The Phantom*? To begin with, these magazines, unlike newspapers, were distributed nationally and could reach audiences well beyond metropolitan centers, thus ensuring that *The Phantom* circulated among a genuinely national read-ership. Even though these magazines were ostensibly meant for women, they were frequently read by most members of the "typical" family household. By the late 1950s, market research had confirmed that *The Australian Women's Weekly* was read by one husband in three (Davies and Encel, 1965: 224), while anecdotal accounts from retailers disclosed that husbands and sons fought over the latest issue of the *Women's Weekly* just to read *Mandrake the Magician* (Harvey, 1945: 570). There is little reason to suggest that similar scenes did not occur in households that received the *Woman's Mirror* instead. Eileen Gomm recalled how, as a child, she used to "read my mother's copy of the *Woman's Mirror* and anxiously check-up on The Phantom's adventures" well before the character appeared in his own comic magazine (1997: 97). Anders Yngve Pers's 1966 study of the Swedish press claimed that 25–30 percent of most Swedish women's magazine readers were male (1966: 16, 18).[7] So even though *The Phantom* may have been initially promoted as "adult" entertain-ment, principally intended for a female readership, it scored an avid following among adult male household members and young children, too.

The *Illustrated Weekly of India*, however, was never intended to be exclu-sively for women; its publisher, Bennett, Coleman & Co., chose to reach that market through the movie magazine *Filmfare* (1953) and *Femina* (1959), an upmarket women's magazine comparable to *Vecko-Revyn* (Natarajan, 1997: 256–57). A brief survey of the issue cover-dated February 24, 1952 (in which *The Phantom* first appeared) indicates that the *Illustrated Weekly* aimed for a broader, more inclusive readership. Joining such regular features as the cross-word puzzle, book reviews, and astrology forecasts was a special report on the death of King George VI, the serialized life story of Lady Mountbatten, and photographic essays about Rhodesian tobacco farms and the temples of Ang-kor Wat. The magazine's advertisements, for such varied products as home-tuition courses, men's business shirts, chocolate biscuits, and hair-removal products, indicate that it was intended largely for a prosperous (English-speaking) middle-class, family readership. Comic strips like *The Phantom*, therefore, were ostensibly included for the benefit of children, rather than adults — but it would not be unreasonable to suggest that at least some adults also read *The Phantom*, if only as a guilty pleasure to be savored when no other family members were present.

The Phantom became an integral part of all three magazines for decades thereafter even as they changed their demographic focus or altered their format. The Phantom's continued exposure in these magazines would yield promotional dividends for the character's eventual transition to comic books after World War II, but it also ensured his popular status in other, more subtle ways. The Phantom's inclusion in these conservative mass-market magazines meant he received an unspoken endorsement as a "wholesome" character who appealed to the entire family in ways that other American superheroes (largely confined to "disreputable" comic books) could rarely hope to match.

The international syndication of *The Phantom* comic strip does, at first glance, seem to conform with the "largely one-directional flow of information from core to periphery" which was central to the enduring conception of American cultural imperialism (Schiller, 1976: 6). Yet as we have seen, the international acceptance of American comic strips was far from assured, and was fraught with commercial risk and uncertainty. Foreign intermediaries were needed to tailor American comics for domestic tastes and to identify media outlets unique to their respective markets, which were prepared to gamble on their success. This unpredictable, and sometimes chaotic, process meant that few—if any—of the companies which invested in *The Phantom* comic strip could have anticipated its eventual success. Nor could they have foreseen how the Phantom would spur the development of domestic comic-book industries in Australia, Sweden, and India in ways that allowed these countries to become both "centers" and "peripheries" in the global circulation of American comics culture.

CHAPTER FOUR

THE "YANK COMICS" INVASION

arroll Rheinstrom's job was to sell superheroes to the world. As the head of MacFadden Publications International, Rheinstrom acted as the overseas distributor for National Periodical Publications, whose roster of comic-book characters included Superman, Batman, and Wonder Woman. Yet not even their incredible powers could overcome foreign publishers' early indifference to American superheroes. After making his first trip to Sweden in the late 1940s, Rheinstrom recalled:

> I was turned down by every publisher I visited. When I returned to my hotel, my Swedish interpreter, a clerk from the American embassy, told me, "Mr. Rheinstrom, I'm only a clerk. I think these publishers are all crazy. These magazines would be terrific money-makers. Don't laugh at me, but someday I will be your publisher in Sweden." And one year later, he was. (Quoted in Marx, ed., 1985: 19)

Unbeknownst to Rheinstrom, the self-effacing embassy clerk, T. Armas Morby (1909–1980), had established his own public relations company in 1938 and had made invaluable American contacts in his capacity as press and publicity liaison for Allied armed forces' newspapers during World War II (Berglund, n.d.; Gustafsson and Rydén, 2010: 262). After the war Morby formed a new publishing company, Press & Publicity AB, to launch his first comic book, *Seriemagasinet* (*The Comic Strip Magazine*), in January 1948. Capitalizing on its early success, Morby launched Swedish editions of *Superman* (*Stålmannen*, 1949) and *Batman* (*Läderlappen*, 1951), their popularity cementing Press & Publicity's position as Sweden's largest comic-book publisher by the mid-1950s (Bejerot, 1954: 82; Gustafsson and Rydén, 2010: 262).

However apocryphal it may sound, this story nonetheless demonstrates the cultural barriers and the commercial opportunities that confronted American newspaper feature syndicates and comic-magazine publishers as they sought entry into new foreign markets. For these American media companies were not so much selling a physical commodity, but the very idea of the comic book itself to countries that had little or no direct experience of this new form of illustrated periodical.

The explosive growth, and attendant popularity, of American comic magazines in Australia, Sweden, and India suggests a narrative of untrammeled commercial success. But as we will see, a combination of economic, regulatory, and cultural factors meant that American-style comic books had to be modified in order to meet the unique conditions of these three countries both prior to and during World War II. While this new generation of American comic books was wildly acclaimed by their intended audience, they were roundly condemned by parents and educators, prompting foreign governments to adopt extraordinary measures designed to curb the publication and sale of "objectionable" comics to children. Contemporary critics were quick to label comic books as a uniquely American phenomenon, one that was alien to the values and aspirations of other nations. Ironically, the popularity of American comics generally, and *The Phantom* in particular, galvanized domestic comic-book production in Australia, Sweden, and India and provided new creative opportunities and commercial outlets for local publishers, writers, and illustrators throughout the postwar era.

Exporting American Comics, 1938–1945

The international circulation of American comic strips during the 1920s and 1930s was made possible through alliances struck between American feature syndicates and their licensed overseas representatives, who in turn sold comic strips to local newspapers and periodicals. American comic books, however, reached foreign shores during the mid- to late 1930s on an infrequent, even ad hoc basis through less formal distribution channels. In some instances, American and international press syndicates collaborated in repackaging American comic strips as periodicals for resale in foreign markets. Although these periodicals tried to convey the appearance of imported American comic books, they nonetheless conformed to local publishing industry conditions and practices that were often quite different from those prevalent in the United States.

Australia's initial exposure to American comic books demonstrates how this new medium fanned outward from America to English-speaking countries prior to World War II. By the mid-1930s, Australia had already become a lucrative market for unsold American magazines that were "dumped" on the local market (Coleman, 1963: 146). Towards the end of the decade, these back-dated magazines were being joined by ever-growing quantities of imported American comic books, which were distributed via railway station bookstalls and newsagents, or through selected discount retail chains, which sold three comic books for one shilling (Ryan, 1979: 150, 154).

These were by no means the first, nor the only, example of children's periodicals available to Australian readers. *Pals* (ca. 1920–25), a children's magazine published by Melbourne's Herald & Weekly Times newspaper group, featured a mixture of illustrated fiction serials and occasional cartoons that was clearly modeled on imported British "children's papers," such as *Gem* and *Magnet* (Lindesay, 1983: 119, 123). Throughout the 1930s, successive Australian children's magazines, such as *The Kookaburra* (ca. 1931–32), *Fatty Finn's Weekly* (1934), and *The Comet* (ca. 1936–37), made greater use of comic-strip serials, but they were not yet "comic books" as we recognize them today (Gordon, 1998b: 6–9).

Having introduced the American adventure-serial comic strip to local audiences, Australian women's magazines would now become pioneering comic-book publishers. Fitchett Brothers (Melbourne) added the American science fiction comic *Buck Rogers in the 25th Century* to its popular women's magazine, *The New Idea*, in April 1936 — just months before the Phantom's debut in the *Woman's Mirror*. Shortly thereafter, Fitchett Brothers released the first issue of *The Adventures of Buck Rogers* in November, making it the first locally published example of an American-style comic magazine. It was the first successful comic book of its kind in Australia, and remained in print until 1953.

Spurred on by his rival's success in this new market, Henry Kenneth Prior unveiled *The Phantom* magazine in May 1938, the front cover announcing its presentation of the "thrilling picture story reprinted from The Australian Woman's Mirror." Sensing that *The Phantom* would, like the *Woman's Mirror*, prove popular with the whole family, the magazine featured content intended for both children and adults. The fourth issue included pro-motions for the *Woman's Mirror*'s "Piccaninnies" children's page, together with advertisements for McKenzie's porridge, Heenzo cough medicine, and the *Woman's Mirror Cookery Book* (young readers were urged to "show this page to mum!"). The magazine's somber covers and black-and-white interiors reflected the austere production values common to most Australian comic books of the period.

Because it did not share a common language with the United States, Swe-den never experienced the physical influx of imported American comic books seen in Australia during the late 1930s. Nonetheless, translated versions of American comic strips figured prominently in many of the earliest Swedish comic books released prior to World War II. They were initially modeled on the popular Christmas album (*julalbum*) that had been a staple children's gift since the late nineteenth century. Today, the oldest surviving *julalbum* is *Jul-stämning*, first published by Åhlén & Åkerlund in 1906 and now published by Jultidnings Förlaget, a division of Bokförlaget Semic (Strömberg, 2010: 25). Featuring illustrated stories, cartoons, and puzzles, these Christmas albums were sold door-to-door by schoolchildren, who received a commission (in the form of money or gifts) from publishers and distributors based on the number of orders they obtained, and this remains a traditional Christmas practice in Sweden to this day.

Åhlén & Åkerlund began publishing Christmas albums featuring Swed-ish comic-strip characters, commencing with *Adamson* (1921), created by Oscar Jacobson (1885–1945) for the humor magazine *Söndags-Nisse* (Ström-berg, 2010: 19). Following the company's acquisition by the Bonnier group in 1929, Åhlén & Åkerlund introduced Christmas albums featuring Amer-ican comic-strip characters, including Popeye (*Karl-Alfred*, 1936) and Walt Disney's Donald Duck (*Kalle Ankas Julbok*, 1941). However, the company's attempts to popularize American-style comic magazines in Sweden were not immediately successful. Launched in 1937, *Musse Pigg Tidningen* (*Mickey Mouse Weekly*) was modeled on the Disney-licensed British magazine of the same name (Gifford, 1984: 52–53). Despite public awareness of both Mickey Mouse and the Disney "brand," the magazine, containing a selection of Brit-ish and Swedish-drawn comic strips, ceased publication in 1938 (Bejerot, 1954: 80; Pilcher and Brooks, 2005: 244).

Bulls Press played a key role in furnishing American comic strips for these

Christmas albums, and it continued to provide Åhlén & Åkerlund with new adventure-serials from King Features Syndicate for subsequent titles, including *Flash Gordon* (*Blixt Gordon*, 1941), *Prince Valiant* (*Prins Valiant*, 1942), and Lee Falk's *Mandrake the Magician* (*Mandrake*, 1945). Yet none of these would ever match the enduring popularity of *The Phantom* album (*Fantomen*, 1944), which continues to be published every year by Jultidnings Förlaget. The first *Fantomen* album contained an edited version of Lee Falk's *Phantom* adventure "The Golden Circle" (Falk and Moore, 1989c [1939–40]: 6–46), which had been previously serialized in *Vecko-Revyn* during 1940–41. Åhlén & Åkerlund used the Christmas album to cross-promote the *Fantomen* comic strip; the 1946 edition urged readers to follow the "excitement-charged adventures" of Fantomen, who appears "like a flash every week in *Vecko-Revyn*."

The use of American comic strips in these early Australian and Swedish comic magazines would have continued unabated were it not for the economic disruptions caused by World War II. Yet the war did not entirely arrest the international circulation of American comic strips; that they continued to appear in overseas publications is perhaps testament to the international popularity of American comic-strip characters, as well as the determination of American feature syndicates and their international partners to pursue their business interests as best they could, regardless of wartime constraints.

The economic consequences of war were already being felt by King Features Syndicate through its exposure to foreign markets, long before the Japanese attack on Pearl Harbor. Shortly after Australia joined Great Britain in declaring war against Germany in September 1939, the Commonwealth government introduced import licensing restrictions that prohibited the importation of "unnecessary goods" (such as printed matter) from non-sterling currency markets — chiefly the United States and Canada (Butlin, 1955: 115–22; Johnson-Woods, 2006: 114). These restrictions, designed to conserve local sterling currency reserves needed for Australia's war effort, led to bans on both imported American comic magazines (*The Argus*, 1940: 11) and syndicated comic-strip artwork intended for publication within Australia (*Courier-Mail*, 1940: 2). These measures were soon followed by the Commonwealth government's decision in 1940 to ration newsprint supplies and ban the production of any new, ongoing periodicals or newspapers (Butlin, 1955: 458–59).

These restrictions jeopardized the supply of content from King Features Syndicate to its Australasian representative, David Yaffa, but such wartime controls were not always rigorously enforced, nor were their effects as onerous as anticipated. For example, in February 1940 the *Woman's Mirror* advised readers that stocks of the fourth edition of *The Phantom* magazine would be limited "owing to paper restrictions." The fifth and final issue of *The Phantom* comic, released in September 1940, urged readers to continue following the character in the *Woman's Mirror*. *The Phantom* magazine was presumably canceled so that Henry Kenneth Prior could preserve his newsprint allocation for producing the *Woman's Mirror* and *The Bulletin* instead.

Despite the embargo on syndicated American comic strips, *The Phantom* continued to appear in the *Woman's Mirror* for the duration of the war. Nor was this an isolated case; according to the Australian Journalists' Association (AJA), not only did many prewar American comic strips continue to appear in local newspapers from 1940 to 1945, but several newspapers managed to obtain new American features for their comic-strip sections, in blatant defiance of wartime restrictions. The AJA also pointed out that several Australian publishers continued to release new "comic strip magazines" featuring material "imported from America" (ca. 1945: 17–19).[1] That many of the comic strips cited by the AJA—such as *Prince Valiant, Flash Gordon*, and *Mandrake the Magician*—were owned by King Features Syndicate speaks volumes about David Yaffa's determination to ensure the uninterrupted supply of syndicated American press features to his Australasian clients. But enforcing these bans remained difficult, if not impossible; when imported proof-sheets were no longer obtainable, Australian syndicates and publishers simply hired local artists to redraw American comic strips by copying or tracing them directly from U.S. newspaper comic-strip sections (Ryan, 1979: 46).

The Phantom became embroiled in a propaganda war which highlighted the difficult conditions that threatened King Features' commercial interests in the Scandinavian market. Bulls Press had sold *The Phantom* to Norway's *Aftenposten* (*Evening Post*) newspaper, where it appeared as *Fantomet* on November 25, 1939, just a few months prior to the German invasion in April 1940. Following the United States' entry into the war, Norway's commissary government (dominated by the fascist Nasjonal Samling Party) banned the use of American comic strips in Norwegian newspapers in 1942. Bulls Press's Norwegian representative, Einar Wyller, smuggled copies of the latest

Fantomen episodes from Sweden into Norway via boat. The artwork was modified to remove all traces of its American origins prior to being delivered to *Aftenposten* where, in defiance of the newspaper's commissariat-appointed managers, *Fantomet* continued to appear for the duration of the war (Steen, 2011: 337).

However, Bulls Press's decision to circumvent the Norwegian ban on imported American comic strips was driven by economic, rather than political, considerations. Fearful that the war would disrupt access to its Scandinavian markets, Bulls Press used clandestine courier networks to smuggle material to newspapers in occupied territories (Bulls Press, 1994: 9–10). Bulls Press's commitment to its international clients was fueled by deteriorating economic conditions in Sweden. Although Sweden remained neutral during the war, it was not entirely shielded from the political and economic upheavals that arose as the conflict flared across Europe. Germany's naval blockade of the North Sea severed Sweden's vital maritime trade link, leading to sharp reductions of imported goods, which forced the Swedish government to impose widespread rationing in 1942 (Kent, 2008: 234). The war brought mixed blessings to Sweden's newspaper industry; public demand for the latest war news led to increased circulations, but the rising cost of newsprint and printer's ink forced many newspapers to print fewer pages per issue. Many newspapers were thus forced to scrap their weekend supplements and comic-strip sections (Gustafsson and Rydén, 2010: 220), which were key outlets for Bulls Press's syndicated material.[2]

India's wartime experience highlights the informal and irregular channels whereby American comic books circulated throughout the world during the 1940s. India, still under British colonial rule, became a vital source of material supplies and military personnel for Britain's war effort. Following the United States' declaration of war against Japan, India became a strategic operational base for the Allies' South East Asia Command, from where British and American forces launched operations against the Japanese in neighboring Burma (Spear, 1970: 215–16). American soldiers brought with them not only weapons and machines, but comic books as well. Aabid Surti (b. 1935), creator of the famed Indian comic-book hero *Bahadur*, recalled how he received his first-ever comic book (featuring Mickey Mouse) from soldiers traveling through Bombay (Mumbai), who threw copies from the train to children begging for money and food (Sharma, 2011).

There was little evidence of locally published children's periodicals, of any description, in the decade following India's independence from Great Britain in 1947. Aside from the children's supplements appearing in English-language newspapers (such as *The Times of India*), the earliest—and possibly only—example from this period was *Chandamama*, an illustrated "children's paper" edited by the film producer B. Nagi Reddy, and initially published in Telugu and Tamil editions in July 1947 (McLain, 2009a: 158). The bulk of the comic books available to Indian readers following the war would be imported from Great Britain and the United States by local publishers, many of whom had commercial interests in wholesale book distribution and retail bookstalls (Altbach, 1975: 40).

Australia, Sweden, and India would soon become valuable markets for America's comic-book industry, which was now facing some unique challenges arising from its explosive wartime growth. By 1945, approximately 70,000,000 Americans read comic books. While children comprised their largest audience, the Market Research Company of America estimated that 41 percent of men and 28 percent of women between 18 and 30 years of age read comic books as well (Wright, 2001: 57). However, readers abandoned former wartime favorites like *Captain Marvel Adventures*, which once posted sales of 1,000,000 copies per issue in 1943, but saw its sales plummet by 50 percent by 1949 (Goulart, 1986: 17; Wright, 2001: 57). This economic downturn was exacerbated by the demobilization of American soldiers, whose comic-book purchases at military postal exchanges (PXs) had previously exceeded sales of mainstream magazines to service personnel by ten to one (*Newspaper News*, 1946b; Wright, 2001: 57).

American publishers were thus compelled to look abroad in search of untapped foreign markets. Yet attempts to resume the prewar practice of dumping backdated American magazines in English-speaking countries were met with resistance. The Publishers' Export Company, which bought unsold American magazines for international resale, conceded that continuing import licensing restrictions in Australia, New Zealand, and South Africa (which accounted for 25 percent of their sales) greatly hindered its business (*Newspaper News*, 1946a: 1). The changed postwar environment therefore required American comic-book publishers to develop new strategies, and form new international partnerships, that would allow them to circumvent foreign embargoes on imported American magazines.

American Comics in Australia:
The "Peacetime Invasion"

Giving evidence to the Tariff Board inquiry into Australia's publishing industry in November 1945, the Australian magazine publisher Kenneth Murray
acknowledged domestic concerns about the cultural impact of cheaply imported American periodicals. "The Australian mass mind," he argued, "has
unconsciously become conditioned to a foreign sentiment, as the continual
reading of the American viewpoint . . . [induces] contempt for Australian
things" (*Ideas*, 1946: 82). To overcome this problem, Murray suggested that
the Commonwealth government should adopt policies that maintain the
"strict and permanent prohibition of 'dumping' [backdated] magazines in
Australia," as well as encourage "the republication of overseas magazines in
Australia" (*Ideas*, 1946: 81, 83). This would not only create economic opportunities for local publishers and printers, argued Murray, but would foster "the
Australianizing of the publication . . . and the inclusion of purely Australian
material" (*Ideas*, 1946: 83). Murray's anxiety about the influence of American
culture was disingenuous at best. In 1946 Murray commissioned local writers and illustrators to contribute to the acclaimed *Climax Color Comic* series
(1947–48), the first Australian-drawn comic magazine to be printed entirely
in color (Ryan, 1979: 188, 190). High production costs, however, forced Murray to abandon the project in favor of using cheaper American content. And
it was Carroll Rheinstrom's company, MacFadden Publications International,
which furnished Murray with his runaway hit, *Superman All Color Comic*
(1947), which boasted sales of 150,000 copies per issue.

The unprecedented success of *Superman All Color Comic* in many ways set
the parameters for the postwar "boom" in Australian comic-book production.
Eager to satisfy pent-up consumer demand for escapist reading, Australian
publishers scrambled to secure licensing deals with the major American comics publishers and their international representatives. American publishers
overcame the existing ban on imported periodicals by supplying print-ready
artwork (sent through the mail to avoid detection by the Department of Trade
and Customs) to Australian firms, who assembled, printed, and distributed
the comics locally (Patrick, 2012a: 167). By 1949, there were already ninety
individual comic-book titles being published in Australia (*Current Affairs
Bulletin*, 1949: 71). Even though the attrition rates among competing titles

remained high—40 percent of titles available in 1949 had disappeared by 1952 (Connell, Francis, and Skilbeck, 1957: 155)—their numbers continued to swell, reaching 150 titles by 1952 (*Ideas*, 1952: 237).

Ron Forsyth (1907–1991) was well-placed to understand how popular—and profitable—comic books had become in Australia. Prior to the war, Forsyth had joined Frank Packer's Consolidated Press, where he became advertising manager of the *Sunday Telegraph*. After serving with the Australian Army during the war, Forsyth opened a bookstore and commercial lending library in Sydney, where he had ample opportunity to witness the booming comic-book trade firsthand. Forsyth's wife, Sylvia (née Eisen), encouraged him to meet with her friend, David Yaffa, to discuss business opportunities in the comics field. Yaffa informed Forsyth that the only remaining comic strip for which he could offer comic-book publishing rights was *The Phantom*. However, Yaffa stipulated that Forsyth could not reprint any episodes which had been recently published in *The Australian Woman's Mirror*.[3] Undeterred, Forsyth persuaded his brother-in-law, Jack Eisen, along with fellow veterans Lawford "Jim" Richardson (1908–1987) and John Watson, to each invest A£500 to form Frew Publications and purchase the rights to *The Phantom*.[4] The confluence of personal connections, access to capital, and fortuitous timing allowed Frew Publications to thrive in the aggressive business climate of postwar Sydney.

Forsyth assembled the first issue of *The Phantom* at his bookstore premises, which reprinted the 1939 story "The Slave Traders" (Falk and Moore, 1989b [1939]) and went on sale in September 1948. The debut issue reportedly sold out its print run of 50,000 copies, and sales of subsequent issues would climb to 90,000 copies per issue by 1950 (Shedden, 2001; Snowden, 1973: 6). These figures placed *The Phantom* among Australia's top-selling comics, including the local edition of *Walt Disney Comics* (120,000 copies) (*Ideas*, 1948: 190) and the Australian-drawn superhero series *Captain Atom* (100,000 copies) (Ryan, 1979: 190).

The small Australian market made full-color printing prohibitive for all but the largest magazine publishers, and accounted for Frew Publications' thrifty production standards on *The Phantom*, which was printed in black and white and used paper covers instead of the slick, glossy covers common to most Australian comic books of the time. Yet the comic's rough quality seemed to enhance the Phantom's appeal among Australian children, who placed him alongside their favorite heroes from the Saturday movie matinees. As one reader recalled:

> The pictures were simple [and] easy to follow, and left room for the imagination. (I think this is an important contributing factor to The Phantom's long term success). And they were great to color in! The stories were generally interesting and very easy to read . . . As a young boy in the fifties and early sixties, jungle and western adventures in comics and the cinema were top of my—and other boys'—lists. The Phantom fitted into that perfectly, second only to Tarzan! (Male respondent, 50–65 years old, New Zealand, June 19, 2012)

Frew Publications wasted few opportunities to exploit Lee Falk's Australian profile for its commercial advantage. From the outset, *The Phantom* magazine carried the front-cover blurb "By LEE FALK, author of MANDRAKE," to reinforce the author's connection with *Mandrake the Magician*, which was then appearing in *The Australian Women's Weekly*. The company's next major success was *The Phantom Ranger*, an Australian-drawn cowboy comic created by Jeff Wilkinson (1924–2007), modeled on *The Lone Ranger* (Ryan, 1979: 196; Patrick, 2006). *The Phantom Ranger* sold 100,000 copies per issue in Australia, generated a successful range of licensed clothing and accessories, and was produced as a radio serial in 1952 (Jones, 1951: 3; Ryan, 1979: 196; Patrick, 2012a: 168). Frew subsequently chose the Phantom to costar in their new title, *Super Yank Comics* (ca. 1951), to bolster readers' interest in Catman, an American superhero which Frew contracted to be redrawn under license by the Australian cartoonist Lloyd Piper (1922–1983). The success of *The Phantom* provided Frew Publications with the financial means required to expand its publishing activities, and therefore played an indirect, but no less indelible, role in fostering the development of locally drawn comics in postwar Australia.

Of Danish Ducks and Swedish Supermen

The Swedish debut of *Fantomen* (*The Phantom*) in 1950 coincided with the explosive growth of the local comic-book industry, which initially saw American content dominate the output of most Swedish publishers throughout the late 1940s and early 1950s. However, Sweden's unique publishing environment, together with the country's exposure to European publishing trends, shaped both *Fantomen* and the Swedish comics industry in ways that set it apart from the Australian market.

One of Sweden's first comic-book publishers had Danish roots and would eventually dominate Sweden's comic-book industry. Gutenberghus, the publishing company founded by the Danish printer Egmont Petersen (1869–1914), grew rapidly in Scandinavia's flourishing weekly magazine market throughout the 1920s and 1930s. In 1948 Gutenberghus obtained the Scandinavian publishing rights to *Walt Disney's Donald Duck* comic book. Due to paper shortages in Denmark, the company's Swedish subsidiary, Hemmets Journal Förlag, published the first edition of *Donald Duck* (renamed *Kalle Anka & C:o*) in September 1948, whereupon it sold 100,000 copies, making it the most successful comic yet published in Sweden (Engblom, 2002: 61; Dorph-Petersen and Kaster, 2003: 62–63).

Donald Duck's first serious rival, however, was Superman, who led the American superhero "invasion" of Sweden. Rechristened *Stålmannen* (*Man of Steel*) for its Swedish debut in September 1949, the magazine's sales nearly matched those of *Kalle Anke & C:o* (Engblom, 2002: 61). The publisher T. Armas Morby used his comic-book venture to further the expansion of his company, Press & Publicity, in the same way that the success of *The Phantom* allowed Ron Forsyth to turn Frew Publications into one of Australia's largest magazine publishers in the 1950s. Press & Publicity subsequently switched its focus to "cowboy" comics, including *Vilda Västern* (1952), *Prärieserier*, and *Texas* (both 1953). The artwork for many of these titles was supplied by British, Franco-Belgian, and Italian publishers, for whom cowboy comics were as popular as they were in the United States, if not more so (Gifford, 1984: 96–97). By the mid-1950s, Morby's new Centerförlaget imprint controlled 30 percent of Sweden's comic-book market (Gustafsson and Rydén, 2010: 262).

Comic strips had become a popular fixture in many of the Bonnier group's weekly magazines, but some members of the Bonnier family were reportedly wary about the company entering the comic-book market (Bulls Press, 1994: 26). Undeterred, Lukas Bonnier (1922–2006) approached Bjarne Steinsvik, president of Bulls Press, and secured the comic-book rights to *Fantomen*. Despite his father's misgivings about this new venture, Lukas Bonnier remained certain that the character's exposure in Swedish newspapers (such as *Svenska Dagbladet*) would ensure its success (Pilcher and Brooks, 2005:

246). The following anecdote from one Scandinavian reader suggests that Bonnier's hunch was, indeed, correct:

It was my father's favorite comic. He had read it as a child . . . sneaking up to the neighbor's mailbox and reading it from the local newspaper before the neighbor had fetched it. My father is 74 years young now, and we read the Swedish [*Fantomen*] comic book together. (Male respondent, 36–49 years old, Finland, October 8, 2012)

Bonnier appointed Rolf Janson (b. 1925), a commercial artist from Åhlén & Åkerlund's advertising department, as editor of *Fantomen*. Janson, too, enjoyed reading *Fantomen* in the daily press (Bonnier, 2010: 76), but he had to comply with Swedish postal regulations, which stipulated that no single feature could take up more than half the space of any periodical sent by mail to subscribers, in order for publishers to receive discounted postal delivery rates (Pilcher and Brooks, 2005: 246). Therefore, Janson was forced to allocate just twelve pages for the lead Fantomen story, "The Maharajah's Daughter" (Falk and McCoy, 1998a [1944–45]: 34–93). The rest of the magazine was taken up with other translated American comic strips, including *Hopalong Cassidy* and *King of the Northern Mounted*. The first issue of *Fantomen* was printed in color on leftover letterpress machines, after Åhlén & Åkerlund shifted to offset printing, but the old presses could not correctly reproduce the character's costume, which now appeared blue, instead of purple.[5] The debut issue was released in October 1950 and sold 50,000 copies; sales for subsequent editions reached 72,000 copies per issue by 1951 (Pilcher and Brooks, 2005: 246).

Its success vindicated Lukas Bonnier's belief that there were enough young readers who were entranced by the "jersey-clad" hero and his mystical world of the "Deep Woods" (Bonnier, 2010: 76). Under its Serieförlaget imprint, the Bonnier group gradually released a handful of comic magazines using translated American comic strips that adhered to already proven trends and genres, such as domestic comedy (*Blondie*, 1951), jungle adventures (*Tarzan*, 1951), and westerns (*Tom Mix*, 1953). Unlike Frew Publications in Australia, Bonnier seemed unwilling to capitalize on its hero's popularity and refrained from launching companion *Fantomen* titles until the 1970s. This reflected internal disquiet about whether the company should deepen its commitment to this potentially controversial medium — fears that, as it turned out, would be well-founded in the coming decade.

Comics Under Fire, 1945-1955

The Phantom became an undisputed comic-book star at a time when there was a near-insatiable demand for American-style comics in countries like Australia and Sweden. We should not underestimate the sensory appeal these comics held for children living outside the United States, for whom such publications were an unprecedented novelty. The dynamic juxtaposition of words and images which defined the medium synthesized elements from earlier forms of children's entertainment (such as illustrated magazines and motion pictures) in new and exciting ways. Thus, argues Ulf Boëthius, children's avid interest in comic books reaffirmed their historical role as avant-garde consumers, who "pioneer the modern [and] fall upon new media and products" (1995: 48).

Comic books were also affordable and ubiquitous, sold at pocket-money prices, and obtainable through a variety of retail outlets, such as newsagents (Australia), railway bookstalls (India), and tobacconists' kiosks (Sweden). They were also accessible to children in ways that books were not. Comic books' emphasis on visual storytelling appealed to children in countries like India, where illiteracy rates remained stubbornly high; as one child remarked, "You don't have to understand each and every word [in comics] — the pictures tell you quite a lot" (quoted in Bhalla, 1962: 6). This situation was exacerbated by the parlous state of children's book publishing in postwar India, which, according to one observer, remained "dismal" as publishers struggled to recoup high production costs in a retail marketplace which mandated that book prices be kept "within reach of common buyers" (Bhattacharya, 1986: 21). But children's exposure to books was not automatically assured, even in more prosperous countries. A 1953 survey of Australians' reading habits warned that, in communities without adequate public libraries, the consumption of comic books would "persist . . . throughout [adult] life and be transmitted, by example, to a new generation" (*Current Affairs Bulletin*, 1953: 46).

Authors, educators, and other commentators objected to these "American" comics on several grounds. The Indian novelist Khwaja Ahmad Abbas declared his opposition to "the very basic idea of comics," arguing that they prevented children from acquiring a "taste for literature" and thus stunted their "intellectual growth" (1955: 19). The Norwegian author and educator Knut Ingar Hansen argued that superheroes' reliance on physical strength and deadly weapons to resolve conflicts embodied values that "we do not [want to] promote in our society" (quoted in Jensen, 2010: 57). This view was echoed by the Swedish child psychologist Nils Bejerot, who argued that masked (American) heroes like the Phantom embodied the kind of lynch mentality historically associated with the Ku Klux Klan (1954: 120). John Metcalf, chief librarian of the Public Library of New South Wales, pointed out that American comic books were no longer "comical" in the original sense of the word, and that many of those now printed in Australia were "originally designed for adults" (*Woman*, 1954: 12). Such distinctions were lost on most adults, who felt that comic books were entirely inappropriate for children; a Morgan Gallup poll conducted in 1953 found that 69 percent of Australians favored "censored control of children's comics" (Mayer, Garde, and Gibbons, 1983: 166).

The intensity of public debate surrounding comic books provoked governments in Australia, Sweden, and India to introduce legislation which policed the production and dissemination of comic books, especially to minors. The controversy reached the highest levels of India's government after Prime Minister Jawaharlal Nehru, appalled by the contents of a "horror comic" given to his grandson, called for them to be "suppressed ruthlessly" (*Times of India*, 1955: 7). The Indian Parliament's Lok Sabha (House of the People) unanimously passed the Young Persons (Harmful Publications) Bill in November 1956 (*Times of India*, 1956: 9), which prohibited the production and sale within India of any publication which used illustrations to portray "acts of violence or cruelty" or "incidents of a repulsive or horrible nature" (Ministry of Home Affairs, n.d.).

Australia's federal government amended the Customs (Prohibited Imports) Regulations in 1952, which now banned the importation of comics which "unduly [emphasized] matters of sex, horror, or crime [and were] likely to encourage depravity" (Patrick, 2011: 140). Several state governments throughout Australia introduced measures to further control the publication and distribution of comic books within their jurisdiction. Victoria and New South Wales passed laws which held magazine wholesalers liable for the publication and distribution of "obscene" literature (Iliffe, 1956: 134–39). Gordon & Gotch, Australia's largest magazine distributor, sought to protect itself from prosecution under these new laws by instigating a secret censorship program, whereby publishers were required to submit forthcoming magazines distributed by the company for review prior to publication (Harty, 1959: 12). *The Phantom* was not spared; throughout 1954–58, Frew Publications removed all traces of knives and whips from villains' hands, and altered some of Diana Palmer's revealing costumes to make them more modest (Stubbersfield, ca. 1989: 4–7).

Nevertheless, *The Phantom* comic magazine benefited from the character's ongoing appearance in *The Australian Woman's Mirror* during this heated period. The character's popular association with this conservative women's magazine lent him a "wholesome" luster which helped shield *The Phantom* from the worst criticisms leveled against comic books. In fact, the Phantom's virtue and bravery proved sufficient to overcome even the sternest parental objections to comics, according to this Australian reader:

> I am an avid collector of *Phantom* comics . . . I found out recently that both my grandfathers also read *The Phantom*. My mum's father was of the opinion that comics were a waste of space (it was the 1950s, when comics were first looked upon as trash, apparently), but he would allow my mum, her sisters, and her brothers to read *The Phantom*, as he saw him as a moral character, and therefore a good role model for his children. (Female respondent, 36–49 years old, Australia, July 16, 2012)

The Phantom's comic-book stablemates were not always so fortunate; the Federation of Victorian Mothers' Clubs singled out Frew Publications' cowboy series, *The Phantom Ranger*, as an example of the kind of "trash [which] polluted children's minds" (*The Argus*, 1950: 7).

Public anxiety about comic books was no less evident throughout Scandinavia, where teachers and librarians, as the recognized experts on children's reading and "appropriate" juvenile literature, played a pivotal role in shaping the public debate about comics (Jensen, 2012: 260–63). However, unlike Australia and India, the political response to the comics controversy in Sweden was tempered by broader concerns that any attempt to censor comic books posed an unacceptable threat to press freedoms (Larson, 1958: 24), which were protected under the Freedom of the Press Act (1766) (Hadenius and

Weibull, 1999: 130). Motions were raised in the Riksdag (Swedish parliament) throughout 1953–54 calling for investigations into children's literature and reading habits, with a particular focus on the "destructive influences" of comic books and detective magazines. The Straffrättskommittén (Criminal Law Committee) proposed amendments to the Swedish penal code which made the publication and sale of literature which, through words or pictures, "brutalized" children a criminal offense, punishable by fines or prison sentences (Bejerot, 1954: 202).[6] Some of the Swedish comics industry's leading figures took steps to deflect its critics' charges of placing profits ahead of social responsibility. Bjarne Steinsvik, president of Bulls Press (and one of the industry's major content providers), insisted that all "curse words" and references to alcohol be removed from any comic strips it syndicated, while scenes of excessive violence were to be modified or deleted entirely (Bulls Press, 1994: 8).

American Comics: Emulation or Domination?

The initial postwar success of *The Phantom* comic-book franchise in Australia and Sweden seems like yet another instance of American media corporations exploiting their vast economies of scale to syndicate cheap content to overseas media outlets, typically to the detriment of domestic rivals in foreign markets. By purely statistical measures, this would seem to be the case; in 1954 it was estimated that two-thirds of the comic books published in Australia used material "originating [from] America, but printed here under license" (Bartlett, 1954: 8). Similarly, the published output of Sweden's six largest comic-book companies was dominated by translations of American comic-book series, or syndicated American newspaper comic strips (Bejerot, 1954: 80).

But American comic-book publishers and feature syndicates deserve some credit for providing the economic and creative stimulus for postwar comic-book production in countries like Australia, India, and Sweden, where there had been little or no such publishing activity beforehand. Admittedly, American firms achieved commercial dominance in foreign markets by offering publishers a guaranteed supply of ready-made artwork that could be easily reformatted for use in comic magazines, at a fraction of their original production costs. While the economics of using cheap American content were undeniably compelling, when it came to publishing adventure-serial comics, foreign publishers initially had little choice but to use American material, as there were few (if any) locally produced equivalents available to them.

This becomes apparent when considering the haphazard development of Australia's comic-book industry during the early 1940s. The wartime ban on imported American magazines effectively handed Australian publishers a captive market. The first companies to dabble in this largely untested market —such as the New South Wales Bookstall Company and Frank Johnson Publications—were usually forced to rely on individual cartoonists to assemble an entire comic magazine. However, most established Australian cartoonists at that time were schooled in the tradition of single-panel "gag" cartoons and were unfamiliar with the narrative techniques of comic magazines. Despite their often primitive quality, these early Australian-drawn comics were snapped up by children hungry for escapist wartime reading.

Following the war, new American comic-book titles, now available as print-ready artwork to Australian publishers, fueled the dramatic expansion of domestic comic-book production. Australia's newspaper conglomerates leveraged their combined publishing, printing, and distribution networks to achieve commercial dominance of this new market. However, surging consumer demand for comics ensured there was also scope for newer, smaller firms—such as Frew Publications—to establish themselves (Patrick, 2012a: 165–66).

American comic books also provided Australian publishers with new characters, genres, and concepts that might be successfully emulated using local writers and artists. Kevan Hardacre (b. 1927) recalled how he produced his own jungle hero comic, *Char Chapman–The Phantom of the East* (1951), after Peter Gormley, a Sydney press agent, asked Hardacre to "do something like *The Phantom*" for his client, Young's Merchandising, on the grounds that *The Phantom* was "the biggest-selling comic then published" (quoted in Patrick, 2008). Even Frew Publications attempted to duplicate their initial success with *The Phantom*; the staff artist Peter Chapman (1925–2016) accompanied publisher Ron Forsyth to see a psychoanalyst to try and identify the reasons for the Phantom's popularity. "He didn't tell us much more about The Phantom than we didn't already know ourselves," Chapman recalled, "but we partly based our next [comic-book hero], *Sir Falcon*, on the explanation that he gave us" (quoted in Patrick, 2007c).

But such trends were not always evident in other countries. In Sweden, for example, the growing popularity of *Fantomen* did not appear to inspire the same degree of imitation seen in Australian comics following the release of *The Phantom* in 1948. A notable exception was *Kilroy*, the translated version of an Italian comic-book series, *Amok–Il Gigante Mascherato* (*Amok–The Masked Giant*), a *Phantom* "knockoff" created by Cesare Solini and Antonio Canale in 1947, which made its Swedish debut in *Seriemagasinet* in the late 1940s (Bono, 1999: 91). It was no accident that Press & Publicity should recruit an Italian-drawn superhero to compete with *Fantomen*, given the apparent dearth of Swedish writers and artists skilled in producing "American-style" adventure comics. Aside from a few short-lived historical adventure (*Münchhausen-Bravader*, 1933) and science fiction strips (*Allan Kämpe*, 1943) appearing in Swedish magazines during the 1930s and 1940s, the Swedish comics historian Fredrik Strömberg maintains that the "realistic adventure genre has never been really big" among local cartoonists (2010: 43). As the 1950s progressed, Swedish-drawn comics would find greater acceptance in broadly humorous genres, or in publications geared towards young children. It seemed that Swedish readers were—for now, at least—content to let imported comic-book heroes slake their thirst for adventure.

Comic books came relatively late to India and, as such, locally drawn comic books did not really captivate Indian audiences until the 1960s and 1970s, long after the postwar comic-book "craze" had subsided in Australia and Sweden. Despite India's large population, imported British and American comics still only reached a relatively small readership. In 1962 one Indian distributor said that although demand for imported comic books had grown by 25 percent in the previous decade, his company still only imported a rather modest 25,000 comic magazines per month (Joshee, 1962: 6). These were miniscule sums given that, by 1966, approximately 12,000,000 Indians were deemed to be "literate in English" (Altbach, 1976: 41). Domestic magazine publishing was further stymied by the scarcity of imported newsprint, the allocation of which was controlled by the Office of the Registrar of Newspapers for India during the 1960s (Kasbekar, 2006: 113).

When set against this challenging backdrop, the eventual success of *The Phantom* comic-book franchise in India seems all the more remarkable. Yet just as it was with the birth of America's comics industry during the mid-1930s, economic concerns drove the birth of India's comic-book industry in the early 1960s. Anant Pai (1929–2011) was a junior executive in Bennett, Coleman & Co.'s book-publishing division at the time when his supervisor, P. K. Roy, remarked that the company's printing presses lay idle after orders were met for India's calendar production season. Roy thought they could be used to print comic books to keep them operating at peak capacity, and initially suggested that *Superman* would be a suitable title. Pai, however, recommended the company choose *The Phantom* instead, on the grounds that its "steamy tribal . . . milieu" would be more familiar to Indian audiences (Rao, 2001: 38).

The Phantom thus became the designated "star" of the company's first comic magazine, *Indrajal Comics*, which also contained locally produced educational features (*Our New Age of Science*) and humorous comic strips (*Little Raju*). Bennett, Coleman & Co. marketed the comic in *The Times of India*, promoting it as a "modern, educational comic" that was "specially designed for Indian children" (*Times of India*, 1964a: 14; 1964b: 6). Mindful of the anti-comics furor which convulsed India in the 1950s, the first issue also contained an editorial which emphasized its positive contribution to the nation's modernization drive:

> The truth is that the medium of comics is an EXCELLENT one, and, there are GOOD COMICS and BAD COMICS . . . The medium of COLOUR COMICS could be . . . effectively employed in a variety of ways in our country and made to serve the cause of the eradication of illiteracy and of imparting education through entertainment. ("Chitrak," 1964: n.p.)

Indrajal Comics was launched in March 1964, printed in color and simultaneously published in Hindi, English, and Marathi-language editions. The magazine's Indian provenance was reinforced by Govind Brahmania's striking cover illustrations which utilized the flat, two-dimensional aesthetic common to Indian calendar art to great effect (Joshi, 1986: 216–17; Jain, 2007: 34, n.376). Brahmania's illustrations emphasized the faux-Indian trappings common to many of Lee Falk's stories; as Falk himself later disclosed, he invented the Phantom's Afro-Indian domain partly to indulge his desire to write stories featuring rajas and Bengal tigers (Sanghvi, 1999). The first issue contained Falk's 1954 story "The Belt" (Falk and McCoy, 1999b [1954]: 54–71), but this had to be modified to appease local readers' sensibilities. The Phantom's fictional country, "Bengali," was changed to "Denkali" on the grounds that readers would have been confused by the presence of Bandar pygmies in what they presumed was meant to be the Bengali region of northeast India. Furthermore, the name of the pirate who murdered the Phantom's father in "The Belt" was changed from "Rama" to "Ramalu" in deference to the Hindu deity (Salinkumar, 2010). These changes, according to one Indian reader, greatly enhanced the comic's appeal to local audiences:

> Most of the success of The Phantom lies in the fact that *Indrajal Comics* was able to sanitize and reinterpret this [fictional] world to suit the life and times of India at that time. [The] inking and print quality was top notch (as compared to . . . later [series], like Diamond Comics). (Male respondent, 18–35 years old, India, December 4, 2012)

King Features Syndicate remained the chief content provider for *Indrajal Comics* throughout the 1960s and 1970s, supplying *Flash Gordon* and *Mandrake the Magician*, which gradually alternated with *The Phantom* as the magazine's headline features. Despite the magazine's initial success, the Phantom's influence over India's comic-book industry would not become apparent until much later.

Despite sharing the visual makeup of newspaper comic strips, the comic magazine — or "comic book," as it became known in the United States — was an altogether new type of illustrated periodical which chiefly used images, rather than words, to tell new kinds of dynamic, exciting stories. But whereas imported American comic strips had been successfully incorporated into foreign newspapers during the 1920s and 1930s, selling American comic books abroad proved more difficult. Physically "dumping" American comic magazines onto foreign shores was often not practically feasible, commercially desirable — or even legal. Once again, American publishers and newspaper feature syndicates would align themselves with foreign intermediaries that would tailor their product to best meet the needs of overseas markets. These business alliances became ever more vital to ensure the continued syndication and publication of American comics abroad during World War II. Nor did their importance lessen with peacetime, as American publishers continued to rely on their overseas affiliates to help them exploit the resurgent postwar demand for comics in Australia, Sweden, and India. Thanks to its continued exposure in newspapers and magazines throughout the war, *The Phantom* now became a successful comic book series in each of these countries, easily matching the popularity of other imported rivals like Superman in ways that it was never able to achieve in the United States. *The Phantom* proved capable of withstanding the public outcry against American comics throughout the 1950s, but new challenges would await "The Ghost Who Walks," as comics soon faced an even greater threat from the advent of television. The consequences for *The Phantom* comics franchise would be far-reaching and unexpected.

CHAPTER FIVE

BECOMING "FANTOMEN"

F licking through the July 1963 edition of *Fantomen* reveals much about the tastes and preoccupations of Sweden's youth at the dawn of that turbulent decade. Three of the magazine's comic-book features were westerns, which both attested to European audiences' perennial fascination with the American West and reflected the popularity of American television shows like *Gunsmoke* and *Bonanza* being broadcast in Sweden at the time (Björk, 2001: 309–21).[1] These westerns' inclusion in *Fantomen* further highlighted the globalization of postwar comics publishing: *Svarta Bågen* was a translated version of *Blackbow the Cheyenne*, a British comic strip; *Baronens Revolvermän* was originally published by the American firm Atlas Comics (the forerunner of Marvel Comics); and *Texas Jim* was a Swedish series illustrated by Göte Göransson. But growing up at the height of the space race, Swedish readers also delighted in the latest episode of *Dan Dare*, the British science fiction hero renamed *Dan Drake* for his appearance in *Fantomen*. Keeping with the futuristic theme, the comic included a cutaway diagram of Telstar, the world's first communications satellite, launched in 1962.

The magazine, of course, opened with the latest *Fantomen* adventure, which saw the Phantom thwart a criminal gang's plans to rob the Skull Cave's treasure room. But keen-eyed readers, accustomed to the style of the American cartoonist Wilson McCoy, may have noticed something unusual about this particular story. What set this story apart from previous installments had less to do with the plot than the artwork, which, although unsigned, was drawn by the Swedish illustrator Bertil Wilhelmsson. When viewed in isolation, this story is an editorial curiosity that is of interest to no one except perhaps devoted *Fantomen* readers. When seen in its historical context, however,

99

this story takes on far greater significance. It appeared at the end of a tumultuous period for Sweden's comic-book industry, which had been buffeted by
public outcries over the allegedly harmful effects of comic books on Swedish
children's intellectual and moral well-being. Adding to the industry's woes
was the commencement of television broadcasting in 1956, which threatened
to lure young readers away from comic books altogether.

This same narrative, whereby comic-book publishers found themselves
subject to both intense public scrutiny and competition from television, was
also being played out in Australia and India throughout the 1950s and 1960s.
What distinguished publisher Åhlén & Åkerlund's response to these events
was the company's commitment to reinvent *Fantomen* as a comic book palatable to Swedish tastes, and thus counteract claims that comic books embodied an alien American culture seemingly at odds with Scandinavian values.
Åhlén & Åkerlund's decision to produce Swedish-drawn *Fantomen* stories
showed that it was far more adept in responding to these challenges than its
Australian and, to a lesser extent, Indian counterparts. More importantly,
this Swedish publisher would become a key production node that would fundamentally alter the commercial and creative dynamics of the international
Phantom media franchise.

Comic Books in the Television Era, 1955–1970

Television's growth as a mass medium throughout the 1950s compounded the
difficulties facing the comic-book industry in the United States, and the early
indications of television's impact on comic-book sales were, frankly, chilling.
By the early 1960s, it was estimated that the annual total circulation of comic
books in the United States had slumped to 350,000,000, from their wartime
peak of 800,000,000. The number of publishers had declined by 75 percent,
and most of the industry's advertising revenue, like many of its readers, had
crossed over to television (Wolseley, 1969: 275).

The debut of television in Australia, inaugurated with the launch of
TCN-9 (Sydney) on September 16, 1956, proved no less catastrophic for the
local comic-book industry. John Dixon (1929–2015), who created a new series
of *Catman* comics for Frew Publications in the late 1950s, recalled that the
average circulations for many Australian comics fell from 80,000 to 10,000

soon after the arrival of television (O'Brien, 2011: 29). In Sydney alone, it was estimated that 52 percent of households owned a television set by 1959 (Campbell and Keogh, 1962: 14). Australia boasted twelve separate television stations serving over 500,000 households in most mainland capital cities by 1960 (Elliot, 1960: 268, n.280). Television's effect on Australians' reading habits was as undeniable as it was detrimental. A survey of Sydney households throughout 1956–59 found that recreational reading among adolescents from households that owned television sets declined by 20 percent (Campbell and Keogh, 1962: 111–12).[2]

The Department of Customs and Excise estimated that annual sales of locally published comics totaled 14,000,000 copies in 1959 (National Archives of Australia [Adelaide], 1959), indicating a massive slump from the industry's postwar peak of 60,000,000 copies in 1954 (Connell, Francis, and Skilbeck, 1957: 155). This dire situation was compounded by the abolition of import licensing restrictions in February 1960, which allowed for the direct importation of American comic books into Australia for the first time in twenty years. Many small publishers, whose cheaply printed comics compared unfavorably with glossy, full-color American comic books, quit the industry, leaving the Australian market to a handful of larger publishers such as K.G. Murray, which relaunched many of its titles as 100-page "supacomics" (*The Observer*, 1960: 5–6).

Swedish television broadcasting commenced in 1956, but was subject to regulatory controls which ensured that its growth was far slower than in Australia. The reigning Socialdemokraterna (Social Democrat) government granted a monopoly broadcasting license to the private company Sveriges Radio (SR). The service, confined to a single channel, was expected to emphasize education ahead of entertainment and would not carry advertising; revenues would instead be raised through government subsidies and license fees levied on television sets.[3] The number of television set licenses purchased by Swedish households leapt from 8,900 in 1956 to 599,000 in 1959, while broadcast transmissions gradually expanded from just 9 hours per week in 1956–57 to 28 hours per week by 1961–62 (Björk, 1999: 151–52). SR launched a second television channel in 1970, by which time broadcasts reached 90 percent of Sweden's population (Rosengren, 1994a: 27). The tightly controlled expansion of Swedish television services arguably spared local comic-book

publishers from the degree of upheaval experienced by their Australian counterparts immediately following the launch of television. Media scarcity further shielded comics from the competitive threat of television, as this Swedish reader points out:

> There was no other media when I started to read [*Fantomen*], besides
> the radio. We didn't [buy] a TV before the [mid-1970s]. (Male respon-
> dent, 36–49 years old, Sweden, November 23, 2012)

Nor did the increased output of television broadcasts diminish children's
interest in comic books. A survey of Swedish households found that although
the volume of children's television programming tripled throughout 1964–72,
children's rate of television viewing only doubled during this same period
(Filipson, 1976: 23). This same study also found that 95 percent of Swedish
children surveyed either bought or read comics, with parents buying comics
for their children in most instances (Filipson, 1976: 39).

While reading comic books remained a popular pastime among Swedish
children, the same could not be said for Australian youth. A 1970 survey of
Sydney adolescents' leisure activities revealed a marked decline in comic-
book reading among high-school students. Whereas over 60 percent of boys
and girls aged 13–14 years regularly read comics in 1952 (Connell, Francis,
and Skilbeck, 1957: 158), these figures had dropped to 45 percent for boys and
30 percent for girls in the same age group by 1970. These figures fell even
further as adolescents grew older; by 1970, the portion of 17–18-year-old boys
and girls who read comic books on a regular basis stood at just 5 percent and
10 percent respectively (Connell et al., 1975: 175–76). For the generation of
Australian children growing up in the glare of the television screen, comic
books had largely ceased to be part of their "everyday consciousness" (Possamai, 2003: 110).

Television came to India in 1959, when it was launched as an experimental
service, but regular daily broadcasts only began in 1965 (Singhal et al., 1988:
224). The expansion of domestic television services was hampered throughout the 1960s and 1970s by the comparatively high cost of television sets and
the lack of electricity supply to rural areas (Dhawan, 1973: 525–26). Even
if these obstacles had been removed, the reportedly dull quality of India's
state-owned television broadcaster did little to entice viewers. As one critic
remarked:

It is not surprising that those viewers who live on India's edges often tune in to more enjoyable programs, including western films, broadcast from Pakistan, Bangladesh, and Sri Lanka . . . There is little encouragement for [Indian] writers and artists, the financial rewards are poor and production facilities old-fashioned and bad. (Fishlock, 1987: 122–23)

India's burgeoning comic-book industry would, in fact, have little to fear from television until the 1990s, when technological advances and regulatory reforms would transform the broadcasting sector beyond all recognition.

Creating a Swedish Phantom

During the early 1950s, Åhlén & Åkerlund made changes to its Serieförlaget (The Comics Publisher) division which it hoped would appease public concerns about children's taste for comic books, and help cement the company's dominance of the Swedish comics market. Serieförlaget published the first entirely Swedish-drawn comic book, *Tuff och Tuss* (1953), a decidedly "wholesome" magazine featuring whimsical characters and stories intended for young children. Lukas Bonnier, keen to produce a uniquely Swedish humor comic, oversaw the successful relaunch of the 1930s comic strip *91:an* as a comic magazine in 1956 (Engblom, 2002: 63; Gustafsson and Rydén, 2010: 262–63). Each of these publications was designed to provide parents and children alike with an acceptable Swedish alternative to "American" comic books. More importantly, their success demonstrated the commercial viability of Swedish-drawn comic magazines, and enabled Serieförlaget to develop the editorial infrastructure required to reinvent "The Ghost Who Walks" for Swedish audiences.

Fantomen underwent numerous changes throughout this period. The magazine changed from color printing to a black-and-white format in 1955 and switched from a fortnightly to a monthly schedule in 1960, with the reduced frequency offset by its expanded 68-page format. But whereas *Fantomen* previously had to serialize Lee Falk's stories over several issues, the magazine could now feature complete episodes in a single issue. This proved popular with readers, but it created new difficulties for Åhlén & Åkerlund Youth Magazines, as the company was now known. *Fantomen* required 12 complete episodes to fill its revised publishing schedule, yet Åhlén & Åkerlund could only anticipate receiving 2–3 new Lee Falk *Phantom* stories per year. This shortfall was exacerbated by the company's policy of reserving Falk's Sunday episodes of *The Phantom* for the annual *Fantomen julalbum*.

This difficult situation was only made worse by the death in 1961 of Wilson McCoy, the American cartoonist who had illustrated *The Phantom* newspaper strip since the early 1940s. McCoy's successor, Seymour "Sy" Barry, brought a dynamic, realistic style to the series, which gave *The Phantom* a fresher, "modern" appearance. But even King Features expressed some reservations about their newly chosen artist, as Sy Barry later recalled:

> I delivered my first week of work, they [King Features] called me and said, "Sy, this looks like *Flash Gordon*. It doesn't look like *The Phantom*. It's beautifully done, but it's not at all like McCoy's style." They wanted me to try to duplicate his style . . . They were worried that the editors would see such an extreme change that they could lose papers as a result. (Quoted in Stroud, 2015)[4]

Åhlén & Åkerlund was reluctant to use Barry's work at first, fearing that it, too, would alienate Swedish readers accustomed to McCoy's simpler—and undeniably popular—interpretation of the character. Åhlén & Åkerlund opted instead to negotiate a licensing agreement with Bulls Press, which allowed the company to commission new *Fantomen* stories using Swedish writers and artists. The first Swedish episode, "Skatten i dödskallegrottan" ("The Treasure in the Skull Cave"), was illustrated by Bertil Wilhelmsson (1926–1992) and was published in *Fantomen* no. 8 (July 1963). These all-new episodes were supplemented by updated versions of earlier Lee Falk stories (originally illustrated by Ray Moore and Wilson McCoy) redrawn by Swedish illustrators, which appeared in *Fantomen* from 1965 onwards. This editorial transition helped prepare Swedish audiences for Sy Barry's modern interpretation of the Phantom. More importantly, it gave Åhlén & Åkerlund the opportunity to give the series an incremental Swedish makeover, as American episodes redrawn by local artists were now peppered with visual references to Swedish newspapers and automobiles. With these small steps, the transition from the (American) Phantom to the (Swedish) Fantomen had begun.

Twilight of the Adventure Heroes

Sy Barry's appointment as artist on *The Phantom* came at a turbulent time in the history of adventure-serial comic strips. Even though America's newspaper industry faced intense competition from television, few newspaper editors seemed willing to actively "sell" their daily and weekly comic-strip sections, despite their reputation for being one of the most widely read features in any newspaper. Compared with television networks, which constantly promoted their forthcoming shows, Philip Porter (feature editor for the *Cleveland Plain Dealer*) claimed that editors rarely promoted their most popular comic strips in "high-traffic" areas of the newspaper, such as the front page or the sports section. This approach, Porter argued, could be particularly suitable for promoting comic-strip serials:

> Why not make a virtue out of our own soap operas and hint at what's going to happen next to Dondi or Rex Morgan, or The Phantom or Steve Canyon? The readers are looking for them—why make them work so hard? (Quoted in Erwin, 1962: 10).

Yet there were signs that adventure-serial comic strips were already falling out of favor with the public. A 1959 survey of 1,360 adult American newspaper readers found that "adventure" and "soap opera" features (such as *Dick Tracy* and *Mary Worth*) accounted for 50 percent of the 15 most popular Sunday newspaper comic strips (Robinson and White, 1962: 39–40). However, the survey also noted that "satiric sophisticated humor" comic strips (such as *Peanuts*) were more popular among college graduates (Robinson and White, 1962: 39, 41). The generational and demographic distinctions between the rival newspaper audiences for adventure-serial and sophisticated humor comic strips grew more pronounced with each passing decade. A 1979 readership poll conducted by the Allentown (Pennsylvania) *Evening Chronicle* found that although its three "adventure-continuity strips" (*Dick Tracy*, *Alley Oop*, and *Captain Easy*) scored the most negative ratings from the overall survey group, they were highly ranked as favorites among their core readership of adult males aged fifty-five years and over (Subber and Schweitzer, 1980: 42–43).

Throughout the late 1960s and early 1970s, rising newsprint costs forced many newspapers to reduce the space allocated to comic strips from five columns down to three or four columns. As Robert Gillespie (from the Chicago Tribune-New York News Syndicate) explained, "with the space shortage, publishers have been cutting down on features rather than on advertising and news" (quoted in Culhane, 1974: 39). Joke-a-day comic strips, with their simpler illustrations and punch-line dialogue, could adapt to these constraints. Adventure-continuity strips, which relied on detailed scripts and intricate artwork to convey drama, suffered by comparison.

Television, too, had an inadvertent but no less decisive impact on the dramatic appeal of adventure-continuity comic strips. George Wunder, who had illustrated the *Terry and the Pirates* comic strip since 1947, reflected on the series' cancellation in 1973:

> [People] get an average of three or four complete stories a night off the boob tube. There's no reason why they should hang around anywhere from 8 to 12 weeks to find out just how one [comic-strip] story came out. (Quoted in Van Gelder, 1975: 403)

The demise of many of the pioneering adventure-serial comic strips from the 1930s was hastened by the death and retirement of their creators during the 1970s, for whom no suitable replacements were found, nor, in some cases, were such successors actively sought by the feature syndicates that once championed the strips.

The Phantom was spared from this dismal fate thanks to its global popularity; in 1966, King Features stated that *The Phantom* appeared in 583 newspapers, "including 261 foreign newspapers," and claimed that only Chic Young's *Blondie* comic strip had a greater worldwide readership (Mullaney, ed., 2015: 185). Nevertheless, Lee Falk was compelled to readjust his approach to the series in light of the reduced space now allocated to comic strips. When asked about the sparse dialogue he now employed, Falk replied:

> A strip used to have six columns [across a newspaper page] . . . Through the years, they were cut to four, which makes [the strip] smaller. So I tried to cut the amount of words to make room for the art . . . The reason is mechanical . . . to make room for the drawing. (Quoted in Rhoades, 2011: 259–60)

The variable quality of Falk's scripts, which became more evident throughout the 1970s, also owed much to his reliance on "fantastic" story lines, which were far removed from the series' original premise. These changes were not universally welcomed by longtime readers, who drew unfavorable comparisons between Falk's later work and his earliest *Phantom* stories:

> I am a big fan of the earliest Falk/Moore stories . . . [which were] fast-paced and exciting, blending action with romance . . . As much as I loved Falk's earlier work, I could not stand his later stories. When he started writing about aliens, witches, dinosaurs, [and] robots . . . I lost interest. (Male respondent, 18–35 years old, Australia, May 31, 2012)

The economic pressures confronting feature syndicates and newspaper publishers now threatened to undermine the appeal of even the most popular comic strips. The Newspaper Features Council argued that not only were older readers were "turned off" by the reduced size of comic strips that were difficult to read, but that cartoonists now "lost the chance to draw attractively," thus jeopardizing the medium's very survival (quoted in Astor, 1986: 33). Conversely, international demand for syndicated American news stories and features outstripped the sluggish U.S. market during this same period. According to Sid Goldberg, vice president of United Media, "the American comic strip sets the standard for comics in the world, just like Hollywood does for movies." American feature syndicates that had proven strengths in text features and comics would, he added, "sell more comics abroad." The Editors Press Service, which represented several American feature syndicates in foreign markets, reported that its annual sales had increased by over 20 percent, with comic strips accounting for 75 percent of its overall business (Astor, 1991: 38). Reports such as these only underscored American feature syndicates' growing reliance on international markets, which would prove crucial for the future longevity of adventure-serial comic strips, such as *The Phantom*, which were now falling from favor with American newspaper readers.

The Phantom Prevails

Sy Barry took over the artistic reins of *The Phantom* newspaper strip shortly before the character made a belated return to the American comic-book field.

The Phantom received his first self-titled magazine, published by Gold Key Comics, in November 1962. *The Phantom* showcased new stories (adapted from Lee Falk's newspaper story lines) illustrated by Bill Lignante (b. 1925) and prepared exclusively for the comic book.[5] Gold Key was best known for its licensed television comic-book franchises (such as *Bonanza* and *The Twilight Zone*), but *The Phantom* was one of the company's newer titles, such as *Doctor Solar—Man of the Atom* (1962) and *Magnus, Robot Fighter* (1963), which blended superhero and science fiction themes. Gold Key no doubt hoped that the Phantom would benefit from the revival of costumed superheroes, heralded by DC Comics' modernized version of its 1940s-era heroes, the Flash (1956) and the Green Lantern (1959), and further invigorated by Marvel Comics' new generation of emotionally charged superheroes, such as the Fantastic Four (1961), the Incredible Hulk (1962) and the Amazing Spider-Man (1963). Despite the company's best efforts to capitalize on renewed public interest in superhero comics, Gold Key's licensed film and television properties—such as *Walt Disney's Comics and Stories*—remained their top-selling titles. Even among the company's modest suite of action-adventure titles, *The Phantom* remained a comparatively poor seller and was canceled in 1966.

In Australia, Frew Publications reprinted two Gold Key stories in *The Phantom* (no. 236, 1962), but the shorter American episodes could not adequately fill the Australian comic's longer 32-page format (which contained far fewer advertisements), and were not used again until 1991.[6] Frew Publications was one of the handful of Australian comic-book publishers left standing by the early 1960s, thanks largely to *The Phantom*, which, according to *The Observer*, continued to exert a "phenomenal grip on the juvenile market" (1960: 6). The company's remaining Australian-drawn comics—*The Phantom Ranger*, *The Shadow*, and *Sir Falcon*—had by now lapsed into reprinting previously published stories.[7] Frew Publications switched *The Phantom* from a monthly to a fortnightly publication in 1960, but unlike their Swedish counterparts, the company did not commission Australian-drawn stories to meet its expanded publishing roster. Instead, Frew Publications published the latest Lee Falk/Sy Barry *Phantom* stories soon after they concluded their appearance in American newspapers. The character's new look under Sy Barry helped give *The Phantom* comic a modest visual facelift, but Frew could only count on receiving 2–3 new Falk/Barry stories annually from the Yaffa Syndicate. The company therefore adhered to its practice of recycling previously published *Phantom* stories every 5–7 years, believing that the magazine's casual readership turned over regularly within this time frame, and the repetition would thus go unnoticed by newer readers (Patrick, 2012b: 143).

As Frew Publications' business steadily contracted throughout the 1960s, Åhlén & Åkerlund Youth Magazines' operations underwent significant expansion. The company was renamed Semic Press after acquiring 60 percent of its largest competitor, Press & Publicity, in 1969 (Gustafsson and Rydén, 2010: 263).[8] The purchase included assets from the company's Centerförlag comics division, most notably *Seriemagasinet*. Ebbe Zetterstad (1924–2012), a former editor of *Fantomen*, was appointed managing director of Semic Press. Zetterstad now allocated two editors to *Fantomen*; one editor was responsible for overseeing each issue's "Fantomen" story, while the other editor assembled the rest of the magazine. Taking the former role was Janne Lundström (b. 1941), an ex-journalist and cofounder of Seriefrämjandet (The Swedish Comics Association, est. 1968). By 1968, Semic Press had begun using *Phantom* stories produced by the Italian publisher Edizioni Fratelli Spada, which Lundström was required to edit, rewrite, and, where necessary, commission new artwork to adapt them for use in *Fantomen*.[9] Dissatisfied with the quality of the Italian material, Lundström invited members of the Seriefrämjandet fan organization to submit synopses for new *Fantomen* episodes which, if suitable, he would assign to Semic's freelance writers to develop into full-length scripts. This was an unprecedented collaboration between a comic-book publisher and Swedish comics fandom, as yet unheard of in either Australia or India.[10]

Shortly after Lundström began writing his own original *Fantomen* stories,[11] he was joined by Magnus Knutsson (b. 1944), who had previously worked as an editor on the magazine. Dismayed by the excessive violence of the Italian stories, Knutsson proposed writing a new story that involved the Phantom liberating slaves being held in the neighboring African state of Rodia (later "Rhodia"), a fictional amalgam of Southern Rhodesia and South Africa (Knutsson and Vallvé, 1972: 3–24). "It was a good way to make The Phantom a better hero by fighting for the oppressed," explained Knutsson, "which helped make this 'Swedish' version of The Phantom a positive reinterpretation of American culture."[12] Lundström, who regarded Knutsson as a "kindred spirit," said that the story's progressive political themes demonstrated that it was possible to make "good Swedish comics," which challenged the prevailing view that American comics were violent, sexist, racist, and offensive to Swedish sensibilities—a view that Lundström himself partly shared.[13]

The injection of "real-world" politics into *Fantomen* reflected many of the then-current preoccupations of Sweden's broadsheet press, where, according to Richard F. Tomasson, "the plight of the world's unfortunate peoples is given special attention" (1970: 281–82). The political rehabilitation of *Fantomen* received favorable press coverage in the mainstream press, in Sweden and elsewhere (Mosey, 1981: 54; Hockney, 1984: 11). But others were not so readily impressed; the author and critic Lars Peterson argued that the series' basic premise—wherein African natives required the protection of a white ruler—remained essentially racist (1976: 132). Furthermore, Peterson argued that Swedish writers' determination to "reform" the comic's colonial-era politics was undermined by the magazine's inclusion of earlier American- and Italian-drawn episodes, which only reinforced negative perceptions of Africa and Africans (1976: 137). Undeterred by such criticisms, both Lundström and Knutsson continued writing stories that championed progressive social causes. Lundström pitted the Phantom against the rapacious (white) owners of a jungle trading post, while helping a Bengali tribe establish their own cooperative store (Lundström and Wilhelmsson, 1973: 3–27). Knutsson had Diana Palmer challenge the Jungle Patrol's discriminatory men-only recruitment policy by becoming the first woman to successfully pass their combat training test, achieve the rank of sergeant, and help the Phantom apprehend a gang of criminals (Knutsson and Vallvé, 1973: 3–27).

By the late 1960s *Fantomen* remained one of Sweden's best-selling comic books, with an estimated circulation of 140,000, second only to *Kalle Anka & C:o* (200,000) (Blomberg, 1967: 15). Semic Press capitalized on the character's surging popularity in a series of special-edition gift books, such as *Stora Fantomenboken* (*Great Fantomen Book*, 1973), as well as the *Serie-Pocket* paperback library (1972–86). Further changes were undertaken by Ulf Granberg (b. 1945), who was appointed editor of *Fantomen* in 1972. "There was no expectation [upon me] to change the title," he explained, "but back in those days, you could dive into a sea of [comic strips] and come up with many goodies."[14] Granberg diversified the magazine's supporting comic-strip features in order to broaden its appeal. His inclusion of Stan Lynde's western-comedy drama, *Rick O'Shay* (U.S.), along with Dan Barry's then-current version of *Flash Gordon* (*Blixt Gordon*), proved especially popular and lifted the magazine's circulation even higher.[15] According to Granberg, the anthology format was key to ensuring the magazine's ongoing success:

> Swedish audiences have become used to the more varied type of comic-strip "diet" in *Fantomen*, which is more of a magazine, and not just a comic book with a single character.[16]

Granberg's approach, according to Peter Grännby (marketing manager, Bulls Press), reflected the pivotal role that editors play in the Scandinavian comics industry, who "build up the [self-contained] 'universe' of the magazine."[17] As a consequence, the diverse anthology format championed by Granberg created different groupings among *Fantomen* readers:

> The Swedish *Fantomen* . . . is dedicated roughly to 50% to *The Phantom* and 50% to other comics. The "other comics" are what attracted me at first (*Mandrake* and *Flash Gordon*, for example), and that applies for many Swedish readers. While all readers have different favorites, it is not unusual for *Fantomen* readers to NOT have "The Phantom" as their #1 favorite comic from the [magazine]. (Male respondent, 18–35 years old, Sweden, March 21, 2012)

For one Swedish reader, *Fantomen* became a "marvelous way to find new comics" from Belgium and France, "which I would never have found otherwise" (female respondent, 18–35 years old, Sweden, December 18, 2012). Another Swedish reader maintained that the inclusion of translated foreign comics, such as *Lt. Blueberry* (France) and *The Spirit* (U.S.), was "essential to keep the [*Fantomen*] comic book vital for so many years" (male respondent, 36–49 years old, Sweden, April 1, 2012).

Janne Lundström, who relinquished his editorial role on *Fantomen* after eighteen months, remained a contributing writer to the magazine. His work took a new creative direction with "I Piraternas Våld" ("The Pirates' Prisoner"), the first of seven historical adventures he would write about the Phantom's ancestors throughout 1973–75 (Lundström and Vallvé, 1973: 3–33). Lee Falk had recently rewritten the origins of the Phantom's ancestral dynasty in the 1969 story line "Walker's Table," which overturned the series' original British colonial milieu in order to give his hero a stronger American affiliation

(Falk and Barry, 1992b [1969]: 4–20). But Lundström's historical sagas recast the Phantom as a costumed swashbuckler embroiled in European political intrigues spanning the seventeenth and eighteenth centuries, and thus became the template for many Swedish writers who subsequently worked on the series.

Ulf Granberg used Lundström's historical adventures as the springboard for drafting a new chronology of the Phantom dynasty which blended elements from Lee Falk's original American stories with new characters and scenarios taken from the Swedish stories created expressly for *Fantomen* (Granberg [attrib.], 1975: 5–16). "It was easier to write a historical [Phantom] story," according to Granberg, "because the settings and costumes made it easier for the supporting characters to accept [him] as a contemporary hero."[18] But Lundström, who disliked the character's propensity for violence to solve problems ("It doesn't set a good example"), also tried to reform the present-day Phantom in such stories as "Mjölkdrickaren" ("The Milk Drinker") by making him "more like a detective" who used his intellect to solve crimes instead (Lundström and Vallvé, 1974: 3–26).[19]

The cumulative effect of these incremental changes and editorial strategies transformed the *Fantomen* magazine in commercial and artistic terms. By the early 1980s, the magazine's average circulation had climbed to 170,000 per issue after recording an extraordinary sales spike of 204,000 copies for its publication of "The Wedding of The Phantom" in 1978.[20] These changes were largely welcomed by readers, who felt that the Swedish-drawn *Fantomen* stories frequently surpassed the quality of Lee Falk's work:

> When I first started reading the Swedish *Fantomen* magazine in the early 1970s, it was mainly Italian-produced stories which were [being] published, but when the Swedish team . . . led by Ulf Granberg really began to restructure the whole *Fantomen* world, things got better and better! To be honest, with all due respect, Lee Falk's ideas during the 1980s felt quite outdated in comparison. (Male respondent, 36–49 years old, Sweden, April 11, 2012)

The shortage of new American stories available for the Swedish market created an opportunity whereby the magazine's creative personnel transformed the Phantom into an adventure hero more in the spirit of an Alexandre Dumas novel, rather than a "traditional" American comic-book superhero. In doing so, they created a distinctively Swedish interpretation of the Phantom that was, by turns, both "classic" and "modern," and which would eventually rival the American version of the character, at home and abroad.

The Further Voyages of Fantomen

The success of *Fantomen* in Sweden coincided with Semic Press's expansion into neighboring markets throughout the 1960s and 1970s. Scandinavian editions of *Fantomen* were launched in Norway (*Fantomet*, 1964), Finland (*Mustanaamio*, 1966), and Denmark (*Fantomet*, 1971), either in partnership with local publishers or through Semic Press's subsidiary companies.[21] Semic Press made its first foray beyond Scandinavia when it launched *Phantom* in West Germany, where it was published from 1966 to 1969.[22] The company subsequently bought out its largest domestic rival, Williams Förlags AB (a subsidiary of Warner Communications [U.S.]), in 1975.[23] Just as the Bonnier group came to dominate the periodical press after purchasing Åhlén & Åkerlund decades earlier, Semic Press's acquisition of Williams Förlags AB made it Sweden's largest comic-book publisher.[24]

The Phantom's Scandinavian success was offset by the character's lackluster performance in the United States, where it continued to lose ground against more popular superhero comics. Determined to keep their best-known adventure heroes on magazine newsstands, King Features Syndicate briefly acted as a comic-book publisher, releasing new series of *The Phantom*, *Flash Gordon*, and *Mandrake the Magician* under its own King Comics imprint throughout 1966–67. The short-lived venture ended once King Features Syndicate sold the publishing rights to Charlton Press, which relaunched *The Phantom* comic book in 1969, together with new titles starring various King Features characters, including *Popeye* and *Beetle Bailey*.

Charlton Press began publishing song lyric sheets in the 1930s and established the Charlton Comic Group division in 1945, which eventually accounted for 50 percent of the company's total publishing output (Slezak, 1980: 184, 187). The company was unique in that it operated its own printing plant and a magazine distribution business, the Capital Distributing Company (Slezak, 1980: 184). Yet despite having these resources at its disposal, the Charlton Comic Group remained among the American comic-book industry's worst performers, accounting for just 10 percent of total market share in 1959 (Miller, 2008). Charlton's relaunch of *The Phantom* came towards the end of the company's brief foray into the superhero field during the mid- to late 1960s (Irving, 2000: 25–28). However, the new comic's inconsistent quality not only angered American audiences (Griffin and Griffin, ca. 2002) but also led to complaints from Lee Falk himself, which prompted Charlton to hire better illustrators and use translated *Phantom* stories from the Italian publisher, Edizioni Fratelli Spada (Brancatelli, 1999: 612). None of these efforts could reverse the title's declining circulation, which had dipped below 100,000 by the time Charlton canceled *The Phantom* in 1977 (Shedden, ca. 2002). Nevertheless, the Charlton Comic Group's version of *The Phantom* is fondly recalled by readers outside the United States. One reader remarked that the Charlton series featured "some of the best [Phantom] cover art" they'd seen (male respondent, 36–49 years old, Australia, July 16, 2012)—an opinion shared by another fan, who felt that Charlton artist Jim Aparo's *Phantom* covers "were excellent," while adding that Don Newton—a future *Batman* artist—also "did a good job" on the series (male respondent, 50–65 years old, Scotland, November 30, 2012).

The proliferation of new *Phantom* stories from the United States proved beneficial for Bennett, Coleman & Co., which by this time stood poised to dominate India's surging comic-book market as sales leaped from Rs.1 crore (Rs.10m) in 1978 to nearly Rs.5.5 crore (Rs. 55m) by 1982 (Singh, 1982: 84).[25] The surge in comic-book sales, according to Trevor Fishlock, reflected "a new demand for Indian heroes and stories to take their place alongside James Bond and Superman" (1987: 125). This demand was initially fueled by the founding editor of *Indrajal Comics*, Anant Pai, who left Bennett, Coleman & Co. in order to launch India's first locally drawn comic magazine, *Amar Chitra Katha* (*Immortal Picture Stories*), which retold stories taken from Hindu legends, along with dramatic episodes from Indian history, in pictorial form (Pritchett, 1997: 76–106; McLain, 2009b). *Indrajal Comics*, however, remained the market leader, although its initial sales were solid rather than spectacular. In 1978, after nearly 15 years of publication, *Indrajal Comics* was still selling fewer than 200,000 copies per month; but by 1982 its sales had surged to 580,000 copies per month (Singh, 1982: 84). *The Phantom* remained the magazine's headline feature, thanks largely to the series' atmospheric setting, which struck a chord with Indian readers (as elsewhere), if this comment is any indication:

[I loved] his mysterious outfit, the [mystical] Skull Cave in Deep Woods, and, of course, the 400-year old lineage of crime fighters! In India, he was known to us as "Betal"—[which] means ghost—in the *Indrajal Comics*. (Male respondent, 18–35 years old, India, March 22, 2012)

The magazine's editors drew on a selection of stories from King Features Syndicate, Gold Key Comics, and the Charlton Comic Group to satisfy public demand once *Indrajal Comics* moved from a fortnightly to a weekly release schedule in 1981. The visual diversity of these stories appealed to Indian readers, even if their enjoyment of *The Phantom* was not universally shared by their immediate family:

> I enjoyed all the *Phantom* stories that I read in *Indrajal Comics* . . . I did collect all the *Indrajals* and I had a 3-feet high stack of comics—but one day when I was not home, my mom sold everything to a *raddiwalla* [scrap-paper dealer]. It is [my] single biggest misfortune as far as comics are concerned. (Male respondent, 36–49 years old, India, July 1, 2012)

The commercial success of *Indrajal Comics* proved beyond doubt that there existed a large enough audience capable of sustaining domestic comic-book production. The popularity of American heroes, such as the Phantom and Flash Gordon, gave Bennett, Coleman & Co. the opportunity to use *Indrajal Comics* as a vehicle to promote indigenous comic-book characters. They struck immediate success with *Bahadur* (*Brave*), starring a reformed dacoit (robber) who, together with his girlfriend Bela, led a Citizens' Security Force to defend their village from the notorious Chambal Valley bandits. The series, created by Aabid Sutri and Govind Brahmania, was inspired by the crime wave then sweeping central India and met with immediate acclaim upon its debut in *Indrajal Comics* in 1976 (Khanduri, 2010: 178–79). The success of *The Phantom* provided Bennett, Coleman & Co. with the commercial means to support locally drawn comics, just as it had done so for Frew Publications in Australia in the 1940s.

By this time, however, Bennett, Coleman & Co. no longer retained exclusive comic-book rights to *The Phantom*, which was now being licensed to Indian newspapers and magazines by Advertising Films India (later AFI Features) on behalf of King Features Syndicate. The sheer size and linguistic diversity of India's media marketplace meant that different versions of

The Phantom were published for specific regions, and frequently appeared alongside *Indrajal Comics* throughout the 1970s.[26] *Vidyarthi Mithram Comics*, a Tamil-language magazine published by the Vidyarthi Mithram Press (Kerala), reprinted at least four episodes of *The Phantom* (renamed "Mayavi") in the mid-1970s. While *Indrajal Comics* had begun publishing Tamil-language editions in the mid- to late 1960s, the *Vidyarthi Mithram Comics* series was printed in black and white and, at just 24 pages, was considerably shorter than the 32-page, full-color *Indrajal Comics* editions. *The Phantom* episodes reprinted in this Tamil-language magazine were heavily edited to fit this truncated format, but such cost-cutting measures were often necessary to ensure that Indian comics remained within the financial reach of everyday readers ("Muthufan," 2007).

Muthu Comics, launched in 1971, is historically credited with establishing the popular, widespread demand for Tamil-language comics in India. Published by Muthu Fine Arts (Sivakasi, Tamil Nadu), and edited by Mullai Thangarasan, *Muthu Comics* initially featured translated versions of British comic-book serials, such as *The Steel Claw*, *The Spider*, and *Robot Archie*, originally published by Fleetway Publications (U.K.). *Muthu Comics* subsequently published *The Phantom* (renamed *Mugamoodi Veethalar*, or *The Masked Phantom*) over fifteen issues published between 1977 and 1980. However, the series' appeal may have been hampered by the comic's erratic publishing schedule (Comicology, 2009).

Rani Comics subsequently emerged as India's most successful Tamil-language comics publisher. Launched in 1984, *Rani Comics*, like its chief rival, *Muthu Comics*, relied on using translated versions of British comic-book serials and newspaper strips, the most popular of these being the *James Bond* comic strip, which was originally created for the *Daily Express* (U.K.) in 1958 (Comicology, 2009). *Rani Comics*' success arguably owed much to the wide public exposure it gained from being sold through the extensive distribution channels operated by its owner, the Tamil-language newspaper *Dina Thanati* (*Daily Thanati*). India's newspaper and magazine publishers have historically relied on a complex network of wholesale distributors, regional agents, retail outlets (such as bookstalls and lending libraries), and street hawkers to service vast regional sales territories (Joshi, 1986: 216). *The Phantom* made its debut in *Rani Comics* in 1990 and appeared in every second issue until 1998, but only sporadically thereafter. However, it has been suggested that *Rani Comics*' sales suffered following the departure of its founding editor, S. Ramajayan, which heralded a period of poor-quality translations and an overall decline in production values (Comicology, 2009).[27] Full-color episodes of *The Phantom* appearing in *Rani Comics* from 2003 onwards were apparently scanned directly from old copies of *Indrajal Comics* (Shedden, 2004). Despite switching to full-color printing, and an expanded 84-page format, *Rani Comics* could not stave off declining sales and it ceased publication in 2005.

India's comic-book industry may have been on the cusp of explosive growth by the early 1980s, but the same could not be said for Australia, where comics lost further ground to rival media formats. *The Phantom* was now Frew Publications' sole remaining title, which still posted average sales of 60,000–70,000 copies per issue throughout Australia, New Zealand, and the South Pacific in the mid-1970s. But local publishers now had to contend with color television broadcasting (launched in 1975), which was soon followed by newer forms of audiovisual entertainment, such as videocassette recorders and compact discs. As one Sydney newsagent remarked, "children don't need comics as much as they used to" (quoted in Porter, 1981: 30). Yet children's interaction with comics was changing and was no longer confined solely to magazines. A 1984 survey of junior high-school students' reading habits across three Sydney schools found that they overwhelmingly preferred humorous newspaper comic strips (e.g., *Garfield*), magazines (e.g., *Australian Mad*) and European comic "albums" (e.g., *Asterix*) to other genres. More worryingly for Frew Publications, the survey concluded that "adventure comics" such as *The Phantom* "were not particularly popular" among students (Hunt, 1986: 42–43).

Semic Press's entry into the Australian market at this time occurred almost by chance, but would ultimately prove fortuitous for Frew Publications —although it would not be without controversy. David Yaffa Jr. was representing the Yaffa Syndicate at the Frankfurt Book Fair in Germany in 1980 when he saw a Semic Press display featuring the *Fantomen* magazine. He brought back sample copies to show Ron Forsyth, co-owner of Frew Publications. Impressed by the artwork, Forsyth authorized Yaffa Jr. to purchase the Australasian publishing rights for *Fantomen* stories on behalf of Frew Publications. The first Swedish-drawn *Fantomen* story to appear in Australia was "The Ghost" (Lundström and Vallvé, 1972: 3–30), published in

The Phantom, no. 730 (1981) and translated by Ron's daughter-in-law, Astri Forsyth. Frew Publications promoted it as a "new—different—story fresh from The Phantom's diaries," never before published in Australia, but made no mention of its Swedish origins. The change did not, however, go unnoticed by John Henderson, president of the Phantom Club (Australia)—a fan organization—who made the following comments in the club's *Jungle Beat* newsletter:

> Issue 730 is a new story which I believe originates from Sweden . . .
> While I thought the story was basically a good one, with lots of fast-moving action, I must admit to being a little disappointed with parts of the script and some of the drawing. I think the inexperience of both the writer and artist allowed The Phantom to get himself into situations, and to make comments that he would normally avoid. (Henderson [attrib.], ca. 1981: 6)

Nevertheless, Frew's commitment to reprinting Swedish *Fantomen* stories in Australia allowed the company to overcome its dependence on the slow trickle of new Lee Falk–scripted stories from America and to infuse *The Phantom* with "new" content without incurring the expense of commissioning locally drawn stories. Frew Publications released two further Swedish-drawn stories in 1981 (*The Phantom*, nos. 731 and 732), but waited until 1983 before repeating the experiment.

Australia would eventually become a significant export market for Semic Press's *Fantomen* series. Yet the Swedish company's route to Australia does not neatly conform to the center-to-periphery dynamic that has historically characterized the cultural imperialism model of global media diffusion. This commercial exchange was instigated, not by Semic Press, but through an Australian intermediary (Yaffa Syndicate) acting on behalf of a client (Frew Publications) which occupied a relatively dominant position within its own "peripheral" market (Australia). This repeated the historical pattern of the 1920s and 1930s, whereby foreign media organizations initiated deals with American feature syndicates and facilitated the acceptance of American comic strips throughout international markets. The key difference here was that, by the early 1980s, the center of comic-book production had—in the case of *The Phantom*—shifted from the United States to Sweden.

Frew Publications faced further challenges following the appointment of King Features Syndicate's new Australian licensing representative. While the Yaffa Syndicate still retained the newspaper comic-strip syndication rights to *The Phantom*, its affiliated company — Yaffa Darlington Licensing — lost the comic-book licensing rights to the series in 1987 (*Intellectual Property Reports*, 1991), which were now held by Gaffney International Licensing. The company's founder, Fred Gaffney (b. 1946) — widely regarded as the "father" of Australia's media licensing industry (Jenkins, 2007; Schmidt, 2007) — was reportedly keen to award *The Phantom* comic-book license to Robert Ungar, whose company (Budget Books) had for years successfully repackaged British and American comic strips in paperback editions for the Australian market. Gaffney International Licensing allowed Budget Books to release four *Phantom* comic-strip paperback collections throughout 1985–87. Not only was this a commercially provocative act, but the Budget Books series' superior production values — and use of unedited Lee Falk stories — drew unwanted comparisons with Frew Publications' rather shopworn comic magazine.[28]

In 1987 Ron Forsyth and Lawford "Jim" Richardson approached Sydney journalist and publisher Jim Shepherd (1933–2013) for advice on how to revitalize *The Phantom* and thus defend their business from this wholly unexpected competitor. "They were getting pretty old and, while they hadn't lost interest in *The Phantom*," Shepherd recalled, "they needed someone who could give them a few ideas about what could be done to kick it along a bit" (quoted in Patrick, 2007b). Shepherd flew to New York and secured an extension of Frew's publishing license for *The Phantom* comic book, after outlining his plans for rejuvenating the magazine to King Features Syndicate's international licensing representatives.

Returning to Australia, Shepherd learned that Richardson had died in his absence, while Forsyth had been hospitalized after suffering a stroke. Shepherd bought out Richardson's share of the company and became co-owner of Frew Publications with Ron's son, Peter Forsyth.[29] Shepherd made cosmetic changes to *The Phantom*, such as printing the covers on glossy paper, and introduced his regular "Message from the Publisher" column, along with the "Phantom Forum" letters page, in 1988. Following the retirement of Frew's long-serving cover artist Thomas ("Tommy") Hughes that same year, Shepherd hired Australian artists to design covers that reflected each issue's story—something that Frew Publications had not consistently done for decades.

Shepherd commissioned market research which revealed that the average age of readers (twenty years and upwards) was considerably older than previously thought, and that many fans could remember pivotal scenes from decades-old *Phantom* stories (Power and Pietrzykowski, 1995: 19; Shepherd, 1998: 11). Keen to capitalize on this overlooked audience, Shepherd enlisted the help of Australian fans and collectors to reassemble Lee Falk's earliest stories from the 1930s and 1940s, many of which had never been reprinted in their entirety by Frew Publications. The first of these restored episodes, "The Phantom Goes to War" (Falk, Moore and McCoy, 1988 [1942–43]: 12–111) was, according to Shepherd, a "blockbuster sell-out" (1998: 11). The story's wartime setting resonated with Australian audiences, who, together with Americans, shared the historical experience of battling Japanese forces in the Pacific theater during World War II. Some readers considered it to be a fascinating historical document in its own right, which challenged their perceptions of the Phantom:

The Phantom Goes to War [was another favorite story] because by the time I read that, I was old enough to understand propaganda, which was fascinating. [The Phantom says] "This is war, Diana," after he's just killed (!) a Japanese General. (Male respondent, 18–35 years old, Australia, June 9, 2012)

By now, *The Phantom* was selling nearly 70 percent of each issue's print run (Power and Pietrzykowski, 1995: 21). Shepherd decided to package the forthcoming 1,000th issue of *The Phantom* (no. 972, 1991) as a 290-page "blockbuster" edition, selling for the unheard-of price of A$10.00.[30] Despite reservations from the distributor, Gordon & Gotch—which believed Frew would be lucky to sell 30,000 copies at most—Shepherd gambled on a 45,000-copy print run, which sold out within a fortnight (Patrick, 2007b). Shepherd's success eventually allowed him to bypass dealing with Gaffney Licensing International and negotiate a publishing deal with King Features Syndicate directly—an apparently unprecedented arrangement.[31]

Frew Publications developed an eclectic publishing schedule that combined "classic" Lee Falk stories and new Swedish *Fantomen* stories. But the company remained dependent on Semic Press for most of its editorial content; by 1994, translated *Fantomen* stories accounted for nearly 70 percent of the company's annual output (Frew Publications, 1995: 314). Nevertheless, Shepherd maintained that he was "ultra-selective" when choosing *Fantomen* stories for the Australian market. Swedish stories that focused too heavily on Scandinavian history, or which featured strong fantasy elements, were, he claimed, not popular with Australian readers, and could cost Frew Publications between 5,000–8,000 "casual [reader] sales" for those issues.[32]

Frew Publications' commitment to restoring early Lee Falk stories was therefore a defensive strategy designed to counter frequent criticism of the Swedish *Fantomen* episodes. Shepherd felt compelled to address the issue in the magazine's Phantom Forum letters page:

> We continue to receive . . . letters from readers who are not enchanted with the European stories . . . I have no intention of running letters which are centered exclusively on an anti-European story theme. The point has been raised, all at Frew have noted same, and there the matter will rest. (Shepherd, 1989: 3)

However, the enthusiastic reception that met the rerelease of uncensored, "classic" Lee Falk episodes suggests that Australian audiences had a greater affinity with the politically conservative ethos of *Phantom* narratives from the 1930s and 1940s, which were frequently at odds with the more "progressive" ideals that underscored many Swedish *Fantomen* stories. Therefore, while Frew Publications remained economically dependent on the supply of new Swedish stories, it had to take steps to ensure that it did not alienate its core readership's preferred (American) interpretation of the character.

Why was The Phantom allowed to undergo such a radical transformation at the hands of his Swedish publisher during the 1960s? The answer arises, in part, from the commercial decision taken by Åhlén & Åkerlund to create its own content for the *Fantomen* magazine—a decision precipitated by the death of longtime American artist Wilson McCoy, which threatened to disrupt the flow of stories from the United States deemed acceptable to the Swedish market. Thus, a commercial crisis gave rise to new creative opportunities for the series' Swedish publisher. Swedish authors and illustrators were able to refashion the Phantom as a uniquely "Scandinavian" hero in ways they simply could not achieve with other comic-book heroes (such as Batman or Spider-Man), who were inextricably defined by their "American" outlook and origins. Thus began the process that would eventually see Sweden become an international production node in *The Phantom* comics' franchise. However, the ongoing transformation of the Phantom would also take place far beyond Sweden's borders, nor would it be confined to the pages of comic books. "The Ghost Who Walks" would come to take on many guises in Australia, Sweden, and India in ways that would challenge the wildest imaginings of his corporate gatekeepers.

CHAPTER SIX

ONE HERO, MANY MASKS

I t did not take Diana Palmer long to realize that the "honeymoon" phase of her marriage to the Phantom was well and truly over. Living in the Deep Woods, and coping with the primitive living conditions of the Skull Cave, Diana saw her husband for what he truly was—a costumed layabout who spent his days chasing after nonexistent pirates. Diana reached her wits' end when the Phantom's faithful wolf, Devil, attacked and killed a visiting Avon Lady. Deprived of even these most basic feminine comforts, Diana killed Devil and served up his remains to her unsuspecting husband for dinner.

This scene will not be found in any episode of *The Phantom* comic strip, nor in the pages of *The Phantom* comic magazine. It was broadcast on Australian television in 1978, when comedian Paul Hogan portrayed "The Ghost Who Walks" on his top-rated sketch-comedy program, *The Paul Hogan Show*, long before he became the world-famous star of *Crocodile Dundee* (1986). The episode aired on the Nine Network soon after "The Wedding of The Phantom" (Falk and Barry, 1993c [1977–78]: 70–91) was published in Australia by Frew Publications. That very issue of *The Phantom* comic— titled "Married at Last"—was being read by Hogan's dim-witted housemate, "Strop" (played by John Cornell), at the beginning of the segment.

This televised satire was a clear indicator of the Phantom's entrenched status in mainstream Australian culture. But it was also noteworthy for the way in which it evoked the sexual interplay between the Phantom and Diana Palmer portrayed in the comic strip, only to reduce it to the banal conventions of a television sitcom, wherein the Phantom (Paul Hogan) becomes a henpacked husband, while Diana Palmer (Delvene Delaney) is turned into a nagging, frustrated housewife.

This is but one example drawn from an eclectic array of unauthorized media texts produced in Australia, Sweden, and India which have in turn celebrated, mocked, and interrogated the world of the Phantom. Conveyed through experimental films, television series, and subversive artworks, these sometimes scandalous portrayals of the Phantom nevertheless exhibit a level of fidelity to the original comic strip that has not always been evident in "authorized" media adaptations of the Phantom.

Nor have these transgressive texts existed solely on the fringes of experimental or underground media circuits. On occasion, King Features Syndicate (and its international representatives) have formally sanctioned "alternative" versions of the Phantom which have been at odds with the character's official narrative, or which have even risked alienating loyal fans altogether. Conversely, King Features Syndicate has not hesitated to seek legal recourse against any unauthorized interpretations of the Phantom which threatened its commercial interests. Their conflicting response suggests that there is a tacit recognition, even at the corporate level, of the difficulties in sustaining the stark official/unofficial binary that is frequently cited in order to justify the legal measures used to deter the unauthorized use of trademarked media properties. These subversive texts are nonetheless significant as reflections of the Phantom's popular standing in Australia, Sweden, and India and for their capacity to address the racial, sexual, and political subtexts embedded in the original comic strip, in ways that "official" adaptations seldom have.

The Celluloid Ghost

The resurgence of the "comic-book movie," heralded by the blockbuster *Batman* feature film (1989), might seem like a relatively recent phenomenon, but superheroes flared across movie screens within a few short years of Superman's debut in *Action Comics* in 1938. But whereas Superman's initial fame stemmed from his appearance in comic magazines, the same cannot be said for most American comic-book characters, who today reach new audiences via altogether different routes. As Elisaret Ioannidou observes:

Those outside the [comic-book] subculture [are] most likely to obtain knowledge of the superhero . . . solely by means of their filmic adaptations . . . [These] films introduce themselves to the public as the real deal because ignorance of the comic books' contents prevent direct comparison. (Ioannidou, 2013: 233)

The Phantom remains the exception which proves the rule, despite the fact that he has been the subject of numerous film and television adaptations over several decades. Print media have been chiefly responsible for exposing successive generations of readers in Australia, Sweden, and India to "The Ghost Who Walks," and they still remain the key media outlet for the character. Approximately 80 percent of Australian, Swedish, and Indian fans surveyed for this study first discovered *The Phantom* in a newspaper, magazine, or comic book. Fewer than 5 percent of survey respondents first saw the character on television or at the cinema—in fact, a greater number of fans (8.8 percent) were introduced to *The Phantom* by a family member.

Nevertheless, Hollywood has long recognized the box-office potential of comic-strip characters, whose exposure through newspapers nationwide had already made them household names. In 1923 Universal Studios produced the first of several comedies based on *The Gumps* (created by Sidney Smith), making it the first live-action film adaptation of a comic strip. Their success led to a spate of comedy "shorts" based on comic strips during the 1920s, including *Buster Brown* (1925) and *Bringing Up Father* (1928) (Spears, 1956: 317–19). Adventure-serial comic strips, however, seemed ready-made for the new trend of motion-picture serials, which were screened as "cliff-hanger" episodes over several weeks, thus enticing viewers back to the cinema on a regular basis to follow the drama to its conclusion. King Features Syndicate moved swiftly into this market, enlisting Universal Studios to produce the live-action *Flash Gordon* serial (1936), based on their science fiction comic-strip drawn by Alex Raymond (1909–1956). The company subsequently partnered with Columbia Pictures, which produced a twelve-part serial based on Lee Falk's *Mandrake the Magician* (1939), starring Robert Hull in the lead role. Falk, however, described it as "just terrible . . . Mandrake didn't even wear a moustache, which disappointed me" (quoted in Madison, 1996: 48).

When measured against the meagre production values common to many motion-picture serials of its era, Columbia Pictures' subsequent production of *The Phantom*, released as a fifteen-part "chapter-play" in 1943, is a relatively superior example of the genre. Tom Tyler (1903–1954), a physically imposing actor described by some as "the Gary Cooper of B-films" (Harmon and Glut, 1973: 268), was cast as the Phantom, following his starring performance in *The Adventures of Captain Marvel* (Republic Pictures, 1941), the first live-action screen adaptation of a comic-book superhero. *The Phantom* was directed by veteran filmmaker B. Reeves Eason (1886–1956), whose credits dated back to the silent film era. The screenplay, written in part by Victor McLeod (1903–1972) and Leslie Swabacker (1885–1955), adhered closely to Lee Falk and Ray Moore's original conception of the character.[1] While only 13 percent of survey participants had seen the Columbia Pictures serial, the majority of fans seemed to enjoy it as the distinctive product of a bygone era:

> The serial is great for what it is, quite dated, but still a lot of fun. Tom Tyler was a good Phantom in every way, and it is quite faithful to the source material. (Male respondent, 18–35 years old, Norway, March 23, 2012)

The Phantom serial enjoyed a long afterlife following its original cinematic release, judging by this reader's account:[2]

> I have a vague recollection of the serial which was re-screened in my hometown cinema in the fifties. Lots of running around in the woods! The character looked right, and must have made an impression, because I remember dressing up and playing the part in my backyard! (Male respondent, 50–65 years old, New Zealand, June 19, 2012)

The Phantom, however, endured a checkered screen career for several decades thereafter. In 1961 Tele-Screen Productions, together with King Features Television, produced a pilot episode of *The Phantom* starring Roger Creed (1915–1997), but the series was never picked up by American television networks. The Phantom later appeared in *Popeye Meets the Man Who Hated Laughter* (1972), a bizarre and crudely produced animated telemovie screened on the ABC network. The show, produced by King Features Entertainment, was designed to showcase the company's best-known comic strip characters, including Flash Gordon and Mandrake the Magician, but as one critic later remarked, "most of these characters were already well past their peak of popularity by the time this film was made" (Hall, 2006).

"The Ghost Who Walks" would be reunited with his comic-strip compatriots in *Defenders of the Earth* (1986), an animated television series developed by King Features Entertainment as a promotional vehicle for its "big three" adventure-strip heroes: Flash Gordon, Mandrake the Magician, and The Phantom. Set in the then-futuristic world of AD 2015, the series pitted its stars against Flash Gordon's arch-nemesis, Ming the Merciless, whose army of Ice Robots threatened to plunder Earth's vast natural resources. The Phantom underwent an extreme makeover for the series. Taught the secrets of the jungle by the Bandar natives of the Deep Woods, The Phantom now uttered a single phrase— "I need the strength of ten tigers"—to temporarily acquire super powers. However, The Phantom was stripped of his Colt .45 pistols, and his Skull Ring now emitted a laser beam which left a "skull mark" on their skin instead.

In a radical departure from their established comic strip scenarios, Flash Gordon, Mandrake the Magician, and Lothar (Mandrake's crime-fighting companion) were accompanied by their on-screen children: Rick Gordon (an athletic computer genius); Kshin (an Asian orphan adopted by Mandrake, and proficient in martial arts); and L. J. (Lothar Jr., a "streetwise" high-school student). The Phantom now had a teenage daughter, Jedda, who could communicate telepathically with animals and possessed telekinetic powers. Their inclusion, however improbable, was considered crucial to the show's success. Bruce Paiser, the president of King Features Entertainment, acknowledged that comic strips like *Mandrake the Magician* and *The Phantom* "were dropping out of newspapers at a fearful clip" and were dismissed by many as "yesterday's mashed potatoes" (quoted in Schwed, 1986: 6). Setting *Defenders of the Earth* in the space-age future, and making the main heroes' children central to the story line, was deemed essential in order to attract a "younger audience" (Schwed, 1986: 6).

Defenders of the Earth was seen by nearly 15 percent of survey respondents, but its portrayal of the Phantom was roundly criticized by most fans, who otherwise enjoyed the series:

> [It] was nothing special to remember, but I enjoyed watching it nonetheless. [I] did not like the "strength of ten tigers" bit about The Phantom, as it contradicts [the] comic book character [who has no super powers]. (Male respondent, 18–35 years old, India, March 21, 2012)

Yet some fans acknowledged that, whatever its faults, *Defenders of the Earth* arguably helped make the "television generation" aware of the Phantom in ways that King Features Entertainment no doubt hoped it would:

[It] would have been great when I was eight years old, but is hard to watch for adults. Though some of the Phantom-centered episodes are good fun, and it's a nice way of introducing the character to kids who don't read comics. (Male respondent, 18–35 years old, Norway, March 23, 2012)

Comments such as these only reinforce how central electronic media had become in the everyday lives of children, who had once been considered the primary audience for comic books. This trend was now becoming evident in Sweden, where, according to the editor Ulf Granberg, sales of the *Fantomen* comic magazine began plummeting by 5,000–10,000 copies per issue during the early 1980s. This was, he believes, a reflection of the rapidly changing media environment:[3]

Comics were once a staple of Swedish children's entertainment diet . . . [but] in the 1980s, the picture of entertainment started to change . . . children could rent a video for the cost of a comic book . . . and music became more and more popular among [Swedish] children, who spent more money on music [than on comics].[4]

Similar changes in the leisure habits of children and adolescents were already apparent in Australia, and would gradually take hold in India throughout the 1990s. Making the Phantom relevant and appealing to the "video generation" would continue to test the ingenuity of film and television producers for years to come.

If Columbia Pictures' production of *The Phantom* was made at the commercial peak of Hollywood's studio system, the feature-film version of *The Phantom* (1996) was the product of an altogether different moviemaking era. The story behind its development not only highlights the globalization of American film production, but the project's Australian genesis also underscores the character's entrenched popularity "Down Under." The Australian businessman Bruce Sherlock—a self-confessed *Phantom* fan—and Peter Sjoquist (production manager on the Australian film *Crocodile Dundee*) purchased film rights to *The Phantom* from King Features Syndicate after meeting Lee Falk in 1987. Village Roadshow Pictures, an Australian firm with extensive interests in hardtop cinemas and film and video distribution, came on board as a production partner with Paramount Pictures (U.S.). The film would be partly shot at the former company's Warner Roadshow Movie Studios based in Queensland, Australia, which—thanks to then-favorable currency exchange rates between the U.S. and Australian dollars—became a cost-effective, offshore production site for American film studios throughout the 1990s (Patrick, 2015: 19–35).

Despite the film's multimillion-dollar budget, *The Phantom* was in many ways a throwback to the spirit of the Columbia Pictures "cliff-hanger" serial. The film's screenwriter, Jeffrey Boam (1946–2000), whose credits included *Indiana Jones and the Last Crusade* (1989), explained why he chose to set the story in the comic strip's original 1930s milieu:

> The Phantom . . . holds to old-fashioned values like honor and integrity, loyalty and courage . . . [The film] had to be in that period, because I don't think a lot of those ideas translate well into the present. (Quoted in Scapperotti, 1995: 8)

The film's star, Billy Zane, who first read the comic while filming *Dead Calm* (1989) in Australia, publicly embraced the Phantom as a positive role model (Paramount Pictures, 1996, n.p.). Simon Wincer, a veteran Australian filmmaker and lifelong *Phantom* reader, was chosen to direct the film. Despite the cast and crew's enthusiasm for the project, *The Phantom* was a box-office failure, earning just $16,000,000 in ticket sales from its American theatrical release against its $45,000,000 production budget (Hindes, 1996: 10).[5]

Nevertheless, *The Phantom* feature film arguably remains the best-known screen adaptation of the character produced to date. Nearly 42 percent of survey respondents had seen the film, but their opinions were often starkly divided. Some Swedish fans, for example, felt it was at odds with the overall tone of the *Fantomen* comic, which was increasingly pitched towards an older audience by the mid-1990s:

> The movie is very much a matinee adventure, and as such, I like it. In Sweden, The Phantom [comic] then tried a darker, more grown-up attitude, which this movie didn't really fit, but I think it connected well with the feel of the eighties' [Swedish comic]. (Male respondent, 36–49 years old, Sweden, April 23, 2012)

Boam's screenplay drew heavily on Lee Falk's earliest comic-strip episodes, "The Singh Brotherhood" (1936) and "The Sky Band" (1936–37), but some fans still felt the film took too many liberties with Falk's original conception of the character:

> [The film was] pretty lousy. Five minutes into the movie, The Phantom had injured or killed people (not just shoot any guns out of their hands), ordered beer in a bar (instead of just milk), and showed his eyes without the mask. These have been important characteristics in the magazine, and the movie just made The Phantom into any other superhero in a silly suit. (Female respondent, 36–49 years old, Sweden, July 12, 2012)

It is doubtful that King Features Syndicate would have been unduly concerned with the objections raised by a vocal and articulate minority of die-hard fans. It is far more likely that the company would have been vitally interested in the film's potential to generate wider public interest in the character's moribund "brand," which—if successful—would have generated further revenues from the sale of licensed *Phantom* merchandise produced to coincide with the film's release. That the film clearly failed to do so would have mattered far more to the company than the passionate critique of comic-book fans.

Policing the Screen

The Phantom feature film may have strayed from fans' collective vision of the character, but it was nevertheless an official adaptation of the comic strip, formally sanctioned by its trademark owner, King Features Syndicate. The same could not be said, on legal or aesthetic grounds, for the Phantom's controversial reincarnation on Indian television. *Betaal Pachisi* was a Hindi-language television serial directed by Sunil Agnihotri, which aired on the Doordarshan 2 (DD2) television network during 1997–98. Betaal Pachisi (played by Shabaaz Khan) was a mysterious masked hero who rose from the grave every 100 years to reclaim his secret "bat cave," deep in the fictitious Indian jungles of Dongralu. Donning his red body costume, cowl, and black eye-mask, Betaal Pachisi, accompanied by his white stallion and loyal Alsatian hound, confronts his arch-nemesis, Heeralal, the "devil king." Romantic complications arise when the beautiful Sonu (Sonu Walia) falls in love with Betaal, to the annoyance of her archaeologist companion, Harry (Tom Alter), who secretly yearns for her.

Sunil Agnihorti willingly conceded that his television series owed a considerable debt to Lee Falk's original creation:

> I was inspired by The Phantom, I admit. When I first read these comics, I used to wonder why no one was making a film about them, because they had all the elements of a good film—love, action, adventure, and an exotic atmosphere. (Quoted in Pinto, 1996: A7)

But as the series' premiere drew closer, Agnihorti chose his words more carefully. While admitting that he originally hoped to produce an adaptation of *The Phantom*, this did not eventuate due to protracted "legal wrangling" (Sharma, 1997). With Doordashan now committed to broadcasting the series, Agnihorti said he decided to "completely [forget] about the original Phantom and [create] my own character" (quoted in Sharma, 1997).

While few television critics were swayed by Agnihorti's claims about the originality of *Betaal Pachisi* (Pinto, 1996: A7; Sharma, 1997), the series, in a roundabout way, evoked the Phantom's prewar Indian setting. It did so through more than just boasting an Indian cast and crew, or by virtue of its distinctive "Bollywood" aesthetic. (A dance sequence featuring Sonu Walia, surrounded by pygmies, was seen in the first episode [Pinto, 1996: A7].) Agnihorti had his hero forsake the Phantom's "skull" emblem for the swastika, a symbol common to Indian Buddhist worship. *Betaal Pachisi* can be viewed as a parallel interpretation of *The Phantom* which amplified the Afro-Asian setting and quasi-mythical aspects of the original text.

King Features Syndicate, however, took a less charitable view and filed a lawsuit against Sunil Agnihorti with the Delhi High Court in April 1997. King Features sought a permanent injunction preventing Agnihorti from either making or releasing any television serial or cinematographic film entitled either *The Phantom* and/or *Betaal*, and sought damages to the value of Rs.5,00,500 ($91,000), with legal costs to be awarded in their favor (*King Features Syndicate vs. Sunil Agnihorti & Ors*, 1997: 1–2). This lawsuit needs to be understood in the context of the dramatic changes sweeping India's comic-book industry at that time. Throughout the 1990s, Bennett, Coleman & Co. began implementing severe cost-cutting measures, which led to the closure of *Indrajal Comics* in 1990 and the subsequent demise of *The Illustrated Weekly of India* in 1993. Competition from television no doubt drove such changes; not only had the number of household television sets increased eightfold to

30,800,000 by 1991 (Bhatt, 1997: 154), but there was now greater diversity of programming. Local cable television operators transmitted foreign satellite telecasts (such as Hong Kong-based Star TV) directly to Indian households for a small fee, thus bypassing the monopoly, state-owned broadcaster Doordarshan (Manchanda, 1998: 138). Indeed, Doordashan 2 was launched as an entertainment channel in response to competition from rival Hindi-language satellite broadcasters, such as Zee TV (Ninan, 1995: 154–175). Rina Puri, editor of the *Amar Chitra Katha* comic book, recalled that when "the Cartoon Network [TV] channel came to India [it] pretty much halved our sales" (quoted in *The National*, 2011).

Despite this challenging environment, the New Delhi-based publisher Diamond Comics purchased the comic-book rights to *The Phantom* from AFI Features, which was now King Features Syndicate's Indian representative. While Diamond Comics was best known for violent, nationalistic action heroes like Dynamite (Rao, 1996: 41–42), the company's managing director, Gulshan Rai, maintained that *The Phantom* nevertheless appealed to its working-class, Hindi-speaking audience: "The stories were simple, [offered] interesting adventures and [were set in a] jungle environment."[6] The company repackaged *The Phantom* for its popular *Diamond Comics Digest* series, which was published in Hindi, English, and Bengali editions. In an affidavit filed with the Delhi High Court as part of King Features' legal proceedings, Gulshan Rai stated that annual sales of *The Phantom* comic magazine exceeded 4,000,000 copies by 1996, which underscored this emerging market's economic value to King Features Syndicate. Because the Hindi-language edition of *The Phantom* was titled *Betaal* (meaning "ghost" or "specter"), Rai argued that any planned broadcast of *Betaal Pachisi* would confuse television viewers, who might think that the series was based on the comic magazine (*King Features Syndicate vs. Sunil Agnihorti & Ors*, 1997: 6).

King Features' lawsuit enumerated many points of similarity between the two works, even claiming that the swastika symbol shown on Betaal's belt buckle in the television series strongly resembled "the peace sign" (i.e., the "Good Mark") ring worn on the Phantom's left hand (*King Features Syndicate vs. Sunil Agnihorti & Ors*, 1997: 6). King Features also expressed concern that *Betaal Pachisi* would further infringe their copyright and trademark ownership of *The Phantom* feature film, which was scheduled for staggered release in international cinema markets throughout 1996–97 (*King Features*

Syndicate vs. Sunil Agnihorti & Ors, 1997: 2). The Delhi High Court, however, ruled in favor of the defendant, Sunil Agnihorti. While acknowledging that the defendant had used ideas and "materials" contained in the plaintiff's comic magazines, the court found that defendant had "[used] them for a different purpose" as a television serial, rather than a comic magazine. The key difference in the opinion of the court was not so much the originality of the idea itself, but the form in which that idea was expressed. Therefore, the presentation of *Betaal Pachisi* as a television serial did not represent an instance of copyright infringement (*King Features Syndicate vs. Sunil Agnihorti & Ors,* 1997: 17).

King Features Syndicate could only have been dissatisfied with this outcome. The company's decision to seek an injunction against any broadcast of *Betaal Pachisi* suggested a renewed corporate awareness of the character's economic potential as a multimedia licensing franchise, spearheaded by the release of *The Phantom* motion picture. King Features' financial commitment to *The Phantom* was arguably now greater than ever before, and necessitated legal measures designed to prevent others from "passing off" imitations of *The Phantom* as original works. The controversy surrounding *Betaal Pachisi* suggests that King Features Syndicate clearly felt that this television serial, produced for a state-owned broadcaster capable of reaching millions of viewers, warranted a forceful legal challenge.

Ersatz Visions

The distinctions between authorized and unlawful interpretations of the Phantom have not always been so starkly delineated—at least not within the context of Indian cinema. Such ambiguities are evident in *Bundal Baaz* (1976), a Hindi-language romantic comedy directed by Shammi Kapoor (1931–2011). The story concerns a young daydreamer, Rajaram (played by Rajesh Khanna), who longs to escape his poor village and pretends to be wealthy so that he can marry his sweetheart, Nisha (Sulakshana Pandit), whose father wants her to marry a famous boxer, Ranjit (Gopal Bedi). The film's remarkable opening scenes reveal Rajesh Khanna dressed as the Phantom, pursuing a gang of bank robbers (led by Gopal Bedi) and chasing their getaway car along a tree-lined boulevard before apprehending them in some nearby backstreets. This "dream sequence" ends with Rajaram suddenly awakening in a student cafeteria, poring over copies of *Indrajal Comics*, and awkwardly explaining to his sweetheart Nisha why he admires the Phantom. Whether Bennett, Coleman & Co. knew of this "adaptation" is unclear, as they are not listed in the film's production credits—but it is difficult to imagine they would have disapproved of such generous publicity for *Indrajal Comics*.

This same affectionate spirit was evident in *Fanta* (1973), an experimental film directed by the Australian painter and "underground" filmmaker Garry Shead (b. 1942). The film opens with a young man, played by artist Peter Kingston (b. 1943), purchasing a copy of *The Phantom* from a newspaper kiosk as he boards a Sydney Harbor ferry. As he furtively reads the comic, he fantasizes about becoming the Phantom and dreams of rescuing a beautiful female passenger, recast as the gangster's moll, "Baby Jane" (played by Wendy Whiteley, b. 1941), from the clutches of another passenger, transformed into the evil crime boss "Alva Blowfoot" (Michael Hobbs). Briefly overpowered by Blowfoot's henchmen, the Phantom is tied to the tracks of a railway overpass but is rescued by Baby Jane, and he eventually apprehends Blowfoot and his gang. His mission accomplished, the film closes with the Phantom, now dressed in his civilian guise of "Kit Walker," disembarking from the ferry.

If the television series *Betaal Pachisi* tried to conceal (however poorly) its similarities to the Phantom, Garry Shead's *Fanta* constantly drew attention to its source material. The film is interspersed with close-ups of Frew Publications' *Phantom* comic magazine, as the voice-over narration recites the legend of "The Ghost Who Walks." Peter Kingston, as the Phantom, knocks out his opponents with a single punch, leaving a distinctive skull mark on their jaw. But *Fanta* was as much a tongue-in-cheek protest as it was a fond tribute to the original comic strip, as Peter Kingston explained:

> We're rebelling against emotionalism in the character. We like our [Phantom] to be in the old, sterile mold. Today's masked man interests me less than the character he was years ago. (Quoted in Symons, 1973: 90)

Fanta was thus a nostalgic evocation of its creators' preferred interpretation of the Phantom, as recalled from the comic books of their childhood. Yet the film never once discarded its "underground" patina, and was first screened by the Sydney Filmmakers' Co-op at the New Theater (Sydney) in 1973 (Symons, 1973: 90). Even though *Fanta* and *Bundal Baaz* were made within a few years of each other, they were the products of two entirely different filmmaking aesthetics. Nevertheless, both films celebrate the idea of an "everyman" figure who dreams of becoming the Phantom. Perhaps these creators each sensed that their audiences identified—on some level—with The Phantom, who stood in opposition to implausibly "fantastic" superheroes endowed with powers from extraterrestrial forces (Superman), or via freak accidents (Spider-Man).

Guerrilla Image-Makers

During the 1960s, American painters such as Andy Warhol, Roy Lichtenstein, and Mel Ramos were among the key exponents of the Pop Art movement who appropriated comic-book imagery in ways that drew attention to both the banalities of mass media and the pretensions of "high art." This practice was adopted by alternative newspapers and magazines, which—together with agitprop image-makers—freely plundered "official" *Phantom* narratives to mount radical critiques of contemporary political and social issues.

Puss Magazine (1968–74) was a Swedish "underground" newspaper which reveled in notions of political and sexual liberation, but which rarely shrank from criticizing Sweden's left-wing political groups. It published a full-page collage of comic-book images, which depicted Superman (*Stålmannen*) and The Phantom (*Fantomen*) being pursued by reactionary forces for inciting proletarian rebellion. The sequence ends with the Phantom behind bars, declaring "Long live Marxism. Long live the people" (Davidson, 1982: 94–95). *Puss Magazine*'s portrayal of the Phantom as a revolutionary Marxist hero did, in a bizarre way, anticipate subsequent efforts made by Swedish writers to infuse *Fantomen* with progressive, social democratic values during the 1970s. However, it was unthinkable that Semic Press (as a subsidiary of the Bonnier media conglomerate) would have ever allowed its flagship comic magazine to denounce "Yankee imperialists" as "dangerous animals [who] have dug their own grave," as *Puss Magazine* freely did so (Davidson, 1982: 94–95).

Frew Publications' promotional campaign for *The Phantom* took on an altogether different meaning when it, too, was reimagined through the prism of radical politics. In the late 1970s, the company designed a new poster to promote *The Phantom* in newsagents, comic-book shops, and other retailers. The poster's image of a benign, smiling Phantom posing against a lush jungle backdrop was quickly adopted by an Australian activist group calling itself Without Authority. Under their hands, the Phantom swapped his skull emblem for an anti-uranium symbol and recited a radicalized version of the "oath of the skull":

> I swear on the skull of my anti-uranium badge to devote myself to the overthrow of Fraser, and to spend my life in the destruction of capitalism and the state.

Without Authority resituated the Phantom at the forefront of environmentalist and left-wing political groups' opposition to the decision made by Australia's reigning Liberal-National Party coalition government (led by Prime Minister Malcolm Fraser) to permit uranium mining in northern Australia in 1979.

This group's actions superficially conform to Henry Jenkins's conceptualization of media fans as "textual poachers" who "appropriate texts and reread them in a fashion that serves different interests" (Jenkins, 2013: 23). Through borrowing and reinterpreting images taken from "mass culture," Jenkins argues that these fans are attempting "to articulate to themselves and others unrealized possibilities within the original works," and addressing concerns "which often go unvoiced within the dominant media" (Jenkins, 2013: 23). Fans' creative endeavors, whether it be publishing newsletters or writing fan fiction (fanfic), typically reflect their shared enjoyment and appreciation of a popular media text, such as *Star Trek* or *Beauty and the Beast*, to use Jenkins's own examples. Where groups like Without Authority differed from self-styled "textual poachers" is that their appropriation of the Phantom had less to do with any sentimental affinity with the character, and arose out of political urgency instead.

Such conflicting impulses were on abundant display in *Ghost Who Walks Can Never Die*, a visual survey of comic-book superheroes in contemporary Australian art held at the Newcastle Region Art Gallery in 1977. Peter Kingston's array of wooden cutouts portraying various comic-book characters was a centerpiece of the exhibition. The Phantom, too, remained a central focus of Kingston's work, as he later explained:

> [These cut-outs] followed the love of comic books I shared with Garry Shead—and when you look at it, The Phantom is a very 2-D character. When you try to make them 3-D, I don't think it works. I thought The

Phantom and all those crooks were extremely 2-D, so it was a perfect cross-over to cut-out sculpture. (Quoted in Wilson, 2004: 62, 64)

Kingston's cut-out diorama, *The Wedding* (1977)—like Paul Hogan's televised comedy sketch—paid tribute to the Phantom and Diana Palmer's wedding, with the happy couple flanked by Hero, Devil, and the Bandar pygmies' chieftain, Guran. The work's deliberately naive quality evoked the "primitive" wood carvings of the Afro-Asian tribal cultures that lurked at the periphery of the Deep Woods (Newcastle Region Art Gallery, 1977: 9).

While Kingston's work is steeped in his abiding affection for the Phantom, the work of the French-born artist and printmaker Franck Gohier (b. 1968) is deliberately provocative and subversive. Gohier incorporates images from British and American comic books to comment on his experience of life in the "far north" of Australia, where he has lived since the mid-1970s (Angel, 2005: 72, 74). He frequently refers to the Phantom in his work to comment on the historical tensions between European settlers and Aboriginal Australians. *It's For Your Own Good* (ca. 2009) conveys a menacing ambiguity, as The Phantom—with guns blazing—looms over a huddled group of "native" children. But Gohier's work also frequently undercuts the Phantom's status as the unelected ruler of the jungle. *Big Boss* (ca. 2012), for example, portrays the Phantom slumped on the ground, impaled by a large hunting boomerang —presumably hurled by an unseen Aboriginal warrior—and becoming the victim of his own brutal brand of "jungle justice."

The visual appeal of comic-book imagery, along with the public recognition of the Phantom in particular, percolated down to community organizations and government agencies throughout Australia. In 1988, the Department of Community Services and Health commissioned Redback Graphix (Sydney) to design an AIDS-awareness poster for Torres Strait Islander communities in northeastern Australia. Collaborating with indigenous health care workers, Redback Graphix produced a poster design based on *The Phantom* comic, which was "popular with the locals" (Zagala, 2008: 80). The poster depicted a black superhero, Condoman (wearing a costume closely modeled on the Phantom's uniform), who brandished a packet of condoms, and urged people to practice safe sex using the motto: "Don't be shame, be game—use condoms!"[7]

This provocative reimagining of the Phantom as a virile, sexually active superhero is perhaps no less surprising than the character's portrayal as a radical political activist. Yet the simple act of foregrounding a black man in the role of a "superhero" also draws attention to just how infrequently African characters have appeared on the covers of the Australian edition of *The Phantom* comic book, except as hostile "savages," or as urban lawbreakers —a trend which has also been observable in both *Fantomen* (Sweden) and *Indrajal Comics* (India) for several decades.

The visual representation of Condoman, clad in his skin-tight costume, highlights a further sexual dimension of the superhero genre. Gillian Freeman's sardonic review of mass-market erotic literature acknowledged that, for most children, comic-book heroes like Batman "merely wear curious and exciting clothes" (1967: 178). But when juxtaposed against adult sadomasochistic literature, they convey an altogether different image:

> In almost every comic there now appears to be an equivalent male [to Batman], masked or goggled, booted, dressed in rubber, studded with brass or steel, sometimes the enemy, often the hero. Analogous with every form of fetishism, the comic-strip characters could appear unchanged in deviationist literature. (Freeman, 1967: 179)

Scenes of sadomasochism were a regular occurrence in Lee Falk's earliest *Phantom* stories. In "The Sky Band" (Falk and Moore, 1996 [1936–37]), the Phantom found himself caught in a sexual tug-of-war between the Sky Band's icy blonde leader, the Baroness, and her seductive lieutenant, Sala. However, when the Phantom rejects the Baroness's sexual overtures, he soon feels the lash of her whip.

The Phantom dynasty relies on the eldest male of each generation fathering an heir to carry on the eternal crusade against piracy, greed, and cruelty. "The Ghost Who Walks" therefore refutes the notion of sexual renunciation common to many comic-book superheroes, who, according to John Shelton Lawrence and Robert Jewett, typically devise strategies for "segmenting the element of sexual need out of their personalities"—most notably in Clark Kent's refusal to disclose his true identity to Lois Lane, who remains infatuated with Superman (2002: 42–43). However, some texts have speculated about the level of sexual frustration that lurks beneath the Phantom's stony demeanor. The Australian humorist Robert M. McGuinness, in his comic-book satire "The Bantam," shows him overcome with lust when Guran tells him of a white woman, lost in the jungle, who seeks his help: "Hmm . . . ! I haven't seen a white woman in a long time now" (McGuinness, 1965). McGuinness tapped into the subterranean sexual themes which, according to Gerald Early, were key to the popularity of the "jungle comics" genre:

> Jungle comics were . . . constantly teasing the reader with his own adolescent fantasy about the jungle as a lawless place where interracial sex or, more accurately, interracial rape, may break out at any moment. (Early, 2006: 66)

The Phantom newspaper comic strip was never allowed to match the sexual suggestiveness common to many American "jungle comics" of the postwar era, but Lee Falk nevertheless relied on plots which employed the threat —sexual or otherwise—that dark-skinned "savages" posed to defenseless white women who strayed too far into the jungle. The Phantom was also frequently shown "taming" rebellious women by placing them across his knees and spanking them. Carl Johan de Geer (b. 1938), the avant-garde Swedish artist, filmmaker, and former contributor to *Puss* magazine, produced the lithographic print "Fantomen i Skanör" (1978), a sado-erotic collage of "spanking" images taken from the *Fantomen* comic strip, which also played on the city of Skanör's popular reputation as "the St. Tropez of Sweden."

Sanctioned "Poachers"

The erotic aspects of *The Phantom* comic strip, which had been progressively watered down by Lee Falk over the years, were brought to the fore in an exhibition held at the DC Art Gallery (Sydney) in February 1991. It was therefore doubtful that many of the people visiting this exhibition had ever seen the Phantom portrayed in such a provocative manner. *The Australasian Post* magazine, best known for its bawdy humor and pinup girls, filed this report:

> Although the comics portray The Ghost Who Walks as a clean-living chap who never indulges in sexual high-jinks, many artists were eager to explore The Phantom's sexuality. (*Australasian Post*, 1991)

David Nelson's painting, *Take That . . . Phantom*, showed the purple-clad hero, hands bound tightly behind his back, being flayed with a riding crop by a buxom blonde—a scene that would not have looked out of place in the comic strip's earliest installments. Ron Waugh's untitled painting, however, was even more provocative, as it showed the Phantom cupping another man's face, leaning in to kiss him, while his wolf, Devil, looked on in bewilderment. Although such works openly reveled in sexual transgression, they gave no clue about the corporate imperative behind the Phantom Art Show being held at the DC Art Gallery. This exhibition was mounted as part of an extensive public relations exercise branded "The Year of The Phantom," launched to commemorate the fifty-fifth anniversary of *The Phantom* comic strip. The campaign, orchestrated by Holt Public Relations, was designed to boost public awareness of *The Phantom* franchise, which was held by Gaffney International Licensing.[8] These transgressive images of the Phantom were deliberately exploited in order to generate media coverage, and to further the commercial ambitions of the character's Australian franchise owners (Holt Public Relations, ca. 1990). These nominally "subversive" artists had, in effect, become officially sanctioned "poachers."

Gaffney International Licensing had previously authorized the use of the Phantom in ways that were far removed from the original comic strip. The Australian Electoral Commission (AEC) obtained permission to use the Phantom in a series of educational comics intended for Aboriginal and Torres Strait Islander communities. Their decision to use the Phantom, ahead of other comic-book superheroes, acknowledged the character's popularity among indigenous communities throughout Australia. As the Aboriginal lawyer and land rights advocate Noel Pearson (b. 1965) recalled:

> When I was a kid, the old and . . . young read comic books, cowboy stories and magazines . . . [which] would make their way around the village . . . The Phantom was, of course, premium. (2009: 37–38)

The AEC published two comics, *The Phantom Enrols & Votes* (1988) and *Vote 1 Phantom* (1990), which were designed to help readers understand how they could enroll to vote and cast ballots in Australian elections. The scripts were written by Alistair Legge (AEC) and the stories illustrated by members of Garage Graphix, a community arts organization based in western Sydney, which trained and employed Aboriginal women as arts workers and screen printers (Hall, ca. 1988: 12–13). The comics were crudely drawn and the images of the Phantom himself appear to have been copied directly from the comic magazine. What is remarkable about these comics is how they deliberately relocated the Phantom (along with his Skull Cave) to outback Australia, where he is portrayed as a respected participant in the affairs of indigenous Australians.

The comics occasionally poke fun at "The Ghost Who Walks"; when he admits to Dot, an Aboriginal woman, that he doesn't know how to complete his ballot paper, Dot muses: "Phantoms are all the same, big on muscle, small on brains" (Legge [attrib.] and Garage Graphix, 1988: 5). But the comics do, however, address the vital political concerns of indigenous voters that seldom trouble the "mainstream" (white) electorate. Disillusioned by local councilors' willingness to let "outsiders" destroy their land, the community urges the Phantom to stand as their candidate. Hitting the campaign trail, the Phantom addresses a public gathering:

> Are you sick of people destroying your land? Are you tired of outsiders ripping you off? Then do something about it! Vote for me, and I'll do my best to put it right. (Legge and Garage Graphix, 1990: 5)

The Phantom wins the election and warns his fellow councilors that the days of "business as usual" are over, and that he would ensure that the council would "look after" people and give them what they want (Legge and Garage Graphix, 1990: 14).

The Family Court of Australia commissioned a similar educational comic book, *The Wisdom of The Phantom* (1997), to provide Aboriginal and Torres Strait Islander communities with information about the court's counseling services. The Phantom returns "home"—now situated somewhere in northern Australia—and learns from his wife, Diana, that their friends Pug and Ruby have separated and are in dispute over custody rights to their children. The Phantom urges Pug and Ruby to seek advice from the Family Court's counselors, reassuring them that the court employs people "who know us and our ways" and who will "respect our traditions" (Abbott et al., 1997: 6–7). Not only has the Phantom been transplanted to outback Australia, but he now identifies with his adoptive community and also regards its indigenous culture and customs as his own.

The original version of *The Phantom* comic magazine has also been adapted to serve the educational needs of Australia's Aboriginal communities. In the early 1990s, the Wangka Maya Pilbara Aboriginal Language Centre (Western Australia) translated a *Phantom* adventure into the Manyjilyjarra language as a learning aid for younger readers, to supplement its indigenous language preservation scheme (Wangka Maya PLC, 2007: 14). Their chosen text was a Swedish *Fantomen* episode, taken from the Phantom Chronicles, which told of the Phantom's battle against slave traders in Bengali during the 1850s (Guaraz and Bess, 1985)—a story which the organization arguably felt might resonate with its intended audience.

These educational comics raise an intriguing issue. The basic premise of *The Phantom*—"that a white man in the jungle protects the simple savages by spreading law and order" (Strömberg, 2003: 81)—in many ways echoes Aboriginal Australians' historical experience of European colonization. Why, then, should such a "paternalistic" hero as the Phantom remain so popular with indigenous Australians? Garry Kinnane, an Australian author and literary biographer, may have touched upon one possible explanation when he recalled his encounters with Aboriginal musicians in northern Queensland during the early 1960s:

> A number of the Aboriginal guys play guitar, sing cowboy songs. I wish they would learn some Australian folk songs, but . . . it doesn't speak to them as much as . . . Country and Western music does, which is not so culturally specific, or being American, has nothing to do with the white Australian culture that they feel excluded from. With this non-Australian material, they feel free to make the sentiments in them their own. (2012: 186)

The Phantom, being of American origin (although not always identifiably "American" in appearance or outlook), is perhaps sufficiently removed from mainstream Australian popular culture that it allowed Aboriginal readers to similarly interpret the character according to their own schema.

Frew Publications was by now also taking steps to make *The Phantom*, if not more "Australian," then at least to steer it away from the Eurocentric focus of the *Fantomen* series, and closer to the spirit of Lee Falk's stories. In 1990 the company published the first *Phantom* episode to be conceived entirely in Australia, "Rumble in the Jungle," which pitted the Phantom against the world heavyweight boxing champion, Mike "Typhoon" Turner (Shepherd and Chatto, 1990a). The story, written by Jim Shepherd, reflected his former background as a television sports broadcaster and was illustrated by Keith Chatto (1924–1992), a veteran Australian comic-book author and illustrator of the 1940s and 1950s, who had since worked as a television cameraman. "Rumble in the Jungle" was, according to Frew's cofounder, Ron Forsyth, "a traditional Phantom story in which good triumphs over evil," which did not rely on "fantasy [and] special effects" (Forsyth, 1990: 2).

Shepherd and Chatto collaborated on two further stories, "Return of the Singh Brotherhood" (1990b) and "The Kings Cross Connection," which brought the present-day Phantom to Australia for the first time—and featured a cameo appearance by Australia's then-serving prime minister, Robert Hawke (1992: 275–302). Despite being among Frew's top-selling issues in their year of release, Shepherd later maintained that the stories' prohibitive production costs made it financially impractical to commission further Australian-drawn episodes.[9] Whereas Semic Press could offset the cost of producing new *Fantomen* stories through foreign syndication sales, no such avenues were apparently available to Frew Publications. Thus, the economics of global comics publishing continued to favor American and European companies with international exposure over their Australian counterparts.

There have been other formally sanctioned portrayals of the Phantom which have taken the character far from seriously. In 1984, Semic Press published a satirical "sealed section" in the *Fantomen* comic magazine, titled "A Secret Life" (Leppänen, 1984). This piece gleefully ridiculed the Phantom as a muscle-bound buffoon who turns the simple errand of greeting his mother-in-law's ship at the Morristown docks into a disastrous farce, giving President Luaga of Bangalla the perfect opportunity to secretly meet Diana Palmer for a romantic tryst.

The Australian comedian "Austen Tayshus" (Jacob "Sandy" Gutman, b. 1954) released a hit record, "The Phantom Shuffle" (1984), which was accompanied by a suitably irreverent music video clip (Fitzgerald and Murphy, 2011: 156). Bored with life in the Deep Woods, the Phantom (as portrayed by Austen Tayshus) heads off to Sydney, where he dreams of becoming a superstar rapper, only to be dismissed as a costumed freak. "The Phantom Shuffle" was duly advertised in *The Phantom* comic magazine, but Austen Tayshus's status as a chart-topping performer was of greater commercial value to *The Phantom* media franchise. The runaway success of his first comedy record, *Australiana* (1983), would ensure that his new single (and accompanying music video) would gain high exposure on Australian radio and television stations, and promote the character to the youth consumer market.

King Features Syndicate has, as with the case of *Betaal Pachisi*, tried to prohibit or otherwise "control" unauthorized portrayals of the Phantom. But the company has also taken steps to manage the international circulation of competing versions of the Phantom which have been licensed for different territorial markets. In the early 1990s, Marvel Comics (U.S.) commissioned two Australian comic-book illustrators, Glenn Lumsden (b. 1964) and Dave De Vries (b. 1961), to produce a new miniseries, *The Phantom: The Ghost Who Walks* (1995), to be sold via specialty comic-book stores in the United States. Lumsden and De Vries were allowed to reimagine the Phantom as a hi-tech, urban warrior, but Marvel Comics stipulated that they must play down the original comic strip's colonial outlook. According to De Vries, "having The Phantom sitting on his throne in the bush ruling superstitious natives . . . just won't wash anymore" (quoted in Abbott, 1993: 47).

But King Features Syndicate stipulated that Marvel Comics' miniseries could only be sold in Australia via comic-book stores, where it would not directly compete with Frew Publications' edition of *The Phantom*, which was distributed nationally via newsagents and convenience stores. While De Vries was disappointed with the decision ("We'd like to see [it] in areas where there aren't any comic shops" [quoted in Harvey, 1995: 7]), Jim Shepherd, managing director of Frew Publications, was understandably happy with the outcome:

> [De Vries and Lumsden's version] doesn't make any sense, he's an en-
> tirely different Phantom, he's carrying all these weapons, and he's a real
> tough guy, which has nothing to do with the Phantom tradition. I'm
> delighted King Features took the stand they did. (Quoted in Harvey,
> 1995: 7)

The legend of the Phantom is based on a lie. For centuries, the Walker family dynasty has fabricated the myth that the Phantom is immortal. But readers worldwide know all too well that the role of the Phantom has been played by twenty-one men for over 400 years. These men, the eldest male of each generation of the Walker clan, have surrendered their own identities to ensure that the world believes that there is only one true Phantom—"The Ghost Who Walks, Man Who Cannot Die." Similarly, countless writers and artists from the United States, Australia, Sweden, and India have sustained *The Phantom* franchise through their own interpretations of the character, which have challenged, extended, and sometimes rewritten the series' "official" narrative history. Under their creative guidance, there has been not one, but many "Phantoms."

So, which version of the Phantom, if any, is the real one? For decades now, filmmakers and visual artists of all stripes have created their own versions of the Phantom — sometimes with the approval of the character's legally recognized owners, but more often than not without their formal blessing. But the absence of any legal imprimatur does not make these works any less valid, nor do they necessarily diminish the character's popular appeal. Even at their most critical or subversive, these works are testimony to audiences' affection for the Phantom, especially in Australia, Sweden, and India. The character's corporate handlers have come to recognize the unintended benefits such exposure might bring to their trademarked property, and have only selectively challenged "unofficial" versions of the Phantom that were deemed a direct threat to their commercial interests. The Phantom truly is, to borrow Joseph Campbell's phrase, "the hero with a thousand faces" (1975). But which of those faces can ever be said to be his true countenance depends entirely on those who create it, and those who look upon it, and the unspoken exchanges that take place between them.

CHAPTER SEVEN

FANS OF THE PHANTOM

S
ometimes, reading *The Phantom* comes with a heavy burden of responsibility—as Lee "T. J" Hooker of Sydney, Australia, found out. Walking along a busy city street, Hooker saw a man pin his girlfriend by the throat against a shop wall. Armed with only an umbrella and some barely remembered martial arts lessons, Hooker intervened and helped the woman escape, but not before receiving some well-aimed punches for his trouble. Hooker initially berated himself for not "[breaking] the guy's face," but he later shared the following thoughts with his fellow Phantom fans:

> Okay, so I didn't have "fists of steel" . . . but when it came to the crunch, The Phantom in me jumped out and took over . . . You may come face-to-face with the forces of evil, and you won't know what to do, but if you are a fair-dinkum Phantom person, that little spark of Phantom inside will decide for you. (Hooker, 1986: 11)

This is, perhaps, an extreme example of fan loyalty to a comic-book hero. But it nonetheless illustrates both the heroic qualities that readers find most admirable about the Phantom himself and the extent to which fans—or some of them, at least—personally identify with the character.

This book has, until now, been preoccupied with examining the political economy of global comics production by documenting the roles that institutional actors (e.g., newspaper feature syndicates and publishers), along with media industry professionals (e.g., editors, writers, and illustrators) have played in sustaining *The Phantom* media franchise in the United States, Australia, Sweden, and India. While this approach helps us better understand the mechanics and economics of media production, it cannot explain why readers like Lee "T. J." Hooker sometimes act the way they do. Nor can it articulate individuals' often intense level of personal identification with media texts. In order to understand the actions of Hooker and others like him, we must now ask who, in fact, reads *The Phantom*—and why?

This chapter will begin to address these and other questions by drawing on the findings of the *Phantom Comic Book Survey*, which gathered demographic data from hundreds of readers from Australia, Sweden, and India. One of this survey's key aims was to determine whether the popularity of *The Phantom* in these three countries was attributable to the intrinsic appeal of the character himself, or if it owed as much to the comic strip's shared publishing history in Australia, Sweden, and India. Such a complex question can, as it turns out, only be answered by canvassing readers' opinions, along with insights from the comics' creators themselves, and placing them against the backdrop of the international comics industry which was beset by challenges and changes throughout the 1980s and 1990s.

Studying Comic-Book Audiences

These survey findings take on greater significance after considering the development of audience studies research, along with the discipline's engagement with comic books and their readers. The formal study of audiences —particularly *media* audiences—evolved alongside the proliferation of mass communication media throughout the twentieth century. The direction of audience studies has frequently veered between competing (Anglo-American) theoretical and methodological approaches that are used to understand how audiences interact with mass media. The roving intellectual focus of audience studies has been influenced by cultural and political shifts within academia itself, the advent of new media technologies (cinema, radio, social media), and the "discovery" of active audience formations (e.g., media fandom).

These factors have also directed the study of comic-book and comic-strip audiences since the 1940s. The first great outpouring of academic studies of comic-book readers coincided with the medium's explosive growth during the 1940s and 1950s, particularly in the United States.[1] The dwindling number of comic-book audience studies published since the 1950s is a telling indicator of the medium's diminished cultural status, which has seen comics supplanted by television and successive forms of household audiovisual entertainment. The relative dearth of American studies of comic-book readers published in the last 15–20 years attests to comic books' relegation from a mass medium to what is merely a fan-centered subculture.[2]

Audience studies can nevertheless draw attention to issues of audience agency and oppositional behavior that might otherwise be overlooked in sociopolitical analyses of mass media and communications. Revisiting Martin Barker's case study of the controversial 1970s-era British comic *Action* demonstrates how audience members can be discerning, self-aware cultural consumers. In 1986–87, ten years after the magazine's cancellation, Barker sought out former *Action* readers to discover what "they thought about [the] comic" and compare their views with *Action*'s critics (1989: 51), and he received 137 responses to his three-page questionnaire (1989: 314–17; 2002: 68). Barker found that, while the comic's "casual/regular" readers chiefly enjoyed *Action* as "mindless" entertainment, the magazine's "committed" readers valued *Action* because it was "punkish," anti-authority, and thought-provoking (1989: 60). Barker concluded that when discussing *Action* as a comic book, its readers were in agreement; but when asked to consider *Action* as a social document, they evaluated it quite differently (1989: 60).

The following discussion of survey findings will demonstrate that Australian, Swedish, and Indian respondents were equally capable of making articulate, reflective (and frequently humorous) observations about *The Phantom* and their own role as fans. It will reveal how people from three distinct national cultures can embrace and interpret a shared media text—which itself is the product of another "foreign" culture—in surprising and frequently unexpected ways.

Who Reads the Phantom?

The findings presented in this chapter—and featured elsewhere throughout this book—are taken from an international, online survey of *Phantom* fans which obtained both demographic and qualitative data from a targeted sample of comic-book readers (aged eighteen years and over) in Australia, Sweden, and India. The goal was to invite readers from these three countries to share their opinions about *The Phantom*, their exposure to the character in different media, and (where relevant) their participation in comic-book fandom. The survey was conducted online from March 18, 2012, to March 16, 2013, and received 595 completed questionnaires during this twelve-month period.[3]

The majority of respondents came from Australia (50 percent), followed by Sweden (39 percent) and India (6 percent). A further 5 percent of survey participants came from outside these three countries, the most numerous being from—in descending order—Finland, the United States, and Norway. The comparatively small number of Indian respondents seems at odds with the character's longevity in that country. This author posted messages on *Phantom* fan websites and message boards, inviting Indian readers to share their thoughts about this apparent statistical anomaly. One Indian participant of the Phantom Phorum website based one possible explanation on their own family's engagement with *The Phantom*:

> While there are many comics readers in India, there are very few "fanatic fans" of a particular character . . . For example, if buying or reading *Phantom* comics, or following his strip in [the] newspaper, are criteria for calling a person a "Phantom fan," then there are four such "fans" in my family. Still, I am the only one who knows about [this] survey, and has participated. Then there's the problem of how many Phantom readers are netizens, too? . . . Kids who spend a lot of time on the Net are not into [*The Phantom*], while those ["netizens"] who still read *The Phantom* . . . may not be visiting any comics-related [websites]. (Phantom Phorum, 2012)

On the surface, this seems an entirely reasonable explanation, but it does not account for the proliferation of English- and Hindi-language websites dedicated to *The Phantom* and/or *Indrajal Comics*, nor those broadly dedicated to Indian comic books.[4] This reader's explanation does, however, raise intriguing questions about how different levels of reader interest in a particular comic book might define their relative status as "passive" or "active" comic-book fans.

The vast majority of survey participants were male (85 percent). The proportion of female participants (15 percent) may seem low, but these figures nevertheless indicate that *The Phantom* attracts a larger female readership than most comparable American superhero comics, which, according to U.S. industry sources, has hovered between 5 and 10 percent since the 1990s (Nyberg, 1995: 205; Healey, 2009: 145, 160). Readers aged 18–35 years accounted for 38 percent of survey respondents, followed by those aged 36–49 years (34 percent). Yet this survey also attracted a relatively high number of respondents aged 50–65 years (22 percent), who might not otherwise conform to the popular image of comic-book "fans." Indeed, as one 75-year-old survey participant wryly noted:

> My wife thinks I'm crazy buying this silly comic every fortnight [and] she wants to know what to do with my collection when I pass away. SELL them, my love. (Male respondent, Australia, August 2, 2012)

This high level of survey participation by older readers suggests that *The Phantom* continues to captivate readers who might have otherwise stopped reading comic books altogether.

Most survey participants could best be described as "rusted-on" readers, with 82 percent of readers indicating they had been reading *Phantom* comic magazines for ten years or more. Among those *Phantom* comics currently published outside the United States, the Australian edition of *The Phantom* was the most popular (31 percent), followed by the Swedish *Fantomen* magazine (24 percent), and the Swedish *Fantomen* Christmas annual, or *julalbum* (14 percent).

Readers' interest in *The Phantom* was not confined to those comics currently published in Australia, Sweden, and India. Nearly 13 percent of respondents indicated that they also read "foreign" editions of *The Phantom* comic, particularly those previously issued by Gold Key Comics, the Charlton Comic Group, and other American publishers. This might help explain a statistical discrepancy, wherein the number of survey participants who claim to have read Indian editions of *The Phantom* (128 [21 percent]) clearly exceeds the number of respondents who nominated India as their country of residence (35 [6 percent]). Thus we have comic-book fans living outside India who actively acquire "foreign" examples of *Phantom* comics for their collections.

Readers' interest in foreign-language comics has undoubtedly been fueled by the proliferation of *Phantom*-related websites, blogs, and message boards since the mid-1990s. The most popular of these among survey participants were Fantomen.org (Sweden, 28 percent), The Deep Woods (Australia, 27 percent), and ChronicleChamber.com (Australia, 17 percent). Internet auction sites such as eBay have also made it easier for *Phantom* fans worldwide to purchase international editions directly from fellow collectors. Although fans frequently upload and share scanned images taken from *Phantom* comic magazines and newspaper strips via websites, blogs, and social media platforms, only 17 percent of survey participants stated they had downloaded digitally scanned copies of old *Phantom* comics. The demand for "pirated" digital editions may not be so great in countries such as Australia and Sweden, where back-issue *Phantom* comics remain relatively plentiful, even if they are not always affordable.[5] Yet this still seems at odds with the widespread perception of younger media consumers' avowed preference for digital technologies. However, just as fans regard *The Phantom* newspaper comic strip and comic-book narratives as the "definitive" version of the character (against which all others are measured), their enjoyment of these same narratives appears inextricably linked to the tactile experience of reading them in printed formats. To "read" *The Phantom* in any other way is, perhaps, unthinkable.

The Phantom's Former Fans

"The Ghost Who Walks" can exert a vise-like grip on his most loyal followers, many of whom have spent much of their adult life in his company. But not everyone who grew up reading *The Phantom* remained loyal to the series. Of the 595 readers from Australia, Sweden, and India who participated in the survey, approximately 167 respondents (28 percent) were identified as former *Phantom* comic-book readers. Many of them could also be described as "rusted-on" fans, with 62 percent of this group claiming they had read *The Phantom* for ten years or more. So why did they stop reading after all this time? Fifty-four respondents (41 percent) stated they had either "outgrown" or became "bored with" the comic, while a further 46 respondents (27 percent) said they had stopped reading comics altogether.

Some fans grew disenchanted with the series after publishers made unwelcome changes to the comic itself. In its attempt to revive sales, Semic Press repackaged *Fantomen* as a full-color magazine to coincide with the comic's fortieth anniversary issue, which was distributed with a facsimile copy of the first issue from 1950. But the move was not universally welcomed; one Swedish reader said they "really hated [it] when the comic started to be in color" and stopped reading *Fantomen* altogether (male respondent, 18–35 years old, May 2, 2012). Even loyal readers who kept buying the comic in the wake of these changes still had their reservations:

The transition to color was painful, but necessary. The people who [are responsible for the] coloring [have] to shape up and look at the old black-and-white issues to bring back the magic [of] The Phantom. (Male respondent, 36–49 years old, Sweden, November 23, 2012)

Similar complaints were made about the Australian edition of *The Phantom* comic magazine. One reader's decision to cease buying the comic was also bound up in the growing distaste for the dramatic premise of the comic strip. "The poor production quality of Frew's comics was a factor. [They had] horrible covers," the reader said. "I also think that the premise of *The Phantom* is dated and racist" (male respondent, 18–35 years old, Australia, May 31, 2012).

Most former readers, however, gave more prosaic reasons for no longer reading *The Phantom*. These included undertaking college-level studies, the pressures of raising a family, or no longer being able to afford purchasing *Phantom* comics on a regular basis. One reader in particular found more compelling distractions in life than reading *The Phantom*: "[I] got my motorcycle license and discovered women with loose morals" (male respondent, 18–35 years old, Australia, August 31, 2012).

Why Do They Like the Phantom?

The story of the Phantom has unfolded over several decades and has been crafted by many hands across several nations. It has therefore evolved into a rich, complex narrative which can appeal to readers on entirely different levels. Some readers enjoyed the character's visual makeup, while others felt the Phantom's appeal was strongly tied to his fantastic Afro-Asian world. Many survey participants also cited his mythic status as "The Ghost Who Walks" as a key reason for his enduring popularity. These disparate responses are best summarized in the following reader's comments:

> It's hard to say what I like best about The Phantom . . . I like the originality of The Phantom and his world . . . The theme of the man who cannot die, yet is mortal . . . I like the idea of a hero who is a stern and deadly foe of evildoers, a mysterious masked avenger whose symbol is the skull, while being a true hero and protector of the innocent . . . Most of all, I like his exotic & mysterious home in the Deep Woods, where civilization has not yet reached . . . I love the jungle stories, and the

stories of the mountain princes next to the jungle. (Female respondent, 50–65 years old, Australia, July 27, 2012)

Even when readers singled out a specific aspect of the Phantom's persona or remarked on a particular aspect of his fictional world, it was only to highlight the singularity of Lee Falk's creative vision.

Fans frequently took the opportunity to prove that the Phantom was the first comic-strip superhero, whose influence on the genre has—in their eyes at least—never been sufficiently acknowledged. "He is the original superhero —[he has] no powers, just wit and strength," according to one reader. "He is noble, but with a harder edge, kind of like a Batman of the jungle" (male respondent, 18–35 years old, Australia, May 31, 2012). Others drew on their detailed knowledge of the strip's history to prove that the "Caped Crusader" was modeled after the Phantom:

> It should be noted that the idea of a secret identity was pioneered by [Lee] Falk with The Phantom, and that Bruce Wayne could have been modeled on Falk's original candidate for The Phantom's secret identity, Jimmy Wells. (Male respondent, 50–65 years old, Australia, January 25, 2013)

In many respects, the Phantom is a "fantastic" comic-book hero possessing physical strength and agility developed to an almost extraordinary level, but one who remains essentially plausible:

> He was essentially a "normal" man who was highly trained, with lots of cool resources. "If the same thing happened to me," I thought, "I could be The Phantom." I mean, there was no way I was going to let a [radioactive spider] bite me [like Spider-Man], and I wasn't going to zap myself with radiation [like the Hulk]. (Male respondent, 36–49 years old, Australia, May 31, 2012)

The Phantom was a superhero without super powers, a mortal being who was destined to be killed in the line of duty. It was this sense of "normality" which allowed readers to identify with the Phantom in ways they simply could not do with other comic-book superheroes.

Other readers, of course, simply like the Phantom because he was an un-complicated, two-fisted action hero. For one Indian reader, who complained of being overfed with "Gandhian morality" during his childhood, seeing "the Phantom kicking ass was a welcome release" (male respondent, 36–49 years old, November 19, 2012). Others were drawn to the Phantom's embodiment of "old-fashioned" notions of masculinity — he was, as one Australian reader put it, "strong, fast, agile and knowledgeable in 'manly' pursuits, [such as] hunting, gathering, tracking [and] fisticuffs" (male respondent, 18–35 years old, March 24, 2012). Readers also admired the Phantom's adherence to his firm moral code; as one survey participant observed, the Phantom, unlike other comic-book heroes, "never treaded the grey line between right and wrong . . . he knows what's right and lawful, and does his best to uphold it" (female respondent, 18–35 years old, Australia, May 31, 2012). It was for these reasons that another reader suggested "The Phantom is a great role model to any young person who reads the comics" (male respondent, 18–35 years old, Brazil, March 7, 2013).

The Phantom no doubt shared many of the superficial traits common to most American comic-book superheroes which, according to Amy Kiste Nyberg, catered almost exclusively to "adolescent male power fantasies that naturally hold little appeal for women" (1995: 208). Yet some female survey participants confessed that they identified with the Phantom instead of his wife, Diana Palmer, as seen in the following account from one Swedish reader:

> When I was very young, I identified myself with The Phantom, and wanted his life . . . [Diana Palmer] was a cool, UN-employed girl that could look after herself . . . but I always identified with The Phantom . . . I never really thought that I couldn't be him because I was a girl. (Female respondent, 36–49 years old, April 25, 2012)

The series' exotic jungle setting, teeming with wild animals and exotic flora, was a major drawing card for readers. But for one Australian reader, growing up in Papua New Guinea —"very much like the jungle of Bengalla [*sic*]"— provided her with the perfect backdrop that allowed her to imagine herself as the Phantom: "Even though I am a female, I could see myself being a do-gooder like The Phantom, and [fighting] crime, pirates, and baddies" (female respondent, 36–49 years old, Australia, August 15, 2012).

The historic sweep of the Phantom Chronicles allowed both Lee Falk and his Swedish counterparts at Semic Press to create stories which gave female readers the opportunity to truly imagine themselves as "The Ghost Who

Walks." One Swedish reader said she enjoyed the stories appearing in *Fantomen* featuring Julie Walker, the twin sister of the seventeenth Phantom, who briefly took her injured brother's place to become the first female Phantom.[6] "I am a woman," she said, "so maybe I liked the 'feminism' [of those] stories" (female respondent, 18–35 years old, January 21, 2013).

Yet other readers admired the Phantom's dual role as husband and father, and his embodiment of "traditional" family values:

> He's a good bloke. [That he is] a devoted father and loving husband who is now carrying the torch of the family business is probably one of the reasons why I liked him. If one has great respect for their father, grandfather and so on, wouldn't it be reasonable that they are drawn to a hero with the same respect? (Male respondent, 18–35 years old, Australia, August 11, 2012)

Female fans also enjoyed following the turbulent romance between the Phantom and Diana Palmer. One Australian reader said "The Wedding of The Phantom" was among her favorite stories: "After all those years of The Phantom courting Diana, it was a lovely resolution to his old-fashioned wooing" (female respondent, 50–65 years old, April 25, 2012). Stories about the marital interplay between the Phantom and Diana were also popular with another Australian reader, who felt they showed a "softer side" of the Phantom, which "enhances his character and makes it more interesting for the girls" (female respondent, 50–65 years old, August 28, 2012).

The "Adopted" Superhero

The notion that the Phantom somehow stood apart from the costumed superheroes who followed in his wake further enhances his reputation as a "non-American" superhero among survey participants. This made the Phantom culturally palatable to international audiences in ways that Superman or Batman simply were not. Some readers went so far as to endorse the Phantom's personal values as a reflection of their own country's self-image, despite the character's American provenance:

> Ironically, [The Phantom is] part of the Australian cultural image, [even though it isn't] written by an Aussie. I think it's his understated way of doing things, championing [the] weak and looking after a mate, that has

appealed so much to Australians. (Male respondent, 36–49 years old, Australia, June 3, 2012)

Such views were echoed by one Swedish reader who said that in addition to protecting the innocent and being a kind, loyal friend to those who knew him, the Phantom also kept a low profile—"not unlike Swedes in general, I suppose" (male respondent, 18–35 years old, June 15, 2012).

Readers' ability to identify the Phantom as a "home-grown" comic-strip hero was sometimes made easier when it was read alongside American comic strips. One Swedish reader drew comparisons between *The Phantom* and *Johnny Hazard*, an American thriller/espionage strip which appeared in the *Fantomen* magazine for many years, to illustrate this difference:

> [*The Phantom*] is tastefully understated—if such a thing is possible in comic strips—and lacked the ugly American jingoism of [secret agent] comics [like *Johnny Hazard*]. It would not surprise me if the reason why *The Phantom* has been such an international success is that it is, [even] in the Lee Falk stories, in no way US-centric, and appeals equally to people all over the world. (Male respondent, 36–49 years old, October 6, 2012)

The character's tenuous links to American culture might go some way towards explaining how Semic Press was able to infuse its *Fantomen* stories with a distinctively Scandinavian outlook. The gradual transformation of the Phantom into a "Swedish" hero was, according to one reader, a reflection of Sweden's political consensus throughout the 1970s and 1980s which championed "social justice, [the] social democratic state, anti-racism [and] family values" (female respondent, 18–35 years old, Australia, May 31, 2012).

The very ubiquity of *Phantom* comic books in a foreign market also helped convey the impression that it was somehow a domestic, rather than imported, cultural product. As one Indian reader recalled, "The Phantom was so popular in India that many readers used to believe The Phantom was created by an Indian—I know several artists who wanted to 'draw' The Phantom for *Indrajal Comics*" (male respondent, 18–35 years old, November 22, 2012). On a more prosaic level, even the material quality of foreign-edition *Phantom* comics convinced readers that they were purchasing a "local" product:

> For some reason, when I was in my teens, I had always assumed that it was an Aussie comic, not flash and glossy and perfect like [the] US products, but rather rough around the edges—particularly the old newspa-

per strips and [the] Frew Publications [comics] before they [used] glossy covers. So to me, even now, it seems very Australian. (Male respondent, 36–49 years old, Japan, June 2, 2012)

Whereas Semic Press (Sweden) and Bennett, Coleman & Co. (India) initially published the Phantom comic magazine in color, Frew Publications opted to print their version in black and white, using cheaper paper covers, for the Australian market. Although this practice was adhered to for decades, largely as a cost-saving measure, it lent *The Phantom* a frugal, down-market image which further signified the magazine's—and the character's—essential difference from glossy, full-color American superhero comics.

The Pleasures of Reading

While some readers occasionally dreamed of being next in line to occupy the Skull Throne, for others, just reading *The Phantom* was a simple pleasure that offered them a temporary respite from their daily cares: "I still read them after 30 years—a great way to unwind at [the] end of the day" (male respondent, 50–65 years old, Australia, July 21, 2012); "A good 10–15 minute read to turn the brain off from everyday life" (female respondent, 36–49 years old, Australia, August 8, 2012); "The comic is a way to escape from reality for an hour or so" (male respondent, 18–35 years old, Sweden, June 15, 2012). Yet some survey participants forged an emotional connection with the character that went well beyond simply reveling in his adventures:

> The father/son continuity was a big emotional grab for me, as I had lost my father at 14, and The Phantom spoke to this loss I was experiencing (I also liked stories that showed the transition from one Phantom to another). (Male respondent, 36–49 years old, Australia, March 23, 2012)

Just as the mantle of the Phantom was handed down from father to the eldest son in the Walker dynasty, so too was the "family tradition" of reading *The Phantom* frequently passed on from one generation to the next:

> My uncle brought [*Fantomen*] comic books home as a kid during the '70s. His father, my grandfather, disliked this, since he shared a negative attitude towards comics with many others of his generation—but when he started to read the comic himself, he got hooked! . . . Whenever

we visited my grandparents, I knew we could find a bunch of *Fantomen* [comics] between the pillows in the living room sofa . . . It was something that three generations could share an interest [in], and enjoy. (Male respondent, 18–35 years old, Sweden, April 6, 2012)

The joys of reading *The Phantom* were not always uniformly shared within some families. One Australian reader admitted that he only ever read the comic at the insistence of his uncles, "who had all read *The Phantom*, and who took it as a given that I should, too" (male respondent, 18–35 years old, September 4, 2012).

Nostalgia can also be the spur for many forms of fan activity, such as collecting artifacts associated with a media text or a popular pastime. John Bloom's study of adult baseball card collectors in the United States found that, for many collectors, this activity "reflected an effort to find and reestablish a stable sense of order from the cultural symbols of their past" (2002: 70). For these collectors, baseball cards were reminders of their childhood, and thus connoted "a memory that is uncomplicated and straightforward" (Bloom, 2002: 71). Reading *The Phantom* also provided some survey participants with a nostalgic conduit to their own childhood. A 63-year-old survey participant, reflecting on why he still occasionally bought *The Phantom* ("My wife thinks it very odd"), said the magazine allowed him to reconnect with his "very happy childhood growing up in Australia in the 1950s" (male respondent, Australia, September 13, 2012). Nor was this nostalgic impulse confined to readers from the postwar "baby boom" generation, as the following account demonstrates:

Every Thursday after school, we would go with mum and do the food shopping and [visit] McDonalds and I'd buy my [*Phantom*] comic book . . . We'd get home, unpack [the groceries] and I'd run upstairs and put it . . . in order with my other *Phantom* comics . . . and my brother would do the same with his *Conan* comics . . . [Then] we'd eat Maccas [McDonalds] and watch *Friends* on TV as a family . . . I loved the '90s. (Male respondent, 18–35 years old, Australia, May 31, 2012)

But such nostalgic yearning can, over time, be displaced by a sense of obligation. One Australian respondent admitted that he'd read most of the stories many times over, and didn't need to buy any further Frew Publications editions, but he still thought that "not purchasing Frew issues would just seem wrong." Concerned about the company's future prospects, he felt obliged to "keep supporting" the comic book which he declared had made a "big impact" on his childhood (male respondent, 18–35 years old, April 27, 2012). *The Phantom* could also prove to be informative and an educational reading experience for some, especially when it came to the Swedish episodes based on historical events. "Fantomen [contained] a lot of stories based on true historical material," said one reader, "[and] this made me interested in history as a subject" (male respondent, 36–49 years old, Sweden, June 28, 2012). Teachers also acknowledged the comic's educational benefits:

> Another thing I like is . . . the fact that, as readers, we get to delve into [The Phantom Chronicles]. I'm a history teacher . . . and [I] love this idea of a legacy hero, who can essentially travel through time. (Male respondent, 18–35 years old, Australia, July 25, 2012)

The Phantom's historical exploits even inspired some readers to take up unusual athletic pursuits. One Swedish fan, recalling how much the *Fantomen* comic meant to him as a child, revealed that he took up fencing after reading many of the episodes set in the sixteenth and seventeenth centuries which featured dramatic sword-fighting scenes (male respondent, 36–49 years old, June 11, 2012).

Favorite Stories and Storytellers

During the last eighty years, few writers and artists have dared to radically alter Lee Falk's original conception of *The Phantom*. Yet the series has undeniably changed over this long period, sometimes at the behest of Falk himself, and at other times under the direction of those who followed in his wake. But these changes have also been influenced by the commercial directives of feature syndicates and magazine publishers, as well as by changing audience tastes and attitudes. This complex mix of economic and creative pressures therefore has a direct bearing on the different types of comic strips and comic books that are made available to reading publics throughout the world. This became all too clear when Australian, Swedish, and Indian readers were asked to choose their favorite *Phantom* stories. Their choices reveal as much about the prevailing publishing practices in each of these countries as they do about their devotion to "The Ghost Who Walks."

When asked to select their favorite *Phantom* adventures, few readers struggled to come up with a list of their preferred stories, of which the following is but one example:

All the earlier stuff illustrated by Ray Moore was terrific . . . it was moody, atmospheric, and unique. Plus, that era allowed the scripts to be more adventurous and fleshed out . . . instead of the stilted stuff we got in the mid '90s. "Little Toma" and "The Phantom Goes to War" are prime examples. Wilson McCoy's art, although minimalist, was perfect for the character . . . Lee Falk's storytelling really came into its own [with] "The Childhood of The Phantom." (Male respondent, 18–35 years old, Australia, March 24, 2012)

This response, from an Australian reader, is interesting because it refers to both stories and artists taken from the first two decades of *The Phantom* comic strip, a time when many fans felt that Lee Falk was at the peak of his creative powers. It also reminds us how Australian audiences were privy to the earliest *Phantom* stories (drawn by Ray Moore), soon after the series' American debut, and that were continually reprinted by Frew Publications for decades thereafter. This was not the case in either Sweden or India, where local comic-book publishers initially gave preference to later stories drawn by Wilson McCoy or Sy Barry. (In fact, Lee Falk and Ray Moore's first-ever *Phantom* story, "The Singh Brotherhood," was not reprinted in the Swedish *Fantomen* magazine until December 1965.)

While some fans preferred the older, "classic" *Phantom* narratives of the 1930s–1940s era, others chose more recent stories as their favorites, on the basis that these were their first exposure to the Phantom:

The first one [I read] was about Queen Samaris [Falk and Lignante, 1988 (1961–62)], [who] remained young as long as she never fell in love. Eventually she was reduced to ashes when she said she loved The Phantom. A boyfriend (not exactly a boyfriend, I was 10 at the time) had a picture of the ashes in his wallet. (Female respondent, 50–65 years old, Sweden, May 12, 2012)

Swedish readers were more likely to nominate Swedish-drawn stories, since these appeared more frequently in the *Fantomen* magazine than the latest American episodes, which were usually published in the annual *Fantomen julalbum*. But again, Swedish fans' choices were often based on the first stories they had read:

> It is hard to just choose some of the adventures, but I will try to list SOME of my favorites: "Zombiemakaren" ["The Zombie Maker," no. 19, 2000]; "Häxdoktorns Hemlighet" ["The Witch Doctor's Secret," no. 20, 2000]; [and] "Ett dödligat val" ["A Deadly Choice," no. 22, 2000]. I chose these three stories because they were the first *Phantom* comics that I read, and I have bought every number since then. (Male respondent, 18–35 years old, April 22, 2012)

Readers sometimes chose their favorite *Phantom/Fantomen* stories on the basis of their preferred artist. The work of the Spanish-born illustrator Jaime Vallvé (1928–2000) was frequently singled out for praise; one reader described his work from the 1970s as "sublime," and compared him favorably to the American comic-book artist Will Eisner (male respondent, 36–49 years old, Denmark, December 6, 2012).

Vallvé was the first—and, in the eyes of some readers, the best—artist to work on the "historical" Swedish stories that focused exclusively on the Phantom's ancestors, which were presented as untold episodes from The Phantom Chronicles. The factual basis for these stories was especially appealing to some readers:

> I enjoy the stories . . . that are combined with historical themes . . . when [The Phantom] interacts with historically important people and makes a fictive mark in history. It makes an exciting twist. (Female respondent, 18–35 years old, Sweden, November 7, 2012)

Several readers elected "Duel in Venice" (Worker and Leppänen, 2015a [1986]; 2015b [1986]) as their favorite historical adventure, which focused on the transition from the first Phantom to his son, as they fought to defend the island of Malta against the Turks in 1536. As one reader said, "[It had] fantastic [artwork] and a heroic story that really gets your blood pumping" (male respondent, 18–35 years old, Sweden, June 4, 2012).

These historical episodes gave writers the opportunity to "kill off" the

Phantom's ancestors, which, as one survey participant pointed out, gave these stories "a deeper sense of danger." As a result, they were "a little darker in tone," which felt as though they were "more aimed at an adult audience" (female respondent, 18–35 years old, Sweden, June 17, 2012).

Whereas Australian and Swedish readers enjoyed a plentiful supply of new and "classic" *Phantom* stories in local comic magazines, Indian audiences were not so fortunate. Several Indian readers lamented the dearth of *Phantom* comics available to them. "The Phantom [comic] is no longer published in India, other than the random reprint," one reader declared. "It is quite tragic" (male respondent, 36–49 years old, June 28, 2012). Such claims—to be discussed in the next chapter—were not entirely correct, but *The Phantom* was no longer as widely available to Indian readers as it once was through *Indrajal Comics* or *Diamond Comics* during the 1980s and 1990s, thanks, in part, to increased competition from television.

The Phantom, Rebooted

Similar pressures were also being felt by Semic Press in Sweden at this time, which compelled the company to make dramatic changes to *Fantomen* which both excited and alienated readers. These changes were most evident in "Election in Bengali" (Reimerthi and Lindahl, 1994a; 1994b), which several survey participants chose as one of their favorite Swedish episodes featuring the present-day Phantom. This controversial story line came about during a turbulent period for the Swedish *Fantomen* magazine. When Jonas Bonnier (b. 1963) was appointed publisher of Semic Press in 1991, he urged then-editor Ulf Granberg to develop a long-term strategy to improve the comic's sales figures. In December 1992, Granberg convened a two-day summit of writers, artists, and editorial staff to debate the future direction of *Fantomen*. This was the first of the "Team Fantomen" story conferences, where it was decided to make the Phantom more realistic—or, as Granberg put it, to "turn another screw" in order to heighten the drama.[7]

Claes Reimerthi (b. 1955), who had written for *Fantomen* since 1984, proposed an epic story line which would do just that. "Election in Bengali" saw the Phantom's longtime friend, President Lamanda Luaga (who had governed Bangalla for decades), lose the presidential election to a malevolent outsider, Kigali Lubanga, whom Granberg described as a "black Napoleon."[8]

Reimerthi's goal was to overturn readers' familiar conception of the Phantom and his world:

> [My] view back than was that The Phantom's life was too sheltered, that he was too safe . . . I had these seven pillars that The Phantom used as crutches, like the Jungle Patrol [and] President Luaga . . . these made things easy for him, and I wanted [to] make things tough for him . . . We wanted someone who was a bad guy as President, who opposed The Phantom.[9]

"Election in Bengali" cast dark shadows across the Phantom's world, which was being torn asunder by the ruthless President Lubanga. One Swedish reader remarked that "The Phantom [has] never [seemed] so dark and hopeless" and praised the story for its realism (male respondent, 18–35 years old, April 6, 2012). Another Swedish reader enjoyed this long-running story's focus on the "[political] turmoil and conspiracies" which wracked Bangalla following Lubanga's victory (male respondent, 36–49 years old, July 3, 2012).

The story, when first published in Sweden, was supported by a costly and unprecedented marketing campaign which generated enthusiastic media coverage throughout 1994–95. However, "Election in Bangalla" only briefly reversed the magazine's declining sales, which continued unabated once the publicity ceased.[10] Ulf Granberg recalled that readers quickly tired of the story's political intrigue: "They'd complain by saying 'If I want to read politics, I'll watch the [TV] news — please don't put it in *Fantomen*.'"[11] Swedish audiences, it seemed, no longer cared for the intrusion of "real-world" politics that was once the hallmark of *Fantomen* during the 1970s. But even greater changes awaited *Fantomen* in 1997, after the Bonnier family sold Semic Press to Egmont International Holdings, the Danish publisher which owned the rights to Sweden's biggest-selling comic book, *Kalle Anka & C:o* (*Donald Duck*). In keeping with the company's preference for "juvenile" comic-book brands (such as Walt Disney), Egmont gradually tilted *Fantomen* towards a younger age group, which helped stabilize sales at around 35,000–40,000 copies per issue by the late 1990s (Pilcher and Brooks, 2005: 248).

For some readers, these newer Swedish episodes still remained preferable to Lee Falk's work on *The Phantom* comic strip throughout the 1980s and 1990s. One Australian fan stated that he preferred Phantom Chronicle adventures produced by Swedish creators because they were made specifically for comic books:

The older [newspaper] strips are good, but tend to be a little monoto-
nous, and the artwork isn't as interesting, due to the original format in
which they were published. (Male respondent, 18–35 years old, July 25,
2012)

Such comments suggest that readers could make clear distinctions between
episodic newspaper comic strips and self-contained comic-book narratives,
and how the spatial boundaries of each format required different approaches
to visual storytelling. Every episode of an adventure-serial comic strip must
partly recount the previous day's installment, while advancing the plot further, and foreshadowing what is to come in the following day's newspaper.
Such techniques are, according to Kathleen J. Turner, entirely necessary to
"aid the recall of readers who have engaged in twenty-four hours of other
activity since they last read the funnies" (1977: 27). But as the space allocated
to newspaper comic strips gradually shrank, it became ever more difficult
for adventure-serial comic strips to sustain dramatic tension in such a com-
pressed format.

    These constraints became all too obvious whenever Lee Falk's later ep-
isodes of *The Phantom* were collated into comic-book format, which only
emphasized their repetitious tempo and truncated scripts. One survey participant said she almost gave up reading *The Phantom* comic strip during the
1980s due to Lee Falk's "monosyllabic" dialogue and "ridiculously simple"
stories (female respondent, 50–65 years old, Australia, July 27, 2012). Nor
were some fans impressed by Sy Barry's replacements, after the series' longtime artist retired in 1994. "I must say that [the] comics where the artwork is
by George Olesen and Fred Fredericks are woeful to the point of painful,"
confessed one Australian reader. "[Wherever] I see their names, I really struggle to overcome the dreadful artwork to enjoy the story" (male respondent,
36–49 years old, May 2, 2012).

    The death of Lee Falk on March 13, 1999, however, posed considerable
difficulties for King Features Syndicate. Falk had worked on *The Phantom*
until his death, and his wife, Elizabeth Falk, continued writing the comic
strip under his byline until July 1999. Falk's eventual successors would be
drawn from the ranks of Sweden's "Team Fantomen." Claes Reimerthi was
appointed writer for the weekday and Sunday episodes of *The Phantom* comic
strip, a position he held throughout 1999–2003.[12] But it proved to be a challenging assignment for Reimerthi:

There were lots and lots of rules, some I couldn't live with, such as The Phantom had to be in every episode, and you weren't allowed to do flashbacks . . . The "Swedenized" Phantom is easier to write [as] you can swap between jungle, historical, and city adventures.[13]

"Team Fantomen" would, ironically, furnish King Features Syndicate with the American team that would eventually take over the full-time production of *The Phantom* newspaper strip. Tony De Paul (b. 1954), a former journalist who first wrote for *Fantomen* in 1993 (De Paul, Felmang, and Ferri, 1993), occasionally alternated with Reimerthi as writer on *The Phantom* throughout 1999–2003 and eventually became the strip's full-time writer. Paul Ryan (1949–2016), who jointly illustrated *The Amazing Spider-Man* comic strip during 1992–1995, drew his first story for *Fantomen* magazine in 2001 (Raab and Ryan, 2001) and was subsequently hired to replace George Olesen on *The Phantom* comic strip in 2005 — a role he held until his death in 2016.

"Team Fantomen" not only provided a talent pool for King Features Syndicate, but it also infused *The Phantom* newspaper comic strip with elements taken from the *Fantomen* comic magazine. Claes Reimerthi initially adapted his comic-book scripts originally written for *Fantomen* and used them as story lines for the newspaper comic strip. In other instances, writers have "borrowed" aspects of the *Fantomen* continuity and incorporated them into the American newspaper strip. Tony De Paul also made frequent use of the apartheid nation state of Rhodia (originally conceived by Magnus Knutsson for *Fantomen* in 1972) in the daily narratives of *The Phantom* comic strip. He did so to good effect in "The Python Strikes Back," which saw an African terrorist cell fake Diana Palmer's death and have her secretly imprisoned by Rhodian authorities as part of an elaborate revenge plot against the Phantom (De Paul and Ryan, 2011). This epic story line, which originally ran in newspapers worldwide from August 24, 2009, to May 7, 2011, was cited by several readers as one of their favorite recent episodes of *The Phantom*. One Australian reader enjoyed it because "[It took the comic] out of its usual format and challenged The Phantom as a person" (male respondent, 18–35 years old, March 25, 2012).

"The Python Strikes Back" foregrounds the creative and economic links between the Swedish comic magazine and the American newspaper strip. Tony De Paul and Paul Ryan, both former contributors to *Fantomen*, produced this

American newspaper sequence of *The Phantom*, which was then sold by King Features Syndicate (via its international representatives) to Sweden, Australia, and India, where it was serialized in local newspapers and was subsequently compiled and reissued in local editions of *The Phantom* comic magazine. "Team Fantomen" thus made a vital contribution towards sustaining *The Phantom* comics franchise at a critical moment in its long publishing history.

For some people, reading *The Phantom* remains nothing more than a simple form of escapist entertainment. Yet as we have seen here, a good many people did more than just passively "read" *The Phantom*. For some fans, the comic served as a diverting form of moral instruction, offering valuable life lessons drawn from the words and deeds of "The Ghost Who Walks." For others, the comic became a nostalgic gateway to their childhood memories. And more than a few readers from Australia, Sweden, and India felt that the Phantom, in some ways, embodied aspects of their national character in ways that other (American) comic-book heroes simply could not.

These survey findings demonstrate how audience studies can enrich our understanding of how different audience formations engage with media texts. Yet no matter how vital or engaging such insights might be, they cannot be allowed to overshadow the commercial and industrial dimensions of media production and consumption. Ingunn Hagen and Janet Wasko rightly caution that an excessive focus on audiences' active interpretation of mass media risks overlooking a key point—that "media texts are not produced according to the choice of audiences" (2000: 16).

Australian, Swedish, and Indian audiences' engagement with *The Phantom* media franchise has, of course, been influenced by a range of decisions made by newspaper feature syndicates, magazine publishers, and editorial decision-makers, each of which dictate how *The Phantom* has been packaged to meet the demands of international media markets. Sometimes this may become a negotiated process, whereby producers open up channels of communication with their audiences—to hear their opinions and complaints, or to explain their own actions, but always with the ultimate goal of cementing readers' ties to *The Phantom* franchise. In other instances, no such channels are made available to audiences, who must then create their own platforms to voice their opinions and concerns. And it is this complex relationship between comic-book producers and consumers—a relationship that can by turns be symbiotic and antagonistic—that will be the focus of the next chapter.

//

CHAPTER EIGHT

WHO OWNS THE PHANTOM?

A larger than usual crowd had gathered at the Parken Zoo in the Swedish city of Eskilstuna on Wednesday, August 27, 1986. The throng of children and teenagers had come not to see the animals, but to witness Lee Falk, creator of *The Phantom*, officially open the zoo's newest attraction, Fantomen-land. Visitors could have their photo taken on the Skull Throne, inspect the Phantom's secret treasure vault, and visit a scaled-down replica of a jungle village. After being given a guided tour of the theme park by the Phantom himself, Falk was invited to sign the Skull Cave's guest book, before he was mobbed by fans clamoring for his autograph (Swärd, 2011: 206–11).

This scene is significant for several reasons. On one level, it demonstrates how the commercial value of the Phantom could be realized in new forms and physical settings that were far removed from the original comic strip, but which nonetheless drew inspiration from the source texts themselves. The launch of Fantomen-land also signified the character's high public standing among Swedish audiences. The management of the Parken Zoo no doubt believed that the addition of its new Fantomen-land installation could attract a new audience segment that might not otherwise have visited their zoo. Nor, it would seem, was Fantomen-land intended entirely for young children. As one Swedish reader recalled:

In the town where I live, there used to be a theme park about The Phantom at the local zoo when I was younger . . . [I] loved that place, even if I was a little grown-up for it. (Female respondent, 36–49 years old, April 25, 2012)

On another level, the opening of Fantomen-land provided a rare opportunity for Swedish *Fantomen* readers to meet their hero's creator and thus claim a fleeting intimacy with the author of their hero's canonical (American) adventures. Long after Lee Falk's visit, Fantomen-land continued to be a site of pilgrimage for *Fantomen* fans, who took the opportunity to immerse themselves in a physical, "real-world" representation of the Phantom's fictional universe. However, Fantomen-land was only allowed to function in this capacity as long as it successfully met the economic demands of its owners—a fact underscored by the Parken Zoo's decision to close down Fantomen-land in 2009.

The establishment of Fantomen-land demonstrates how media-franchise owners, in partnership with authorized licensees, have actively cultivated "fan consumers" by providing them with new opportunities to engage with a unique media property—in this case, a comic-book character—through retail products or prepackaged "experiences" that are often far removed from its original medium. Yet the closure of Fantomen-land also illustrates how fans' emotional—not to mention financial—investment in fictional characters like the Phantom (Fantomen) ultimately remains subordinate to the commercial interests of media-franchise owners. These tensions are rarely far from the surface in the following examination of the relationship between the Phantom's franchise-holders and *Phantom* fan communities in Australia, India, and Sweden.

To understand why these tensions have occurred, it is first necessary to understand how the historical construction of fan identity has frequently demonized organized media fan movements and their participants. Specific attention will be paid to how *Phantom* "phans" (as they frequently refer to themselves) articulate their own sense of allegiance to the character, and the extent to which the expression of "phan" identity is tied to the consumption of licensed *Phantom* merchandise. A particularly intriguing aspect of this fan community is the extent to which "phans" have borrowed and adapted many of the practices pioneered by earlier iterations of science fiction and media fandom, in ways that maintain both The Phantom's—and their own—"outlier" status within mainstream comics fandom. Finally, this chapter will examine how "phan" communities have sometimes coalesced out of frustration with the perceived indifference of franchise-holders to their particular needs and demands. However, the extent to which these fan groups have been willing to enter into a symbiotic—and occasionally adversarial—relationship with the Phantom's corporate gatekeepers only emphasizes the often lop-sided, and fundamentally unequal, relationship between media producers and media consumers.

Comic-Book Fans and "Deviant" Identity

"The literature of fandom," according to Joli Jensen, "is haunted by images of deviance," and frequently invokes the term's derivation from the word "fanatic" (Jensen, 2001: 301). The term "fan," as it is understood today, first entered common usage in the late nineteenth century and was originally used to describe "keen spectators" of professional sports (such as baseball) before it was gradually applied to organized fan clubs dedicated to popular mass media, such as the cinema and motion-picture performers, that emerged during the 1920s (McKee, 2002: 67). Nonetheless, the specter of the intellectually stunted or emotionally unstable "fan" was already being invoked in some of the earliest academic studies of children's consumption of comic books.

Katherine M. Wolf and Marjorie Fiske's survey of 104 American schoolchildren (aged 7–17 years) identified three types of comic-book reader: "comic-book fans" (37 percent); "moderate readers" (48 percent); and children who were indifferent to, or hostile towards reading comics (15 percent) (1949: 22). Of greatest concern—and scholarly interest—to Wolf and Fiske were

> comic fans . . . whose interest in comics is patently violent and excessive. They prefer comic reading to all other activities and if left to their own devices would apparently do nothing else. (Wolf and Fiske, 1949: 22)

Wolf and Fiske estimated that 50 percent of surveyed children whom they classified as "neurotic"—children "whose [psychological] problems had affected their entire behavior pattern"—could be further labeled "comic fans" (1949: 29). They referred to a twelve-year-old boy who filled his bedroom's bookcase with *Superman* and *Batman* comics as an example of the "neurotic fan" for whom these comics became a "treasured possession" (1949: 22–23).

Similar observations were recorded by Dr. Elwyn Morey, a psychology lecturer at the University of Western Australia, who surveyed comic-book reading patterns among 455 schoolchildren in the early 1950s. Morey reported that, by the time they reached 13 years of age, "one child in every three in the group studied could be classified as a comic 'fan'" who typically read more than 10 comics per week (*West Australian*, 1952: 6). Furthermore, children who "daydreamed excessively," or who came from "insecure" family environments, tended to continue reading comics longer than most "normal" children (*West Australian*, 1952: 6). In both of these studies, the "excessive" consumption of, and desire for hoarding (rather than simply "collecting") comic books evident among "neurotic" children apparently stemmed from some greater psychological disorder. The very act of reading and amassing comic books had thus become a symptom of "deviant" behavior.

Such concerns fueled the international outcry against violent and lurid comic books during the 1950s in the United States (Nyberg, 1998) and elsewhere, including Australia (Finnane, 1989: 220–40) and Scandinavia (Jensen, 2010b: 47–70). Yet decades later, long after the perceived societal "threat" of comic books had subsided, the idea that anyone — let alone adults — would publicly declare their enthusiasm for a comic-book hero by joining a fan club devoted to such a character could still invite derision and ridicule. Media coverage of the launch of the Phantom Club of Australia in 1981 provides some telling examples of these entrenched views. The tireless publicity campaign undertaken by the club's president, John Henderson (who made frequent public appearances dressed in his tailor-made *Phantom* costume), was rewarded with tongue-in-cheek, but otherwise largely positive press coverage (*Daily Sun*, 1982: 13; Walsh, 1984: 4–5). Yet residual suspicion of comic-book "fans" remained evident in some press reportage; Henderson was occasionally portrayed as the president of a "bizarre" organization catering to "Phantom phreaks" (Robson, 1982: n.p.), who were deemed to be otherwise "sane human beings" who had not yet outgrown reading comic books (Kershler, 1987: 3).

But were such characterizations of Phantom "phans" entirely inaccurate, either then or now? Some of the responses submitted to the survey would only confirm such pejorative opinions about "fans" generally — and comic-book fans in particular:

> I love the Ghost Who Walks so much that I named my second daughter Heloise after the 21st Phantom's daughter. My third daughter's middle name is Falk and my own last name was changed to Walker. And when the time finally comes around, my partner and I plan on getting the [Phantom's] "Good Mark" tattooed onto our left arms. (Female respondent, 18–35 years old, Australia, March 23, 2012)

This is, admittedly, an extreme example of one fan's affinity for "The Ghost Who Walks," which, if it were reported in the mainstream media, would no doubt see her condemned as a "Phantom phreak." Yet such a critique might have less to do with the behavior of this particular "phan" than with the object of her adoration. Jonathan Gray, Cornel Sandvoss, and C. Lee Harrington draw a useful comparison in their analysis of the *New York Post's* coverage in 2005 of *Harry Potter* fans, who were dubbed "Potterheads" and were likened to the earlier generation of *Star Trek* fans, or "Trekkies" (2007: 2). The *Post's* condescending account of obsessive, adult *Harry Potter* fans could, the authors argue, be easily applied to sports fans (Gray, Sandvoss, and Harrington, 2007: 4) — for whom, after all, the term "fan" was originally coined (McKee, 2002: 67). Yet as Gray, Sandvoss, and Harrington point out, the *New York Post* would never equate "Potterheads" with their "loyal, pinstripe-wearing readership of New York Yankees fans who are extensively catered to in its back pages" (2007: 4). Therefore, what was under attack in this news story was "not the state of being a fan as such but particular texts as objects of fandom" (2007: 4). The distinctions between socially accepted sports fandom and marginalized comics fandom were deliberately blurred by the Phantom Club of Australia, which proudly announced that its membership list included several Australian sports luminaries, including test cricketer Max Walker and rugby player Wally Lewis (Walker, 1986: 20; Jones, 1986: 131). The de facto endorsement of these (impeccably masculine) sporting celebrities was used to legitimize the status of the Phantom Club of Australia and, by extension, its members' shared passion for the Phantom.

Fan Identity and Media Consumption

Some fans exhibit a degree of self-awareness which acknowledged the sometimes excessive behaviors commonly ascribed to fans of media texts. One Australian fan looked back wryly on attending his first screening of *The Phantom* feature film in 1996:

> [*The Phantom*] movie will always have a special place in my heart, despite its flaws. It came at a time when my passion for *The Phantom* had reached its peak. I was 15 years old and went to see the movie 7 times. The first time was at [the] Greater Union [cinema] in Melbourne, after winning premiere tickets through the *Herald-Sun* [newspaper]. Pretty

sad thinking back to it, but I wore a *Phantom* shirt, hat, socks and my skull ring to the screening. No wonder I didn't get a girlfriend before I was 18! (Male respondent, 18–35 years old, April 27, 2012)

This undeniably sweet anecdote does little to dispel the stereotypical image of comic-book fans as obsessive adolescent male loners. Yet it is arguably more significant for the way in which it demonstrates how the expression of fan allegiance is often inextricably linked to the acquisition and display of licensed merchandise bearing images and motifs drawn from specific media texts. The survey found that nearly 79 percent of respondents have owned some form of licensed *Phantom* merchandise. The most popular *Phantom* product categories were clothing (18 percent); stationery (16 percent); electronic media (13 percent); toys (12 percent); and publications other than comic magazines (10 percent).

Licensed merchandise differs from other categories of consumer goods insofar as it displays a trademarked name, logo, or character/personality in association with a specific product or service. The commercial benefits of such licensing arrangements are, according to trademark consultant Weston Anson, twofold:

Licensees hope that through the use of licensed properties they can create consumer demand for their products and services. Licensors see licensing as an opportunity to gain not only royalty income, but also additional exposure for their properties. (1984: 4)

Anson maintains that it was not until the late nineteenth and early twentieth centuries that licensing deals were struck for an ever-growing number of mass media properties (1984: 4). Richard F. Outcault, creator of *The Yellow Kid* (1895), demonstrated the licensing possibilities of comic-strip characters with his naughty juvenile hero, *Buster Brown*, created for the *New York Herald* in 1902. Outcault successfully licensed the character's image across a wide range of consumer products (such Buster Brown Shoes), a strategy which, according to Ian Gordon, made Buster Brown the first comic-strip character to become a brand name in his own right (1998a: 48–49).

Dan Fleming, author of *Powerplay: Toys as Popular Culture* (1996), suggests that the successful launch of the GI Joe doll by Hasbro (U.S.) in 1964, backed by an award-winning television commercial, signaled a fundamentally new direction in toy manufacturing and marketing:

It was from 1964 onwards . . . that the number of media-related toys seemed to explode exponentially, centered on film and television "character licensing" and TV advertising of toys. (1996: 40)

Until this time, the Phantom had only been intermittently licensed by King Features Syndicate to American toy manufacturers, with little enduring success or impact. However, the character's profile was buoyed by the release of *The Phantom* comic book published by Gold Key Comics in 1962. The comic magazine presaged a relative surge in the production of licensed *Phantom* merchandise in the United States throughout the 1960s—an attempt, perhaps, by licensees to capitalize on the renewed consumer interest in comic-book superheroes sparked by the *Batman* television series (1966–68). *The Phantom* was repackaged as a board game (Transogram), a plastic figure model kit (Revell), rub-on transfers (Hasbro), and a paint-by-numbers set (Ideal, 1967) (Rhoades and Smith, 1997: 111–14).

These products may have generated short-term financial gains for King Features Syndicate, but they only emphasized the character's problematic status as a marketable licensing property. Some comic-strip characters are so boldly defined that their visual appearance reflects their personalities in ways that consumers can easily relate to them, without needing further reference to the medium that spawned them—Buster Brown is simply "naughty," while Popeye is "strong." The Phantom, with his epic backstory and richly detailed fictional world, cannot be easily distilled into a simple "brand" icon.

When compared to the likes of Batman, the Phantom is a "lo-tech" hero who offers little in the way of equipment or accessories that could be successfully marketed as toys. With few exceptions, most licensed merchandise featuring the Phantom divorced the character from his jungle setting altogether, with not even his horse, Hero, or his wolf, Devil, by his side. The only solution to this "problem," it seemed, was to reinvent the Phantom as a marketable commodity. In 1994 Hearst Entertainment unveiled *Phantom 2040*, a futuristic animated television series which showed how Kit Walker, a gifted student at Metropia University, assumed the mantle of "The Ghost Who Walks." Counseled by Guran's grandson, and aided by hi-tech weaponry and equipment, Kit dons his father's uniform to do battle with Rebecca Madison, CEO of Maximum Inc., whose late husband murdered Kit's father—the twenty-third Phantom (Friedman, 1993: 8; Markstein, ca. 2008). The publicity materials for *Phantom 2040* scarcely made any reference to Lee Falk's original comic strip, emphasizing instead the series' "dazzling graphics" and "futuristic technology" designed to "fascinate and stimulate the imaginations of today's computer-age kids" (Hearst Entertainment, 1994: 82).

Hearst Entertainment vigorously pursued new licensing opportunities for *Phantom 2040*, which spanned "staple" children's product categories, such as action figures, Halloween costumes, trading cards, stationery, and clothing (*Playthings*, 1994: 90). However, in keeping with the show's "hi-tech" scenario, Hearst Entertainment licensed the production of *Phantom 2040* video games to Viacom New Media (*Brandweek*, 1995: 14), and made video clips from the series available to CompuServe's and America Online's Internet access subscribers (*Broadcasting & Cable*, 1994: 50). Yet for all its "cutting-edge" excitement, *Phantom 2040* went into reruns after just one season, which suggests it did not resonate with its intended (youth) audience. Diehard Phantom "phans" were, perhaps unsurprisingly, divided in their opinions of the series. One Australian survey participant felt that *Phantom 2040* "had great style" (male respondent, 18–35 years old, March 21, 2012), while a Norwegian fan argued that this "underrated" television show was "well-written and surprisingly intelligent" (male respondent, 18–35 years old, March 23, 2012). Yet some fans felt that it strayed too far from Lee Falk's original vision: "I did not like *Phantom 2040*, (because) it tried to move The Phantom away from his jungle roots and made him more like Batman/Iron Man" (male respondent, 36–49 years old, Australia, July 24, 2012).

The Phantom, it seems, provides insufficient opportunities for commercial exploitation by King Features Syndicate and its licensees, especially when compared to the galaxy of products generated by the likes of Superman or Batman over the last eighty years (Daniels, 2003: 72–75, 142–43). Yet this does not necessarily mean that "phans'" sense of collective identity is not bound up with the consumption of licensed *Phantom* products. If anything, the comparatively small pool of *Phantom* merchandise available to "phans" is, as Vincent Mosco and Lewis Kaye point out, a reminder "that what is available for consumption is often institutionally circumscribed" (2000: 43).

Textual Commodities and Fan Identity

"What 'Makes' a Phan?" This question was posed on ChronicleChamber .com, a *Phantom* fan website, in April 2012. The subsequent online debate suggested that, for some participants at least, *The Phantom* comic strip remained central to both their appreciation of the character and their status as bona fide "phans." The site's moderator, "JoeMD"—who was a fan of both *Doctor Who* and *The Phantom*—made the following observation:

> [For some] . . . to be a "true" phan, you need to have a knowledge of Lee Falk's stories. Thinking on this, I've come to realize that, for me—in regards to both [*The Phantom*] and *Doctor Who*—you need to have, if not a love for, then at least an appreciation of a thing's origins, of "what came before." (ChronicleChamber Forums, 2012)

"Andreas," a Swedish forum participant, challenged this idea by arguing that most Scandinavian *Phantom* fans were probably greater fans of the Swedish "Team Fantomen" stories than of Lee Falk's original comic-strip version ("I wouldn't say that they are NOT fans just because of that, though!" he added). But whatever their country of origin, the comic strip and comic books served as the primary test of "phan" knowledge:

> There are degrees of "fandom" and to be a fan, and not just a casual reader, I don't expect them to have read . . . all that has been produced over the 75-year history of the strip. I would say an entry-level "fan" simply needs to have read a handful of stories (including, but not limited to, [Falk's] stories) and liked the concept. (ChronicleChamber Forums, 2012)

King Features Syndicate and its international publishing partners have gradually realized just how important these canonical texts remain to dedicated "phans." Repackaging these old comic strips and comic magazines has now become a key output for *The Phantom* franchise, one which reflects the shifting cultural and commercial status of the very medium itself.

Even though the Phantom failed to benefit from the comic-book superhero "boom" of the 1940s, the character seemed ideally placed to capitalize on the "pop culture nostalgia" craze that took hold in the United States throughout the 1960s and 1970s (Stedman, 1977: 211–12). Jules Feiffer's sardonic yet affectionate tribute to the comics of his childhood, *The Great Comic Book Heroes* (1965), excited mainstream press interest in the superheroes of yesteryear, culminating with the near-insane heights of "Batmania" which followed the wildly successful debut of *Batman* on American television in 1966

(Spiegel and Jenkins, 1991: 117–48). King Features Syndicate, no doubt keen to exploit the "superhero nostalgia" trend, granted Nostalgia Press (U.S.) the rights to reprint Lee Falk's 1938 story, "The Prisoner of the Himalayas," in a trade paperback edition. The story's prewar, colonial-era politics drew fire from one critic, who denounced the Phantom as a "mercenary running-dog lackey" of British imperialists (Weatherperson [Latimer], 1972: 7)—a charge that would have offended Falk, given his efforts to tone down the strip's racial premise (and derogatory portrayal of Africans) throughout the 1960s.

In 1972, Avon Books (a division of the Hearst Corporation) released *The Story of The Phantom*, a series of paperback novels based on Lee Falk's original comic-strip story lines. The French critic Francis Lacassin wrote (erroneously) that because many early *Phantom* comic strips "have been lost and live only in the memory of their readers," these novels would introduce his earliest exploits "to those who did not know him before" (1975: ix). It is more likely, however, that Avon Books wanted to cash in on renewed public interest in 1930s-era "pulp fiction" heroes, including *The Shadow* (Belmont Books, 1965) and *The Phantom Detective* (Corinth Books, 1965), whose exploits were being successfully reformatted as mass-market paperback novels (Lovisi, 2008: 22–65). *The Story of The Phantom* series brought the character back to its earliest print media roots, reconceived as the modern, adult equivalent of the Big Little Books that introduced "The Ghost Who Walks" to an earlier (and younger) generation of American readers.

There now exists a small cottage industry dedicated to reissuing *Phantom* comic-strip and comic-book episodes in books designed to appeal to adult collectors, rather than children (Johnson, 2006: 47–50). These have ranged from paperback collections of complete, uncensored Lee Falk stories (Pacific Comics Club, 1999–2000, U.S.) to facsimile reproductions of vintage Swedish *Fantomen* comics (2002–present, Egmont Kärnan, Sweden). More recently, Hermes Press (U.S.) has reissued collections of *The Phantom* daily and Sunday newspaper comic strip, in addition to reprinting the Gold Key and Charlton Comics' series of *The Phantom* comic magazines, in deluxe hardcover volumes (2010–present). Eileen R. Meehan argues that such continual recycling and repackaging of "old" content emphasizes the importance that media conglomerates now place on the "cultivation of fans who will purchase any item connected to the title that is sold across . . . secondary markets" (2000: 83). This strategy remains commercially attractive to media organizations, Meehan adds, especially when "the cost of recycling [old content] is less than the cost of new product" (2000: 84).

The Comic Book as Readers' Forum

Comic magazines are today dismissively referred to as "floppies" by many fans who instead now prize glossy paperback collections showcasing their favorite comic-book characters. Yet comic magazines remain a central plank in *The Phantom* media franchise, particularly in Australia, Sweden, and India, where they have also played a pivotal role in providing a forum for "phans." By encouraging readers' participation in sponsored fan clubs, activity pages, and letter columns, these comics have successfully cultivated fan communities centered on the Phantom across these three nations over several decades.

Many of these editorial practices were pioneered by Hugo Gernsback's science fiction magazine, *Amazing Stories*, which first printed a letters page, titled "Discussions," in 1927 (Ash, ed., 1977: 274). Unlike most American pulp-fiction magazines of the Depression era, science fiction magazines like *Amazing Stories* placed greater editorial importance on their readers' letters, which were often published over several pages within each issue (Cheng, 2012: 55). By printing correspondents' addresses, *Amazing Stories* provided readers with a platform that not only allowed them to communicate with Gernsback himself, but with each other as well. It was from this pool of readers that organized science-fiction fandom—fostered by fan magazines ("fanzines"), regional clubs, and national conventions—first emerged throughout the 1930s (Coppa, 2006: 42–43). Comic-book fans would subsequently adopt many of the trappings of science fiction fandom during the 1960s and 1970s, but for those who followed the Phantom, their first contact with fellow "phans" would take place in the pages of the comic magazines themselves.

The Swedish publishers of *Fantomen* initially made greater efforts to court its readers than their Australian or Indian counterparts. *Fantomen* was something of a throwback to the earlier generation of illustrated children's magazines, as its comic-book serials were supplemented by illustrated prose stories, feature articles (particularly about sports stars), and technical profiles on motor cars and aircraft. Within months of its launch in October 1950, *Fantomen* magazine introduced "Fantomen-klubben" ("The Phantom Club"), which offered readers a numbered membership certificate and pin, along with a secret code with which they could read encrypted messages printed in the magazine (Bejerot, 1954: 86–87). New members' details, along with their photographs, were published in each issue. By the mid-1950s, the "Fantomen-klubben" boasted 50,000 members (Bejerot, 1954: 86–87). A new column, "Fantomen Talar" ("The Phantom Speaks"), was added in 1969, inviting readers to submit their questions about the character, which would be "answered" by the Phantom himself.

Throughout the 1970s, the magazine's new editor, Ulf Granberg, expanded "Fantomen-klubben" to include readers' letters and artwork, along with puzzles and quizzes that could be solved for cash prizes. Granberg further involved readers by providing historical information about rare or previously unpublished Lee Falk *Phantom* stories appearing in *Fantomen*, which predated by more than a decade a similar approach used in the Australian edition of *The Phantom*. Granberg also included biographical profiles of the creators responsible for the magazine's supporting comic-book features throughout the 1970s and 1980s, which proved popular with many readers:

> Over the years, I have very much . . . [liked] the editorial comments about the comics and how they [the editors] made . . . changes over time. The Swedish grand old man Ulf [Granberg] has clearly made me more open-minded to this part of the process, and if I feel more involved like this, I'll like [the magazine] as a whole, not only for the specific comic strip in that [issue]. (Male respondent, 50–65 years old, Sweden, April 12, 2012)

These communicative strategies personalized readers' engagement with the magazine, and gave them a glimpse of the editorial process that went into producing each new issue of *Fantomen*.

Granberg's editorial legacy now poses challenges for Mikael Sol (b. 1981), who succeeded him as editor-in-chief following Granberg's retirement in 2011. Sol, a doyen of Sweden's "alternative" comics scene, embodies a generational shift for the magazine.[1] He is particularly conscious of the need to woo a newer, younger audience—seen as vital for securing the magazine's long-term future—without unduly alienating its loyal, older readers:

> I don't have any sentimental feelings about *Fantomen*, [so] I can do things that other people might not . . . [The] old-fashioned appeal of the current *Fantomen* is important to retain . . . So more gradual, in-

cremental change is appropriate, so we can reassure readers, gain their trust — then hopefully we can play around with the stories.[2]

Such changes clearly trouble older, long-term readers who feel they have a privileged relationship with the magazine, fostered under Granberg's long editorial tenure. Their anxieties sometimes came to the fore in their survey responses:

> I'm worried about the future [of *Fantomen*]. The sales figures keep going down and the [magazine] is badly [run]. They don't respond to e-mails, they don't answer phone calls and the new editor is unattainable and totally anonymous. It's pathetic. (Male respondent, 36–49 years old, Sweden, May 17, 2012)

Sol remains aware of the difficulty in reconciling the interests of new "casual" readers and older "phans." "Being an editor is like being God," he explains, "but you can only listen to fan critiques up to a point."[3]

For decades, Frew Publications remained indifferent to its Australian audience; so long as they remained loyal, unquestioning "consumers" of the magazine, Frew Publications clearly saw no reason to publicly recognize or address them as enthusiastic "readers." This policy was sustainable while sales remained relatively healthy, but as circulation figures for *The Phantom* began to steadily drop throughout the 1980s, new thinking was called for. Shortly after assuming managerial control of the company in the late 1980s, publisher Jim Shepherd wrote his first "Message from the Publisher" to accompany the uncensored publication of "The Phantom Goes to War" (*The Phantom*, no. 910A, 1988). This column remained a staple feature of *The Phantom* right up until Shepherd's death in 2013. This first step made towards simply acknowledging readers was warmly received by Australian "phans":

> It is always a pleasure to read Jim Shepherd's editorial on the inside cover and . . . any other editorial content, including the letters to the editor. It is part of *The Phantom* experience to take on board Jim's comments. (Male respondent, 50–65 years old, July 31, 2012)

Frew Publications' decision to introduce a letters page, "Phantom Forum" (*The Phantom*, no. 917, 1988), was driven by a need to clearly establish who, exactly, was buying *The Phantom* comic book. Shepherd also used the "Phantom Forum" to manage readers' debates about the style and contents of the magazine, as well as to justify the company's occasionally contradictory editorial policies. One reader challenged Frew's decision to censor scenes from a Swedish *Fantomen* story depicting naked women, claiming it signaled a return "to the bad old days of censorship" (Shedden, 1996: 96). Shepherd, however, declared that some of the Swedish *Fantomen* stories indulged in "unnecessary titillation" and maintained that Frew Publications would continue to "tidy up any [Swedish] artwork considered [to be] over the top" (Shepherd, 1996: 96). Shepherd further justified this stance by printing letters from readers endorsing his "selective censorship" on the grounds that such scenes were demeaning to women (Furlong, 1996: 34), and that Frew's policy was entirely in keeping with the Phantom's "high moral character" (Davis, 1996: 33). Vigorous debate was therefore permissible in the pages of *The Phantom* magazine—but only in a forum made available at the discretion of Frew Publications, and conducted largely on its terms.

Indian readers were, like their Australian counterparts, rarely granted the opportunity to voice their opinions about *The Phantom* comic magazines published in their country. Aside from staging the occasional essay-writing contest, Bennett, Coleman & Co. seldom encouraged—or published—feedback from *Indrajal Comics*' readers. The same held true for Diamond Comics (New Delhi), which acquired the Indian comic-book rights to *The Phantom* after *Indrajal Comics* ceased publication in 1990. So long as *The Phantom* continued to post strong sales, Diamond Comics—like Frew Publications in Australia—clearly saw little need to court its readers further.

A more inclusive approach was tried with the relaunch of *The Phantom* comic book for the Indian market in 2000, jointly published by Egmont International (Denmark) and the Indian Express Newspapers group (*The Hindu*, 2000). It was closely modeled on the Swedish edition, not least because Ulf Granberg selected all the Swedish-drawn *Fantomen* stories to be translated into English for the new comic (Shedden, 2003). The Indian edition of *The Phantom* ran factual articles about topics raised in each issue's story, such as African wildlife, pirates, and fossils, just as *Fantomen* did during the 1950s. The "Morristown Post" column printed letters from Indian children discovering the character for the first time:

I am a student of class nine. I really like *The Phantom* comic and all its characters. The stories are also interesting. Really! No other comic can compete with you. (Shaikh, ca. 2000: 31)

The Phantom also evidently appealed to adult readers who recalled the character from their own childhood:

When I heard that The Phantom comics [were] back, my mind went back 30–35 years when we used to believe that The Phantom [did] exist. Every issue was a treasure for us and was read by everyone in the family. (Gadre, ca. 2000: 31)

Egmont Imagination (India) prepared a specially priced *Phantom Adventure Kit* (containing three comics and Phantom souvenirs) which was launched with great fanfare during roadshows held throughout India in June 2000 (*The Hindu*, 2000). However, the Rs.30 cover price put it beyond the reach of most Indian children; one reader even wrote to the editor, suggesting they "make the comic price a bit reasonable, so that you may increase the number of readers" (Thakkar, 2000: 31). But Egmont's decision to limit *The Phantom* to English-language editions effectively cut it off from the vast majority of Indian comic-book readers, most of whom were not fluent in English.[4] This new series, which strongly resembled the Swedish *julalbum* format, compared poorly with the riotous aesthetic of Indian comics, and also ignored Indian readers' historical preferences for Lee Falk's original stories. *The Phantom* was canceled in 2002, and Egmont International exited the Asia-Pacific region in 2004 to focus on the Scandinavian market (Amarnath, 2009).

Phantom "Phan" Clubs — Now, and Then

Despite their undoubted enthusiasm for the Phantom, the majority of Australian, Swedish, and Indian readers surveyed for this study (62 percent) have never joined any formally organized *Phantom* fan clubs. Despite being located in different countries and taking on quite different forms, many of these fan clubs were alike insofar as they were often created in response to opportunities and challenges unique to each of these countries, and were founded by organizations and individuals for wildly divergent reasons.

The Phantom Club was, according to founder John Henderson, created to give Australians "the opportunity to express their admiration of The Phantom" (Henderson [attrib.], ca. 1981: 1)—an opportunity that Frew Publications had never extended to its readers. Launched in 1981, the Phantom Club was owned and operated by fans. King Features Syndicate licensed Hendo Industries Pty Ltd. (formed by the club president, John Henderson) to produce and sell *Phantom* merchandise as part of the club's activities throughout Australasia and the South Pacific region (*Intellectual Property Reports*, 1991: 590). The Phantom Club would pay King Features Syndicate either A$1,000 per year, or 7 percent of sales, depending on whichever figure was higher (Robson, 1985: 3).

The Phantom Club was imbued with a distinct moral purpose. New members were asked to sign the Phantom's "Sacred Oath" on their application form, in order to make "phollowers" aware of "the motivation behind every *Phantom* adventure" and to remind them that "they also have a responsibility to society" (Henderson [attrib.], ca. 1981: 2). Henderson, who had read *The Phantom* comic since childhood, declared that "there are many disturbing features of our society that demand attention, and like The Phantom, the club believes it has a duty to help in whatever way it can" (Henderson [attrib.], ca. 1981: 2).

The club's *Jungle Beat* newsletter became a clearinghouse for members to share their knowledge about *The Phantom*. Barry Stubbersfield became a notable contributor by documenting the complex—and hitherto unknown—publishing history of *The Phantom* in Australia (1986: 14–15; 1987a: 5–7; 1987b: 9–11), as well as uncovering Frew Publications' censorship of *Phantom* stories published during the 1950s (ca. 1989: 4–7; n.d. [a]: 4–7; n.d. [b]: 4–6). The *Jungle Beat* newsletter thus became an important site of "fan scholarship," wherein "phans" could undertake academically inclined analysis of their chosen medium or text (Hills, 2002: 11–21). Stubbersfield's expertise later became a valuable resource for publisher Jim Shepherd's plans to revitalize *The Phantom* comic book, which underscored Frew Publications' reliance on the Australian "phan" community to further its commercial ambitions.

While the Phantom Club advertised heavily in *The Phantom* comic magazine to promote its mail-order merchandise and to recruit new members, Henderson frequently used the club's *Jungle Beat* newsletter to criticize Frew Publications' increased reliance on translated *Fantomen* stories from Semic

Press. Dismissing the Swedish stories as "substandard and an insult to both us and The Ghost Who Walks" (Henderson, 1985: 23), Henderson declared that "the Swedes do pose a threat to the real Phantom that generations [of Australians] have come to know and love" and urged "fair-dinkum Phantom people" to act as a "united force" capable of reversing Frew's editorial policy "before it's too late" (Henderson, 1986a: 12). It is not known whether Phantom Club members took up Henderson's challenge; if they did, Frew Publications remained unmoved by any such protests, as it continued publishing translated Swedish stories throughout the 1980s.

Despite these objections, the club remained indefatigable in promoting the Phantom to the wider community, with John Henderson (dressed in his bespoke Phantom costume) doing press and television interviews throughout Australia (*Jungle Beat*, 1987: 8). Bryan Shedden, creator of The Deep Woods fan website, suggested that "much of the public awareness of The Phantom that currently exists in Australia probably owes to the activities of The Phantom Club during those years" (2007a). The club's influence clearly exceeded its modest size; by 1986, the club had 3,291 members worldwide, which was a fraction of the estimated 50,000 readers then purchasing *The Phantom* comic book every fortnight (Henderson [attrib.], 1986b: 14).

The club's license, however, was withdrawn by King Features Syndicate in 1988 due to alleged copyright infringements (Shedden, 2007a). Henderson maintained that the decision, made by "the businessmen in The Phantom head office in New York," boiled down to a philosophical difference. As Henderson saw it, "they were more concerned with the profitability of the character, and we were more concerned with the spirit" (Henderson [attrib.], ca. 1989: 2). Henderson continued to run the organization as the Independent Phantom Fan Club of Australia (ca. 1989–95), but all subsequent club literature clearly emphasized that it was "an unofficial organization and in no way associated with the owners of 'The Phantom' character" (Henderson [attrib.], ca. 1989: 3). The club had grown to 4,788 members worldwide by 1990 (*Jungle Beat*, ca. 1990: 3) and would, according to Henderson, exist as a "secret society" (Kiefer, 1989: n.p.).

Remarkably, Henderson's venture operated for several years as a parallel "underground" organization existing in the shadow of its authorized successor, the Phantom Official Fan Club–Australia (POFCA). The launch of this new fan organization indicated just how lucrative this property had become for its Australian licensor, Gaffney International Licensing. The commercial rejuvenation of *The Phantom* comic book no doubt played a key role in restoring the character's public profile. This in turn enhanced the character's value as a licensing "property," and led to unprecedented volumes of new *Phantom* merchandise being released on to the Australian market. POFCA would cultivate a lucrative secondary market for these products, sold directly to enthusiastic "phans," which meant licensees would not be entirely dependent on the fickle and unpredictable tastes of "mainstream" consumers— or, as Eileen R. Meehan put it, "the dreaded mundanes" (2000: 86).

Gaffney International Licensing awarded the license for this new fan club to Neville Kent Promotions (Melbourne), which also operated licensed Australian fan clubs for Marilyn Monroe and Elvis Presley, along with a retail gift store, Famous Faces (Melbourne) (Shedden, 2007a). POFCA was launched in 1991; advertisements placed in *The Phantom* comic book emphasized that POFCA was "fully endorsed by King Features Syndicate"—an attempt, surely, to distinguish it from John Henderson's unauthorized rival fan club—and offered members an ID card, a quarterly newsletter, and "exclusive PHANTOMANIA product offers" (Phantom Official Fan Club— Australia, 1991a: 35).

Despite promising abundant "historical information" about *The Phantom*, as well as "behind the scenes" profiles on the comic strip's American creators (Shedden, 2007a), POFCA rarely made such content available. It relied instead on subscribers to become *"Phantom* correspondents," an unpaid fan labor force that was encouraged to contribute letters, news stories, and artwork to their new quarterly *Member Newsletter* (POFCA, 1991b: 4). What POFCA did do was to relentlessly stoke consumer demand for licensed *Phantom* products. These were heavily promoted in the *Member Newsletter*, which became a mail-order catalog for the club's nominal retail outlet, Famous Faces. Yet just prior to the release of *The Phantom* feature film, Lee Walsh Licensing (Melbourne) replaced Gaffney Licensing International as King Features Syndicate's licensed Australian representative. This corporate handover coincided with the lackluster box-office performance of *The Phantom*, which signaled the end of "Phantomania" in Australia. POFCA scaled back its operations throughout 1997–98 and ceased trading in 1999 (Shedden, 2007a). POFCA was perhaps too dependent on an anticipated retail "boom" in *Phantom* merchandise and thus ceased to be of value once sales revenues failed to meet the commercial expectations of its operator, Neville Kent Promotions, or its Australian licensor, Lee Walsh Licensing. Members' concerns about the club's future ultimately remained subordinate to its corporate stakeholders' financial interests. Far from being a truly "grassroots" fan club, this was a commercial venture which measured the worth of "phans" in financial terms alone.

The ultimate fate of POFCA was determined not by the "phans" themselves, but by the contractual agreements struck between King Features Syndicate and its foreign licensees. The enthusiastic participation of "phans" alone could not save these organizations—at least, not in Australia. If licensees could not extract maximum revenues from the largest possible number of "phans" on behalf of the franchise owner, the commercial rights to operate such a club could be withdrawn, or reassigned to another company. Australian readers may have held strong opinions about the direction of *The Phantom* comic book and, in the case of John Henderson, created an (officially sanctioned) forum to express these views. Yet even relatively privileged fans like Henderson could exercise little, if any, influence over the management of *The Phantom* franchise. John Tulloch's case study of British and Australian fans of the *Doctor Who* television series, and their fractious relationship with the program's producers, provides a key insight about fan-producer relationships which is equally applicable in this context. Australian "phans" were, to borrow Tulloch's phrase, a "powerless elite," situated between "producers they have little control over" and the "wider public" with whom the long-term survival of most media franchises arguably rests (1995: 145).

"Phans" and Digital Fandom

Perhaps the greatest threat confronting commercially run *Phantom* fan clubs was relevance. By the late 1990s, "phans" throughout the world were no longer reliant on officially sanctioned fan organizations as outlets for expressing their affinity with the character or as a forum for contacting fellow "phans." Instead, many of them borrowed the practices of "mainstream" comics fandom (historically devoted to American superhero comics) to create their own parallel "phan" community—a process made easier by the expansion of online media.

The majority of readers (63 percent) surveyed from Australia, Sweden, and India state that they currently read (or have read) other comics in addition to *The Phantom*. However, a substantially smaller number of survey participants (32 percent) indicated that they took part in comic-book fandom activities that had no connection to *The Phantom*. The most popular of these activities were attending comic-book conventions (34 percent); participating in message boards and other online forums (26 percent); creating websites and/or blogs (12 percent); and producing—or contributing to—fanzines (10 percent). Despite these low participation rates, it would not be unreasonable to suggest that these readers' (limited) engagement with "mainstream" comics fandom has—even on a superficial level—influenced their own practices and activities as Phantom "phans."

The formation of media fandom communities, and the articulation of fan identities, was irrevocably changed throughout the 1990s as the expansion of Internet access services provided people with an unprecedented opportunity to publish and disseminate information on a worldwide scale. The magnitude of the Internet as a communicative platform was not lost on comic-book fans, either—nor on "phans" of *The Phantom*. One of the earliest, and arguably most significant of these online resources was The Deep Woods (http://www.deepwoods.org), an encyclopedic *Phantom* website developed by Bryan Shedden, an Australian "phan." Shedden recruited an international network of *Phantom* fan-scholars from Australia, Sweden, India, and the United States who contributed articles and shared previously unseen images of rare *Phantom* book and magazine covers from around the world. Launched in 1996, The Deep Woods soon established itself as an authoritative fan text about *The Phantom* and elevated Shedden's status as a "fan-scholar" throughout the then-nascent online *Phantom* "phan" community.

The production and reception of The Deep Woods website serves as a useful demonstration of how, according to Jeffrey A. Brown, "the cultural economy of comic book fandom" operates (1997: 26). While conceding that some comic-book collectors "validate" their hobby "by citing the economic value of their [collection]" (1997: 27), Brown maintains that most fans substantiate their participation in fandom by exhibiting their "knowledge of [comic-book] creators, characters and story lines," which is gained through the acquisition of "canonical texts" (1997: 26). The dividend generated by this form of "cultural capital" gained from the specialized knowledge of popular culture artifacts is not, according to John Fiske, measured in economic terms, but instead lies within "the pleasures and esteem of one's peers in a community of taste" (Fiske, 1992: 34). Furthermore, Kate Egan's study of British "video nasty" fan websites found that many of these online resources were—like The Deep Woods—content-rich archives designed to "solidify the [website] creator's identity as a powerful subcultural teacher and historian" (2003: n.p.). Indeed, Shedden's authority as a *Phantom* "expert" was further recognized by Moonstone Books (U.S.), which hired him as an editorial consultant for their new series of *Phantom* comic magazines and graphic novels (ca. 2002–7).[5]

The international dimension of today's online "phan" community is further illustrated by the Scandinavian Chapter (http://www.schapter.org), a Swedish fan organization which has, to some extent, surpassed The Deep Woods as a key online destination for *Phantom* "phans."[6] The Scandinavian Chapter was originally formed as a "sister organization" to the Lee Falk Memorial Bengali Explorers' Club (LFMBEC), which held its first dinner in Sydney, Australia, on April 30, 1999, to commemorate the death of Lee Falk. The event proved so successful that the LFMBEC has continued staging annual dinners, featuring celebrity speakers (including past and present *Phantom* comic artists) and memorabilia auctions, to raise funds for a local children's hospital (LFMBEC, 2005).[7]

The Scandinavian Chapter, like its Australian namesake, considered itself a "Phantom club for adults" (Jensen, 2010a: 253). When Bryan Shedden announced in 2007 that he would no longer be updating The Deep Woods website,[8] the Scandinavian Chapter launched The PhantomWiki (http://www .phantomwiki.org), an international reference guide to *The Phantom* which invited contributions from "phans" throughout the world. The group has also published two books, *Fantomen* (2010) and *Lee Falk, Storyteller* (2011), as tributes to the character and his creator, respectively. The scholarly intent and sophisticated production values evident in these works denote the professional tenor of Swedish comics fandom (Strömberg, 2010: 65–71).

Being based in Sweden has given the Scandinavian Chapter privileged access to writers and artists working on the *Fantomen* magazine, and has allowed it to stage field trips to the offices of Egmont Kärnan and Bulls Press to hold informal discussions about *Fantomen* with magazine editors and newspaper syndicate representatives. Club members were also invited to contribute bibliographical research to *Fantomen* (no. 14, 2006), a special edition commemorating the seventieth anniversary of *The Phantom* comic strip (Jensen, 2010a: 256). So, just as Sweden has emerged as a key production node in *The Phantom* comic-book franchise, Swedish "phans" have now assumed a preeminent position in the international *Phantom* "phan" community. As the Scandinavian Chapter's cofounder, Brian Jensen, observed: "We quickly became more famous than our allies 'Down Under'" (2010a: 253).

Comments such as these draw attention to the internal divisions and rivalries that can undermine fan communities' outward displays of unity and camaraderie. Derek Johnson observes that early studies of fandom, such as Camille Bacon-Smith's *Enterprising Women* (1992) and Henry Jenkins's *Textual Poachers* (2013), typically "stressed unity within fan communities" (2007: 285). However, Johnson argues that there have always been "ongoing, competitive struggles" between rival fan groupings and "external institutions" that seek to legitimize the "fan-text-producer relationship according to their respective interests" (2007: 287). Conversely, Andrea MacDonald argues that this fundamentally competitive and hierarchical conception of fandom is problematic, not least because "fandom views itself as being antithetical to 'mundane' social norms" (1998: 136). Nevertheless, MacDonald states that observable hierarchies do exist within (and between) fan communities. These hierarchies can be delineated by fans' level of (textual) knowledge, participation in formal activities, access to "inside knowledge," and control of venues, be they physical (convention facilities), or virtual (message boards) (1998: 137–38). The Scandinavian Chapter clearly regards itself as the preeminent *Phantom* fan organization; its conveners need only point to the industry of its members (e.g., the PhantomWiki website), the quality of its fan media output (e.g., books, calendars), and its close links with Swedish media organizations involved with *The Phantom/Fantomen* franchise to justify such a claim.

However, the relative prosperity of the Scandinavian Chapter also draws attention to occasionally stark levels of economic disparity between regional and/or national fan communities. The recent formation of *Phantom* fan networks in India has been, in part, a response to the scarcity of media texts in that market. *The Phantom*, like many Indian comic books, had suffered greatly as a younger generation of Indian children spurned comics in favor of new satellite television channels, computer games, and online media. Where a popular comic magazine could once reliably sell 500,000 copies in the early 1990s, average sales figures for most Indian comics had plunged to 50,000–60,000 copies per issue by 2011 (Ahmed, 2011).

Nor have more recent attempts to revive the Phantom in India been met with success. Following the cancellation of *The Phantom* comic published by Egmont Imagination (India) in 2002, the company's Indian executives negotiated a management buyout of the firm, which was renamed EuroKids International (Amarnath, 2009). The company's publishing activities were reorganized under the EuroBooks division, which launched a new series of English-language *Phantom* comics in 2008, available through bookstores and via the EuroBooks website. Printed in full color and priced at Rs.199 (US$3.50), these paperback "graphic novels" sold just 10,000 copies in 2008. "Undoubtedly, the [*Indrajal Comics*] figures would have been better," admitted Uday Mathur, managing director of EuroKids International. "[*Indrajal Comics*] . . . were far more popular, but we're trying to revive interest in [the Phantom]" (quoted in Majumdar, 2009). Yet anecdotal press reports suggest these newer comics hold little appeal for the thousands of adults who grew up reading *Indrajal Comics* in the 1970s and 1980s. These mature-age collectors form the bedrock of an expansive, albeit loose-knit community of Phantom "phans," who scour roadside bookstalls and *raddiwala* (scrap paper) merchants for old copies of *Indrajal Comics*. Readers frequently expressed an almost Proustian pleasure in recalling the very scent and feel of timeworn copies of *Indrajal Comics* (*Times of India*, 2008; Ghosh, 2014).

Paradoxically, the surge in Internet usage and social media which threatened the commercial viability of India's comic-book industry during the 1990s now provided a platform for the "first wave" of Indian comic-book fandom. Ritu G. Khanduri's study of Indian comic-book culture found that, for an older generation of Indian comic-book fans, *The Phantom* remains "a pleasurable childhood memory" (2010: 179). It is through fan-authored "blogs," she adds, that Indian readers now "generate a history of Indian comics and a social network of *Phantom* enthusiasts" (2010: 172).

Indian readers' yearning for the comics of their (pre-television) childhood is most apparent on the Reprint Indrajal Campaign website (http://indrajal .reprintcampaign.com) (est. 2010), which began an online petition lobbying The Times of India media group to reprint *Indrajal Comics*. Their demands are often steeped in nostalgic longing:

> They bring back old memories of childhood. I am sad that I lost my collection and would love to have it back on the market, to be treasured and passed on to the next generation as some of the best things in our lives. (Ghorai, 2010)

Signatories to the petition frequently complained of the scarcity of second-hand copies of *Indrajal Comics* at local bookstalls. Treasured copies of the earliest issues are proudly displayed by "phans" on their blogs and typically command high prices on auction websites, placing them beyond the financial reach of most collectors. Some Indian comic-book collectors have tried to redress this situation by making digitally scanned copies of English- and Hindi-language editions of *Indrajal Comics* freely available for "phans" to download from such sites as the *Indrajal Comics Club* (www.indrajal-comics .blogspot.com) and *Indrajal Online* (http://indrajal-online.blogspot.com).

Despite its whiff of illegality, the online "trafficking" in out-of-print comic books cannot be automatically likened to India's far more lucrative trade in pirated literary works, which accounted for nearly 25 percent of sales in India's retail book trade by 2011 (Mukherjee, 2011). Lawrence Liang and Ravi Sundaram maintain that current debates about copyright piracy in India continue to elevate the "moral and economic claims of rights holders," which are continually juxtaposed against the "illegality and criminality of acts of piracy" (2011: 344). Yet this approach, they argue, frequently overlooks "the ordinariness and ubiquity of piracy in the contemporary media landscape" (2011: 344). Ravi Sundaram explains that since the early 1980s, media piracy "was the dominant form through which [Indian audiences] experienced new media" (2010: 121), thanks largely to the availability of low-cost media reproduction and recording technologies, such as cheap photo-offset printing, and audio and videocassettes (2010: 119). "Pirate culture," argues Sundaram, "allowed the entry of vast numbers of poor residents into media culture" (2010: 112).

Yet in no way could the "phans" responsible for these *Phantom* comic file-sharing websites be thought of as belonging to India's "urban poor." Their blog profiles indicate that they are, for the most part, male, well-educated, and English-speaking and work in India's information technology/telecommunications sector. Nonetheless, their desire to share scarce *Phantom* comic magazines — free of charge — with fellow "phans" highlights the important role that "pirate culture" continues to play in circumventing the institutional and commercial roadblocks that once barred Indian audiences' access to mass media. Overlooked and ignored as consumers by past and present publishers of *The Phantom*, Indian "phans" have used digital media to make rare, analog-era texts available to a geographically dispersed, diasporic online readership. Their commitment to this task further demonstrates how the formation and behavior of comic-book fan communities in different national contexts are influenced by the structures of local media markets, and are often a response to the actions—or indifference—of media franchise owners.

There are many ways in which "phans" can choose to immerse themselves in the world of *The Phantom*. They might follow his exploits each day in their local newspaper, or in a comic magazine purchased from their neighborhood newsstand or kiosk. They can even wear a *Phantom* wristwatch, or pull on a pair of *Phantom* socks, if they so desire. To an outside observer, their identification with *The Phantom* appears explicitly tied to acts of consumption. This image of The Phantom "phan" as a consumerist dupe is both uncharitable and simplistic. To be a "collector," as distinct from a "consumer," requires a level of dedication, organization, and knowledge that is far from passive. True, some "phans" may be omnivorous consumers of *Phantom* merchandise—but there are others who consider themselves more discerning collectors, and may, for example, specialize in collecting original pieces of *Phantom* comic-strip artwork. What links these different types of collectors is a shared desire to accumulate, and demonstrate, a unique form of cultural capital within the broader community of *Phantom* enthusiasts.

Yet the construction of "phan" identity—both individually and collectively—is shot through with conflict and contradiction. On the one hand, "phans" celebrate the Phantom's "cult figure" status within the superhero genre, since it reinforces the character's position (and their own) as outliers on the fringes of comic-book fandom. Nevertheless, "phans" freely plunder the conventions and practices of mainstream comics culture to create their own parallel fan community dedicated to *The Phantom*. But even within this community, there are competing hierarchies and divisions. Some fan-driven enterprises have struck contractual agreements with official licensors, partly to give themselves an "official" platform whereby they might exert influence—ostensibly on behalf of "ordinary" fans like themselves—over the management and direction of *The Phantom* franchise, only to be met with indifference or rejection. The Internet has provided *Phantom* enthusiasts with an altogether easier entry point into organized fandom, one that allows them to bypass their hero's corporate stakeholders entirely, and which has helped foster an international "phan" network. But here, too, conflict and competition are evident. Fan-scholars create online destinations to establish their credentials as authoritative experts on *The Phantom*, while rival "phan" formations jostle for position as the preeminent regional/global *Phantom* community.

Tempting though it might be to dismiss such schisms as adolescent bickering, these divisions nonetheless point to larger debates about the production, consumption, and contested ownership of media properties. The Phantom is clearly much more than a fictional character, but his true "value" can be fluid and imprecise, depending on how that value is defined—and by whom. To his legally recognized owners, *The Phantom* is a commercial commodity which can be repackaged and resold in an infinite variety of ways. To his "phans," however, the Phantom is an almost totemic figure, rich in textual meaning and emotional resonance. The ongoing struggles within, and between, different formations of "phans" are perhaps a reflection of this perennial tension, whereby audiences continually seek new means to define their relationship to media texts—not as consumers, but as "producers" and "owners" in their own right, and on their own terms.

THE ETERNAL CHAMPION

A new statue was unveiled at the Railroad Park, next to Stockholm's Central Station, on September 5, 2014, but it was unlike any of the monuments one normally sees dotted throughout the Swedish capital's parks or thoroughfares. The ceremony was, in a way, a tribute to a Swedish hero, but this wasn't a statue of some long-dead king, or of a valiant general slain in battle. It was, instead, a seven-meter tall aluminum figure of a man dressed in a checked overcoat, his face concealed by a hat and dark glasses, running in hot pursuit of some unseen, distant quarry. The work, according to the artist Jan Håfström (b. 1937), was titled *Who Is Mr. Walker?* Rendered in the style of comic-strip artist Wilson McCoy, the statue portrayed the Phantom's civilian alter ego, and paid homage to Håfström's youthful memories of reading *Fantomen* comics (Bulls Press, 2014).

One need look no further than this brightly colored metallic statue for proof of just how much Swedes regard the Phantom as their own "adopted" national hero. But it is a backward glance to a childhood vision of the Phantom, one that has been supplanted by the work of the many artists who followed in McCoy's wake since the early 1960s. It seems less a tribute than an epitaph for a hero whose time has long since passed.

This sense of melancholy is matched by the elegiac tone evident in the rhetoric of many Phantom "phans" discussed in the previous chapter, which betrayed a collective anxiety about what the future holds for "The Ghost Who Walks." Whereas other media fan communities are actively engaged in producing their own texts, such as fan fiction or amateur films, based on their favorite film or television series, Phantom "phans" instead play the role of archivists and record-keepers, determined to preserve the deeds of their hero (and the work of his creators) for posterity. This is not necessarily the work of "phans" keen to leave their creative stamp on an officially licensed media franchise. Instead, these are the labors of an older generation who perhaps sense that, without them, the Phantom would soon be forgotten.

On one level, such concerns might seem misplaced. Just as the dynasty of the Phantom is renewed with each successive generation, so too has *The Phantom* comics franchise undergone constant renewal. *The Phantom* newspaper comic strip—the canonical text at the heart of King Features Syndicate's "property"—has been reenergized by a cohort of new writers and illustrators since the death of its creator, Lee Falk, in 1999. The comic strip's creative handlers acknowledge Falk's legacy by employing him as a fictional narrator in occasional episodes—but they are looking, not to the past, but to the future of the Phantom dynasty. A recent story line showed the Phantom and Diana Palmer discussing the paths to be taken by their twin children, Kit and Heloise, who would shortly turn fifteen years of age (De Paul and Ryan, 2015–16). While Diana is keen to send Heloise to a boarding school in New York, the Phantom suggests that Kit be sent to a remote school in the Himalayas where the sixteenth Phantom was tutored by a wise man, who gave him the skills needed to become "The Ghost Who Walks." The present-day Phantom must now help Kit prepare to fulfill his destiny, just as he did at his father's deathbed in the Skull Cave, all those years ago (De Paul and Ryan, 2015–16). He will do so under the guidance of artist Mike Manley (b. 1961), who took over as illustrator on *The Phantom* daily newspaper strip following the death of Paul Ryan in March 2016.

Sweden's *Fantomen* comic magazine also underwent a significant transformation in 2012 when its long-serving editor, Ulf Granberg, made way for his younger successor, Mikael Sol, an independently minded comics creator in his own right. But the times when *Fantomen* rivaled *Donald Duck* as Sweden's best-selling comic magazine are a distant memory, and the comic's print run is now just 22,000 copies, with an estimated circulation of 71,000 readers (Gudmundsson, 2015: 7). The magazine was reduced from 68 to 52 pages in 2014, and the number of pages allocated for new *Fantomen* stories was cut back from 32 pages to 22 pages in 2015.

Undeterred by these constraints, Sol has tried to overhaul and update the magazine in order to attract new readers. In 2014 he invited Swedish writers and artists not previously associated with *Fantomen* to contribute to "Fantomens värld" ("The World of the Phantom"), a series of short, self-contained episodes focusing on different supporting characters drawn from the Phantom comic strip. Sol subsequently commissioned a new three-part series, *Fantomen Kids*, starring Kit and Heloise in their own adventures, in the hopes that it would appeal to younger readers, and—if successful—could be spun off into a new stand-alone comic magazine for the Swedish market. While this plan remains as yet unrealized, Egmont Publishing AB (as the company is now known) launched the *Fantomen* software application in 2013, which allowed users to download the latest issue of the comic onto smartphones, tablets, and laptops as part of its ongoing courtship of the "digital generation."

The growing influence of Swedish "phans" in the pages of *Fantomen* has become evident in recent years. Andreas Eriksson (b. 1981), a prominent member of the Scandinavian Chapter fan club, began writing "Fantomens universum" ("The Phantom's Universe") for *Fantomen* in 2015, providing dossier-styled profiles about the series' supporting characters, for the benefit of newer readers. In April 2016 he was appointed acting editor of *Fantomen*, serving as a temporary replacement for Mikael Sol for an eight-month period. His appointment stemmed in part from his in-depth knowledge of Fantomen/Phantom lore, which, coupled with his professional background as a technical writer, made him uniquely suited for the role of *redaktor* (editor). Eriksson acknowledged that his was a largely supervisory role, with the contents of all issues being released during his tenure planned well in advance, but he intended to use each issue's editorial column to put his "stamp" on the magazine (Eriksson, 2016). Nevertheless, Eriksson's temporary elevation to editor further underscores the heightened levels of interaction between media producers and active audiences aligned with popular media franchises.

In Australia, Steve Shepherd—in the best tradition of the Walker family —took over as publisher of *The Phantom* comic magazine following the death of his father, Jim Shepherd, in April 2013. But Shepherd subsequently handed over the publisher's reins to graphic designer Dudley Hogarth in August 2014 so that he could return to his own website and photography business. Jim Shepherd's widow, Judith, stepped down as director of Frew Publications in December 2015—and then, for the first time in the company's history, *The Phantom* ceased publication for nearly two months.

Australian readers' concerns about the future of *The Phantom* comic led to a flurry of speculation among "phans" on social media, but their fears were allayed when former *Phantom* cover artist Glenn Ford announced in February 2016 that he and Rene White (proprietor of The Phantom's Vault, an online retail store specializing in *Phantom* merchandise) had purchased Frew Publications and successfully renegotiated the company's publishing agreement with King Features Syndicate (Ford, 2016). These changes took place within months of Frew Publications having taken its first cautious steps online, launching a website (http://www.phantomcomic.com.au) and a Facebook page, but these were initially designed to serve as retail sales and promotional channels only. Nevertheless, Ford maintained that they would assume greater importance for Frew Publications and Australian "phans" alike:

> We have a lot of ideas, some of which, we hope, will surprise you and some we feel are expected and perhaps long overdue. The most important aspect of all of this, though, is that YOU now have an opportunity to get your voice heard. If we are to grow this business, we need to hear from you. To this end, we intend to make our website and Facebook page a bit more reactive and responsive . . . We are still formulating a lot of this — it's early days — but we are excited. (Ford, 2016)

Dudley Hogarth, who remained as publisher, reinstated the "Phantom Forum" letters page and reprinted readers' comments posted on the company's Facebook page, thus demonstrating the company's renewed desire to engage with "phans," in print and online. Yet even as Frew Publications strives to take *The Phantom* in new creative and commercial directions, Hogarth acknowledged Shepherd's posthumous influence over the magazine:

> The legacy of Jim Shepherd is synonymous with the legend of The Phantom in Oz. Had it not been for his lifelong dedication and effort, there would be nothing to read or collect today. (Hogarth, 2016: 33)

Nevertheless, Frew Publications has made a concerted effort to court its "rusted-on" readers in ways that signal a decisive break from Shepherd's long-standing, and often conservative, editorial approach. The company has begun offering limited-edition comics signed by Australian cover artists, issuing variant covers for the Australian and New Zealand markets, and producing Phantom art folios sold exclusively at Australian comic conventions, and through its online store. These new marketing strategies are, on one level, a tacit acknowledgment that Frew Publications must increasingly cater to the needs of diehard "phans" and collectors in order to ensure the future of *The Phantom* comic magazine.

But Frew Publications is no less affected by the recent cutbacks made to the Swedish *Fantomen* magazine, which remains their chief source of new stories for the Australian edition of *The Phantom*.[1] Like its Swedish counterpart, the Australian edition of *The Phantom* has endured declining sales over time, with average print runs now numbering just 20,000 copies per issue (Lewis, 2016). The reduced length of *Fantomen* stories forced Frew Publications to consider other options to fill out their standard 32-page magazine format. The company initially opted to fill this gap by serializing the epic story line "The Heart of Darkness" (originally published in *Fantomen* during 1994–96) as a backup feature in *The Phantom*, where it has appeared sporadically since October 2015.

Frew Publications' more recent initiatives, however, provide some clues about the company's future editorial direction. Commencing with *The Phantom*, no. 1761 (August 2016), Frew Publications announced plans to publish English translations of "new" *Phantom* stories sourced from Brazil, Italy, Germany, Turkey, and elsewhere, previously unseen by Australian audiences:

> The stories we've found generally date back to the '60s–'80s, when The Phantom was a world-wide newspaper phenomenon, and are accordingly much simpler in their style of story-telling—probably closer to the Lee Falk school of comic-strip writing—and quite far removed from the modern, Egmont-style gritty, multi-part epics. (Frew Publications, 2016)

This statement acknowledges that the era when *The Phantom* comic strip could be legitimately described as a "newspaper phenomenon" has long since passed. Furthermore, it indirectly addresses the generational divide between Australian readers who prefer the "traditional" Lee Falk interpretation of *The Phantom* and those (often younger) readers who favor the "modern" Swedish *Fantomen* stories.

The company has commissioned new, Australian-drawn stories which it undoubtedly hopes will appeal to each of these distinctive audience clusters and, more importantly, entice a new generation of readers to follow the Phantom's adventures. "The Phantom by Gaslight," a new serial written by

Christopher Sequeria and illustrated by Jason Paulos, is set in Victorian-era London, and thus emulates the long-standing Swedish tradition of historical Phantom/Fantomen adventures (ChronicleChamber, 2017a). Frew Publications has also commissioned another series, *Kid Phantom*, which builds on Lee Falk's earlier storyline, "The Childhood of The Phantom" (Falk and McCoy, 1994a [1944–45]: 50–78). *Kid Phantom*, slated to appear as a digest-sized quarterly magazine, will be written by Andrew Constant and is drawn in a distinctively cartoon-like style by Australian artist Paul Mason, not dissimilar from the Swedish "Fantomen Kids" serial, thought to be more appealing to younger readers (ChronicleChamber, 2017b). Each of these series is scheduled to appear in 2017 and, if successful, could presage Frew Publications' elevation as a regional content producer for the global *Phantom* comics franchise.

EuroBooks' ongoing release of new English-language *Phantom* comics, distributed throughout India via bookstores and online retailers, arguably hopes to capitalize on the nostalgic brand awareness of *The Phantom* among older generations of readers as part of its efforts to promote English-language graphic novels as educational aids for children to India's lucrative middle-class audience. This approach has been emulated by other Indian comic-book publishers. Muthu Comics, which previously published Tamil-language episodes of *The Phantom* in the late 1970s, has enjoyed greater success in publishing deluxe-format, graphic-novel collections of European comics (such as the Italian cowboy hero *Tex* and the Belgian espionage thriller *XIII*), which have proved popular with expatriate Tamil audiences in Africa, Australia, France, and the United States (Moorthy, 2016). These marketing and distribution strategies now being undertaken by Indian firms mirror similar efforts made by Western publishers in recent years to reposition comics as "graphic novels," a socially acceptable (and financially lucrative) alternative to the ephemeral and pernicious "comic books" of previous decades.

Despite these signs of editorial innovation and institutional regeneration, there is no denying that King Features Syndicate and its international licensees are confronted with a radically transformed publishing environment, where comic-strip characters like the Phantom no longer command readers' attention as they once did. The challenge confronting each of these organizations—whereby they must strive to make the Phantom attractive to younger audiences without unduly alienating their loyal, older readers—has never been greater, or more urgent.

Newspapers, the original conduit for *The Phantom* comic strip, have struggled to compete with broadcast radio and television for decades, and now face an even greater threat from digital and mobile media. And comic strips, along with other syndicated features, continue to bear the brunt of cost-cutting measures, as newspaper publishers attempt to staunch the flow of retail sales and advertising revenues to online media. Even countries like Sweden, which, despite its small population (currently 9,700,000) once boasted a thriving, diverse newspaper industry, have not been immune from these trends. For example, the number of Swedish newspapers published six days per week plummeted from the postwar peak of 110 titles in 1950 to just over 60 titles by 1998—a decline that first became evident during the first decade of television broadcasting (Hadenius and Weibull, 1999: 135). According to Peter Grännby (marketing manager, Bulls Press), comic-strip syndication suffered further as Swedish newspapers switched from broadsheet to tabloid formats; where newspapers would once carry 6–8 comic strips per day, they could now only fit 4 comic strips in their smaller page format. Nevertheless, Grännby pointed out that, as of 2012, Bulls Press supplied the *Fantomen* comic strip to forty-five newspapers throughout Scandinavia. This was, he suggested, a respectable figure, given that the "adventure [comic] strip is nearly dead."[2]

Demonstrating the kind of innovative thinking borne out of economic necessity, King Features' most recent online initiative denotes a significant break with its historical role as a "content broker" between publishers and readers. Unveiled in 2008, Comics Kingdom (http://comicskingdom.com) goes directly to the consumer by offering annual (US$19.99) and monthly subscriptions (US$1.99) to over ninety comic strips, editorial cartoons, and puzzles. Subscribers can download customized selections of comic strips onto mobile digital devices and share them across social networking sites, thereby furthering exposure for the service. Comics Kingdom aims to cultivate a dedicated online community of comic-strip fans by encouraging subscribers to post questions on the *Ask the Archivist* blog. Comics Kingdom generates new revenue streams from dormant media properties by offering subscribers access to a selection of "vintage comics" (including *The Phantom*) which, the site advises, "are no longer in syndication" and are available exclusively online (King Features Syndicate, 2012). By adopting this strategy, King Features Syndicate effectively takes on the dual roles of content broker for media organizations and that of a bespoke, online publisher for a new generation of consumers who are no longer wedded to reading newspapers.

This snapshot of the challenges and opportunities confronting King Features Syndicate and its affiliates in Australia, Sweden, and India underscores the complex dynamics of global media production, and how much they have changed in the decades since *The Phantom* made its debut in *The New York Journal* on February 17, 1936. Take, for example, Sweden's emergence as a key production node for *Phantom/Fantomen* comics. When Åhlén & Åkerlund (later Semic Press) commissioned locally drawn stories for its *Fantomen* magazine to overcome a shortfall of new material available from the United States, this gave Swedish writers and artists the chance to refashion the Phantom as a nominally "Scandinavian" hero, steeped in European history. Semic Press licensed these Swedish *Fantomen* episodes to Australia and India throughout the 1980s and 1990s, and subsequently provided many of the editorial personnel chosen by King Features Syndicate to briefly take over production of *The Phantom* newspaper comic strip following Lee Falk's death. Thus, the Swedish "periphery" now stands as a regional "center" in the global production of *The Phantom* comics franchise.

But how has *The Phantom* continued to survive when so many of its comic-strip contemporaries have fallen by the wayside? The ubiquity of *The Phantom* comic strip in foreign newspapers, comic magazines, and other print media owes a great deal to the favorable economics of international comic-strip syndication, but the commercial acumen of King Features Syndicate and its international business partners cannot entirely account for the popularity of *The Phantom* in Australia, Sweden, and India. Lawrence W. Levine's assessment of how Depression-era American audiences responded to the mass culture of their day is no less relevant when considering how international audiences might also respond to (imported) American mass media:

> It is important to remember that not all [American] mass culture was popular . . . even if a substantial percentage of what was popular by the 1930s was mass produced. The significance of this is clear: choices were being made; in every popular genre, audiences distinguished between

what they found meaningful, appealing and functional and what they did not. (Levine, 1992: 1373)

Why, then, did Australian, Swedish, and Indian audiences "choose" the Phantom, seemingly above all other American comic-strip heroes? Readers from all three countries have alluded to many reasons why "The Ghost Who Walks" resonated with them in ways that few other "superheroes" ever did. The mysterious ruler of a faraway land, the Phantom himself was neither an identifiably "American" character, nor was he a "superhero" in the modern sense of the word. Although he called the Afro-Asian jungles of the Deep Woods his home, the Phantom's exploits took him to many lands, and, in the pages of The Phantom Chronicles, through time itself. He was, in a sense, a truly universal hero. More than that, as one Australian reader put it, he could be me—or you:

[The Phantom] is more like a persona that the reader can wear . . . His simple, bland costume and his face that lacks pupils help to give this feeling in the reader. In fact, one at no time ever sees The Phantom's, or Mr. Walker's eyes. He's unspecific, so "he could be me, if I was as good as I could be" . . . Even the name "The Phantom" gives a feeling of unsolidity . . . As though he's a spirit floating around in the ether that we, the readers, can access and temporarily put into our own bodies, simply by reading one of the comics . . . In a comic, we must breathe our own voice and movement into the character, [but] in animation or films, the filmmaker does that job for us, so it's different. (Male respondent, 36–49 years old, March 26, 2012)

This reader touches on the importance that the comic-strip medium itself has played in cultivating the image of the Phantom. Once he has been cut loose from the page, the Phantom inexplicably becomes less real when he takes on a more tangible, physical form, especially when he is portrayed by someone who exists outside our own imaginations. But so long as readers worldwide are free to imagine him into existence, he will forever remain "The Ghost Who Walks–Man Who Cannot Die."

THE PHANTOM COMIC BOOK SURVEY-QUESTIONNAIRE

(1) What was your first exposure to *The Phantom*?

☐ Read *The Phantom* comic strip in newspaper or magazine
☐ Read *The Phantom* comic book
☐ Saw *The Phantom* in animated cartoons on TV or DVD
☐ Saw *The Phantom* miniseries on TV or DVD
☐ Saw *The Phantom* movie at the cinema/on TV or DVD
☐ Read about *The Phantom* on the Internet
☐ Heard about *The Phantom* from a friend
☐ Heard about *The Phantom* from a family member
☐ Other: Please specify

(2) What did you like about the Phantom?

(3) After your first exposure to the Phantom, did you follow the character in other media formats?

☐ Yes   ☐ No

(4) If you answered "Yes" to question 3, please indicate which other media formats you used to follow the Phantom series. (You may select more than one answer.)

☐ Newspaper/Magazine comic strip   ☐ Comic book
☐ Television   ☐ Cinema   ☐ Videocassette/DVD
☐ Websites

(5) Do you read any of these currently published Phantom comic books?
(You may select more than one answer.)

☐ *The Phantom* (Frew Publications, Australia)
☐ *The Last Phantom* (Dynamite Entertainment, USA)
☐ *Fantomen* (Egmont, Sweden)
☐ *Fantomen Christmas Album* (Egmont, Sweden)
☐ *Fantomen–Den inbundna årgången* (Egmont, Sweden)
☐ *The Phantom* (Egmont Imagination/Euro Books, India)
☐ None of the above (Proceed to questions 7 and 8.)

(6) How long have you been reading any of the currently published
Phantom comics listed in Question 5?

☐ Less than 1 year   ☐ 1–2 years   ☐ 3–5 years   ☐ 5–10 years
☐ 10 years or more

(7) Have you read any of these previous Phantom comic book series?
(You may select more than one answer.)

☐ *The Phantom* (*Australian Woman's Mirror*, 1938–1940)
☐ *Super Yank Comics* (Australia, early 1950s)
☐ *The Phantom Adventures* (Australia, mid-1950s)
☐ *Giant-Size Phantom* (Australia, 1957–1961)
☐ *Indrajal Comics* (India, 1964–1990)
☐ *Muthu Comics* (India, 1977–1980)
☐ *Diamond Comics Digest* (India, 1990–2000)
☐ *Rani Comics* (India, 1990–2005)
☐ *Serie-Pocket* (Sweden, 1972–1985)
☐ *Fantomen Kronika* (Sweden, 1993–2010)

(8) If you selected "None of the above" in question 5, please indicate how long you previously read Phantom comic books.

☐ Not at all
☐ Less than 1 year
☐ 1–2 years
☐ 3–5 years
☐ 5–10 years
☐ 10 years or more

(9) Do you recall why you stopped reading *The Phantom*? (You may select more than one answer.)

☐ Outgrew reading *The Phantom*
☐ Became bored with *The Phantom*
☐ Didn't like the creative direction *The Phantom* series was taking
☐ Began reading other comic books
☐ Stopped reading comic books entirely
☐ Other (Please specify)

(10) Did you — or do you currently — read any other comic books in addition to *The Phantom*?

☐ Yes   ☐ No (If "No," proceed to question 13.)

(11) Can you recall the name(s) of those other comic books you read, in addition to *The Phantom*?

(12) How does *The Phantom* compare to the other comic-book characters that you've read? Is he different from them? If so, how is he different?

(13) Can you recall any favorite Phantom stories that you enjoyed more than others? Can you remember why you enjoyed them (e.g., story, artwork, characters or plot, etc.)?

(14) Did you ever join an "official" Phantom fan club in your country?

☐ Yes   ☐ No

(15) Have you ever participated in other areas of comic-book fandom that weren't connected to the Phantom?

☐ Yes   ☐ No (If "No," proceed to question 17.)

(16) If you ticked "Yes" to question 15, please specify how you've participated in other comic-book fandom activities. (You may select more than one answer.)

☐ Attended comic-book conventions
☐ Published, or contributed to, fan magazines ("fanzines")
☐ Joined other (non-Phantom) comic-book fan clubs
☐ Created my own comics-related website and/or blog
☐ Participated in comics-related online forums/message boards
☐ Other: Please specify

(17) Have you visited any of the following websites, blogs, or message boards dedicated to the Phantom? (You may select more than one answer.)

☐ Chronicle Chamber (Australia)
☐ The Deep Woods (Australia)
☐ Fantomen.org (Sweden)
☐ Indrajal Online (India)
☐ The Return of Indrajal Comics (India)
☐ Scandinavian Chapter of the Lee Falk Memorial Bengali Explorers' Club (Scandinavia)
☐ Other: Please specify

(18) Have you ever downloaded digitally scanned copies of old *Phantom* comic books?

☐ Yes   ☐ No

(19) Have you ever owned any merchandise featuring the Phantom?

☐ Yes   ☐ No (Proceed to question 21.)

(20) If you answered "Yes" to question 19, please specify what kind of
Phantom merchandise you have purchased or owned. (You may select
more than one answer.)

☐ Stationery (e.g., posters, calendars)
☐ Clothing (e.g., T-shirts, jackets, jewelry)
☐ Trading cards
☐ Food/Confectionery
☐ Toys (e.g., action figures, board games)
☐ Electronic Media (e.g., videocassettes, DVDs, computer games)
☐ Household items (e.g., plates, cups)
☐ Non-comic book publications (e.g., novels, fan club newsletters)
☐ Other (Please specify)

(21) Have you seen any of the following films and/or television shows
featuring the Phantom? (You may select more than one answer.)

☐ *The Phantom*–movie serial (1943)
☐ *The Phantom*–TV pilot episode (1960)
☐ *Defenders of the Earth*–animated cartoon (1986)
☐ *The Phantom 2040*–animated cartoon (1994)
☐ *The Phantom*–motion picture (1996)
☐ *The Phantom*–TV miniseries (2009)

(22) What was your opinion of *The Phantom* films and/or television shows
that you've seen? And how do they compare, in your opinion, to the
comic-book version of *The Phantom*?

(23) Are there any other comments you'd like to make about *The Phantom*
comic book?

(24) Please indicate your gender:

☐ Male   ☐ Female

(25) What is your approximate age-group?

☐ 18–35 years   ☐ 36–49 years   ☐ 50–65 years
☐ 65 years and above

(26) In which country do you live?

☐ Australia   ☐ India   ☐ Sweden   ☐ Other (Please specify)

NOTES

Chapter Two

1. *Puck—The Comic Weekly* proved to be a remarkably successful advertising platform for General Mills, which used its *Inspector Post* comic strip—developed by the advertising agency J. Walter Thompson—to promote its Post Toasties snack product each week, beginning in 1932. Children sent in approximately 3,000,000 Post Toasties box tops as proof-of-purchase required to join the Inspector Post Junior Detective Corps within the first twelve months of the campaign (Asquith, 2014: 25–26).

2. Bob Kane (1915–1998) who, together with writer Bill Finger (1914–1974), created Batman, readily acknowledged the influence of *The Phantom* on his own comic-book superhero. In his autobiography, *Batman & Me* (1989), Kane recalled how he drew copies of *The Phantom* comic strip, which he read in *The New York Journal* as a teenager. Kane, whose original designs for Batman were modeled on the Phantom's grey "form-fitting leotard with a hood and slim black mask," regarded the Phantom as "the forerunner of the superhero" (Kane and Andrae, 1989: 41).

3. *Sheena, Queen of the Jungle* originally appeared in *Wags*, a weekly tabloid comic developed by Editors' Press Service (U.S.) exclusively for overseas English-language markets. *Wags* initially contained reprints of American newspaper comic strips and was launched in Australia in September 1936, with a British edition following in January 1937. *Wags*' British publisher, T. V. Boardman, subsequently contracted the American comic-art studio Universal Phoenix Features (owned by Will Eisner and Jerry Iger) to create entirely new comic-strip features for the magazine. The American cartoonist Mort Meskin (1916–1995) drew the first installments of *Sheena, Queen of the Jungle*, which first appeared in the British edition of *Wags* in January 1938, and were subsequently published in the Australian edition, just prior to the character's American debut in *Jumbo Comics* (September 1938) (Ryan, 1979: 150, 154; Gifford, 1984: 110–11).

Chapter Three

1. David Yaffa also reportedly negotiated many major newspaper deals on Frank Packer's behalf (Griffen-Foley, 2000: 98).

2. It was not until the early 1970s that the first Indian-owned newspaper feature syndicates, such as AFI Features, began operation, promoting locally produced editorial content, including comic strips, to Indian publications (Murthy, 2009: n.p.).

3. In 1975 King Features Syndicate released an advertisement, depicting a laughing face imposed over a papier mâché globe, proclaiming that the company's range of 101 comic strips, panel cartoons, and Sunday comic supplements made "the whole world laugh" (King Features Syndicate, 1975).

4. "Flash" is an old Australian slang expression, typically used to describe someone who is trying too hard to impress others.

5. *Vecko-Revyn* did not, however, have exclusive publication rights to *Fantomen* in Sweden—a situation that arose by chance, rather than design. The Swedish daily newspaper *Svenska Dagbladet* (est. 1884) had purchased Lee Falk's *Mandrake the Magician* from Bulls Press (which it planned to serialize as *Mandragos*), but was mistakenly supplied with *The Phantom* instead. Unable to rectify the mistake at short notice, *Svenska Dagbladet* renamed the strip *Dragos* for its debut on June 8, 1942, which remained in place until 1980, when it was changed back to its "correct" title, *Fantomen* (Eriksson, 2010: 210–12).

6. The company was named after *The Times of India*'s editor, Thomas Bennett, and his business partner, F. M. Coleman (Natarajan, 1962: 170).

7. *Vecko-Revyn* currently maintains that Swedish men comprise 10 percemt of its 117,000 estimated readers (*Vecko-Revyn*, 2015: 1). This indicates a marked decline in both its male readership and overall audience reach in recent years; in 2012, Swedish men accounted for 16 percent of the magazine's 171,000 estimated readers (*Vecko-Revyn*, 2012: 1). However, Swedish men now account for 20 percent of the *Vecko-Revyn* website (veckorevyn.com) audience, which attracted 480,000 "unique visitors" each week (*Vecko-Revyn*, 2015: 1).

Chapter Four

1. One Australian publisher, Ayers & James (Sydney), launched its series of one-off "Yank" comics (e.g., *Popular Yank Comics*, *Gripping Yank Comics*) in 1940, which reprinted American newspaper comic strips, including *Alley Oop* and *Don Winslow of the Navy* (Ryan, 1979: 162; McGee, 1981: 20).

2. Despite these economic constraints, the *Fantomen* comic strip continued to be picked up by Swedish newspapers, including *Nerikes Allehanda* (1943) and *Norra Västerbotten* (1944), throughout the war.

3. Background information on the establishment of Frew Publications supplied by Jim Shepherd, managing director, Frew Publications (e-mail to the author, December 4, 2012).

4. "Frew" was an acronym consisting of the first letter of each partner's surname —*F*orsyth, *R*ichardson, *E*isen, and *W*atson. Eisen and Watson withdrew from the partnership prior to the release of *The Phantom*, but Forsyth and Richardson (having bought out their partners' shares in the business) retained the company name.

5. Åhlén & Åkerlund could not accurately duplicate the purple color scheme of the Phantom's costume on its old printing presses, which came out looking blue instead. The character's trunks—originally colored purple and black—were subsequently changed to red and black diagonal stripes to provide a stronger contrast with his dark blue body costume (*Fantomen*, 1990: 100). This accidental color combination eventually became the "official" Swedish version of the Phantom's costume and is still used in *Fantomen* magazine to this day.

6. The Straffrättskommittén proposal was still awaiting formal response from the Justitiedepartementet (Department of Justice) in 1957, by which time it was widely felt that the comic-book debate had subsided (Björk, 1999: 150).

Chapter Five

1. See Hollick (1992: 17–21) for a historical overview of the relationship between American westerns and European popular culture.

2. This Australian study reported far greater declines in cinema attendance (64 percent) and listening to the radio (54 percent) among Sydney's adolescent population (Campbell and Keogh, 1962: 111–12).

3. Australia's privately owned television stations were allowed to broadcast advertisements, but Australian households were also required to pay an annual television licensing fee, which funded the government-owned Australian Broadcasting Commission's television channel launched in November 1956.

4. Sy Barry's brother, Dan Barry (1923–1997), illustrated the daily version of the *Flash Gordon* comic strip for King Features Syndicate during 1951–90.

5. Gold Key Comics was owned by Western Publishing, the same firm that—through its Whitman Publishing Company subsidiary—also owned the Big Little Books imprint, which produced the children's novels starring *The Phantom* back in the 1930s.

6. The two Gold Key/*Phantom* stories, "The Rattle" and "The Test" (both illustrated by Bill Lignante), were subsequently reprinted by Frew Publications in 1968, 1974, and 1981.

7. Frew subsequently sold the publishing rights for *The Phantom Ranger* and *The Shadow* to Page Publications (a magazine publishing company owned by the Yaffa Syndicate), which continued to produce both comics as giveaway items sold in children's gift bags until the early 1970s (Patrick, 2007a).

8. "Semic" was an amalgamation of the Swedish word *serier* (comic) and the English word "comic."

9. Edizioni Fratelli Spada (est. 1956) commenced publishing an Italian-edition *Phantom* comic magazine, known as *Avventure americane–L'Uomo Mascherato* (1962–80), which contained translated reprints of Lee Falk's newspaper stories, along with episodes from the Gold Key Comics and Charlton Press series of *Phantom* comic books. The company commissioned new *Phantom* stories, illustrated by Italian artists, produced under license from King Features Syndicate, which were reprinted (albeit in edited form) by several publishers throughout Europe.

10. Author interview with Janne Lundström (Sweden, May 23, 2012).

11. Lundström's first *Fantomen* story was "Plantagens hemlighet" ("The Secret of the Plantation"), published in 1971 (Lundström and Wilhelmsson, 1971: 3–26).

12. Author interview with Magnus Knutsson (Sweden, May 22, 2012).

13. Author interview with Janne Lundström (Sweden, May 23, 2012).

14. Author interview with Ulf Granberg (Sweden, May 25, 2012).

15. Ibid.

16. Ibid.

17. Author interview with Peter Grännby (Sweden, May 22, 2012).

18. Author interview with Ulf Granberg (Sweden, May 25, 2012).

19. Author interview with Janne Lundström (Sweden, May 23, 2012).

20. Author interview with Ulf Granberg (Sweden, May 25, 2012).

21. The Danish edition of *Fantomet* was originally published by Interpresse A/S. In 1973 Semic Press acquired a 50 percent stake in the company before purchasing it outright in 1986, when it subsequently became Semic Interpresse.

22. Bastei, a West German publisher, launched a new series of *The Phantom* in 1974, which initially featured translated versions of American, Italian, and Swedish *Phantom/Fantomen* stories. The company subsequently commissioned new stories, many written by German author Peter Mennigen (b. 1952), exclusively for the German/Austrian market throughout the 1970s and early 1980s.

23. Williams Förlags AB acquired 40 percent of Press & Publicity's Centerförlag comics division after Semic Press purchased the majority of Centerförlag's assets. Williams Förlags AB subsequently released Swedish versions of several American superhero comics, including *The Fantastic Four* (*Fantastika Fryan*, 1967–69) and *The Amazing Spider-Man* (*Der Fantastika Spindeln*, 1967–70) (Nederman and Hallin, eds., 2011: 289–336).

24. Semic Press subsequently launched new editions of *Fantomen* in Hungary (*Fantom*, 1988–92), Poland (*Fantom*, 1992–93), Estonia (*Fantoom*, 1993–94), and Russia (*Fantom*, 1992–93) following the end of the Cold War in Europe.

25. Rs.1 crore is equivalent to Rs.10,000,000 (Indian rupees); Rs.5.5 crore is equivalent to Rs.55,000,000 (Indian rupees).

26. The 1971 census identified 281 "mother tongues"—that is, the language spoken in an individual's home during their childhood—with more than 5,000 speakers each (Prasad, ed., 2005: 70). The Eighth Schedule of the Constitution of India currently lists 22 scheduled (or officially recognized) languages spoken throughout India.

27. S. Ramajayam subsequently took his employer, *Varanthana Rani* (*Rani Weekly*), to the Madras High Court in 2008 for wrongful dismissal (*S. Ramajayam vs. The Management of Varanthara Rani, on 4 February, 2008*).

28. Author interview with Jim Shepherd (Australia, July 10, 2012).

29. Jim Shepherd subsequently bought out Peter Forsyth and became the sole owner and managing director of Frew Publications, a position which he retained until his death in April 2013.

30. Due to Frew Publications' often inconsistent numbering system, which included both unnumbered issues and duplicated numbers (e.g., nos. 910, 910A) for double-sized issues, *The Phantom* no. 972 would actually be the 1,000th published issue.

31. Author interview with Jim Shepherd (Australia, July 10, 2012).

32. Ibid.

Chapter Six

1. Victor McLeod and Leslie Swaback had previously worked on the screenplay for Columbia Pictures' 1943 movie-serial version of *Batman*, based on the DC Comics character.

2. The majority of survey respondents who stated they had watched *The Phantom* serial most likely saw it on either VHS videocassette and/or DVD/Blu-ray discs, as copies of the serial have been available in both formats since at the least the early 1990s.

3. These changes were evident from a study of Swedish households' use of audiovisual technologies during the 1980s, which disclosed significant take-up of videocassette recorders (25 percent of households), and even higher levels of household ownership of audiocassette recorders (80 percent) and color television sets (90 percent) (Roe and Johnsson-Smaragdi, 1987: 358, 362). A parallel survey of Swedish adolescents' media consumption patterns held during 1976–87 also revealed that listening to music overtook television viewing as most adolescents' preferred media activity (Rosengren, 1994b: 54–56).

4. Author interview with Ulf Granberg (Sweden, May 25, 2012).

5. *The Phantom* feature film fared better in Australia, where it eventually took A$4,900,000 in box-office receipts, and ranked in 33rd place among the Top 50 highest-grossing films released in Australia during 1996 (Screen Australia, 2012).

6. Author interview with Gulshan Rai (e-mail, August 22, 2012).

7. The Condoman campaign was subsequently overseen by the Queensland Association for Healthy Communities. The character was featured in sex-education comic books, posters, and stationery, as well as in a computer-animated video distributed via the HITnet touchscreen network.

8. Holt Public Relations' media kit for "The Year of The Phantom" suggested further possible story angles for journalists, including the release of the 1,000th issue of *The Phantom* comic magazine, profiles of celebrity Phantom fans, and photos of the new range of licensed Phantom clothing and merchandise (Holt Public Relations, ca. 1990).

9. Author interview with Jim Shepherd (Australia, July 10, 2012).

Chapter Seven

1. For detailed summaries of major U.S. studies of comic-book readers, see *Journal of Educational Sociology* (1944: 250–55); and Witty and Sizemore (1954: 501–6; 1955a: 43–49; 1955b: 109–14).

2. For recent studies of American comic fan culture, see Tankel and Murphy (1998: 55–68); Pustz (1999); Brown (2001: 93–132); Dittmer and Larsen (2007: 735–53); and Gordon (2012: 120–32).

3. See the appendix for further details about the implementation and promotion of the *Phantom Comic Book Survey*, along with the text of the online questionnaire.

4. Shortly after launching the *Phantom Comic Book Survey*, this author conducted an online search in April 2012 which identified seventeen English-language or dual English-Hindi language websites and/or blogs dedicated to *The Phantom*, *Indrajal Comics*, and other historical-fan tributes to Indian comic-book characters and publishers.

5. This is especially true when it comes to scarce, early editions of long-running *Phantom* comics. In Australia, *Johnson's Official Phantom Price Guide* (Johnson, 2006: 14) estimated that a near-mint copy of *The Phantom*, no. 1 (Frew Publications, 1948) would fetch A\$22,000 (US\$16,000). In Sweden, the *Sereisam's Guide Alla Serier i Sverige* (Nederman and Hallin, eds., 2011: 88) valued near-mint copies of *Fantomen*, no. 1 (Serieförlaget, 1950) at SEK25,000 (US\$2,900).

6. The character of Julie Walker, twin sister of the seventeenth Phantom, was introduced in the 1952 newspaper comic strip story line "The Female Phantom" (Falk and McCoy, 1999a [1952]: 7–19). The character was reintroduced in the Swedish *Fantomen* comic in 1985 (Worker and Bess, 1994 [1985]: 3–36), and has since become a recurring character in subsequent historical adventures published in Sweden.

7. Author interview with Ulf Granberg (Sweden, May 25, 2012).

8. Ibid.

9. Author interview with Claes Reimerthi (Sweden, May 28, 2012).

10. Author interview with Ulf Granberg (Sweden, May 25, 2012).

11. Ibid.

12. Several other members of Sweden's "Team Fantomen" worked as uncredited "ghost-writers" on the Sunday episodes of *The Phantom* comic strip, including Ulf Granberg (1999) and Donne Avenell (2000) (Holtz, 2012: 312).

13. Author interview with Claes Reimerthi (Sweden, May 28, 2012).

Chapter Eight

1. Mikael Sol is best known for his graphic novel memoir *Till alla jag legat med* (*To Everyone I Slept With*) (Sol, 2008).

2. Mikael Sol, interviewed by the author (Sweden, May 30, 2012).

3. Ibid.

4. The astonishing growth of India's "periodical press" sector, which had expanded to over 7,800 separate magazine titles by 1986 (Bhatt, 1997: 2, 33), was made possible by the swelling number of readers literate in Indian languages (other than English), which was projected to grow by more than 150,000,000 people throughout 1991–2001 (Jeffrey, 2000: 20).

5. Shedden eventually resigned from this position in 2006 due to "ongoing disagreements [with Moonstone Books] about editorial and scriptwriting decisions" (Shedden, 2007b).

6. Ironically, two of the group's founding members, Brian Jensen and Torbjörn Onegård, first contacted each other via the guest book on The Deep Woods website in 1997 (Jensen, 2010a: 252).

7. The LFMBEC took its name from the Bengali Explorers' Club featured in the 1954 *Phantom* story line "The Belt" (Falk and McCoy, 1999b [1954]: 53–71).

8. Bryan Shedden stated that he would no longer be updating The Deep Woods website because he disliked the quality of recent *Phantom* comic-book stories, which he felt "do not do justice to the legacy of Lee Falk," and would therefore not promote a product that he no longer enjoyed (Shedden, 2007c).

Conclusion

1. Translated Swedish *Fantomen* episodes accounted for 83 percent of all *Phantom* stories published by Frew Publications for the combined Australian/New Zealand market in 2015. However, the number of translated Swedish *Fantomen* episodes used by Frew Publications throughout 2016 dropped to 44 percent, a reflection of the company's growing emphasis on using previously unpublished *Phantom* stories sourced from elsewhere in Europe, South America, and the United States.

2. Author interview with Peter Grännby (Sweden, May 22, 2012).

WORKS CITED

Abbas, Khwaja Ahmad. 1955. "Should Comics Be Banned?" *The Illustrated Weekly of India* 76, no. 27 (July 3): 19.

Abbott, Matthew. 1993. "The Ghost Who Walks Again." (*Good Weekend* supplement.) *Sydney Morning Herald*, May 1: 45–47.

Abbott, Maureen, Lloyd Bray, Kim Hill, Kay Moore, Stephen Ralph, Pat Raymond (script), and Antonio Lemos (artwork). 1997. *The Wisdom of the Phantom.* Melbourne: Family Court of Australia.

Ahmed, Zubair. 2011. "Changing Habits Illustrate Decline of India's Comics." BBC News Asia. November 27. http://www.bbc.co.uk/news/world-asia -15658311.

Altbach, Philip G. 1975. *Publishing in India: An Analysis.* Delhi: Oxford University Press.

———. 1976. "Publishing in a Transitional Society: The Case of India." In *Perspectives on Publishing,* ed. Philip G. Altbach and Sheila McVey, 141–55. Lexington, MA: DC Heath.

Amarnath, Vidya. 2009. "No Kidding!" The Smart CEO. November 15. http:// www.thesmartceo.in/magazine/idea-factory/no-kidding.html.

Ang, Ien. 1985. *Watching Dallas: Soap Opera and the Melodramatic Imagination.* London: Methuen.

Angel, Anita. 2005. "Art at the Frontier: Franck Gohier." *Artlink* 25, no. 2: 72–75.

Anson, Weston. 1984. "A Licensing Retrospective and a Glimpse into the Future." *The Merchandising Reporter* 3, no. 5 (June-July): 4–5.

The Argus. 1940. "Magazines and Comics: Big Import Ban." *The Argus* (Melbourne), April 12: 11.

———. 1950. "Do Your Children Read 'This Trash?'" *The Argus* (Melbourne), December 6: 7.

Ash, Brian, ed. 1977. "Fandom." In *The Visual Encyclopedia of Science Fiction,* ed. Brian Ash, 272–85. London: Pan Books.

Asquith, Kyle. 2014. "Join the Club: Food Advertising, 1930s Children's Popular Culture, and Brand Socialization." *Popular Communication* 12, no. 1: 17–31.

Astor, David. 1986. "NFC Wants Newspapers to Stop Reducing Comics." *Editor & Publisher*, no. 119 (August 2): 33–34.

———. 1991. "Sales Are Booming in Overseas Markets." *Editor & Publisher*, no. 124 (January 26): 38.

———. 1995. "A Look at the State of Comics as They Enter Their Second Century." *Editor & Publisher*, no. 128 (May 13): 39.

Australasian Post. 1991. "Phan-tastic!" *Australasian Post*, March 30: n.p.

Australian Journalists' Association. ca. 1945. *The Case for Australian Authors and Artists*, n.p. Australian Journalists' Association.

Australian Woman's Mirror. 1936. "The Phantom." *Australian Woman's Mirror* 12, no. 41 (September 1): 49.

Bacon-Smith, Camille. 1992. *Enterprising Women: Television Fandom and the Creation of Popular Myth.* Philadelphia: University of Pennsylvania Press.

Badaracco, Claire Hoertz. 1997. "Printing, Publishing and Allied Industries, 27.0." In *Extractives, Manufacturing and Services: A Historiographical and Bibliographical Guide*, ed. David O. Whitten and Bessie E. Whitten, 177–213. Handbook of American Business History, vol. 2. Westport, CT: Greenwood.

Barcus, Francis E. 1961. "A Content Analysis of Trends in Sunday Comics, 1900–1959." *Journalism & Mass Communication Quarterly* 38, no. 2 (June): 171–80.

Barker, Martin. 1984. *A Haunt of Fears: The Strange History of the British Horror Comics Campaign.* London: Pluto.

———. 1989. *Comics: Ideology, Power and the Critics.* Manchester: Manchester University Press.

———. 2002. "Kicked into the Gutters; or, 'My Dad Doesn't Read Comics, He Studies Them.'" *International Journal of Comic Art* 4, no. 1 (Spring): 64–77.

Barker, Martin, and Kate Brooks. 1998. *Knowing Audiences: Judge Dredd, Its Friends, Fans, and Foes.* Luton, UK: University of Luton Press.

Barns, Margarita. 1940. *The Indian Press: A History of the Growth of Public Opinion in India.* London: George Allen & Unwin.

Bartlett, Norman. 1954. "Culture and Comics." *Meanjin* 13, no. 1 (Autumn): 5–18.

Becker, Stephen. 1959. *Comic Art in America.* New York: Simon and Schuster.

Beerbohm, Robert Lee, and Richard D. Olson. 2007. "The American Comic Book: 1929–Present." In *Overstreet Comic Book Price Guide*, 380–90. 37th ed. New York: House of Collectibles.

Bejerot, Nils. 1954. *Barn, Serier, Samhälle [Children, Comics, Society].* Stockholm: Folket i Bild.

Bender, Lauretta, and Reginald S. Lourie. 1941. "The Effect of Comic Books on the Ideology of Children." *American Journal of Orthopsychiatry* 11, no. 3 (July): 540–50.

Berchtold, William E. 1935. "Men of Comics, Part One." *New Outlook* (April): 34–40.

Berglund, Brita. n.d. "T. Armas Morby." In *Svenskt Biografiskt Lexikon* [*Dictionary of Swedish National Biography*]. http://www.nad.riksarkivet.se/sbl /Presentation.aspx?id=9491.

Bhalla, Shakuntala. 1962. "Do Comics Really Warp Child's Mind?" *The Times of India*, September 2: 6.

Bhatt, S. C. 1997. *Indian Press since 1955*. New Delhi: Ministry of Information and Broadcasting, Government of India.

Bhattacharya, Lokenath. 1986. *Books and Reading in India*. Studies on Books and Reading, no. 26. Paris: UNESCO.

Björk, Ulf Jonas. 1999. "From Nick Carter to Perry Mason: A Historical Perspective on the American Media Presence in Sweden." *Swedish-American Historical Quarterly* 50, no. 3 (July): 147–61.

———. 2001. "'Have Gun, Will Travel': Swedish Television and American Westerns, 1959–1969." *Historical Journal of Film, Radio and Television* 21, no. 3 (August): 309–21.

Blomberg, O. 1967. "Fantomens fantastika come-back." *Vecko-Revyn*, no. 22 (May 31): 14–15, 42.

Bloom, John. 2002. "Cardboard Patriarchy: Adult Baseball Card Collecting and the Nostalgia for a Presexual Past." In *Hop on Pop: The Politics and Pleasure of Popular Culture*, ed. Henry Jenkins, Tara McPherson, and Jane Shattuc, 66–87. Durham, NC: Duke University Press.

Boëthius, Ulf. 1995. "Youth, the Media and Moral Panics." In *Youth Culture in Late Modernity*, ed. Johan Fornäs and Göran Bolin, 39–57. London: Sage.

Bold, Christine. 1996. "Malaeska's Revenge; or, The Dime Novel Tradition in Popular Fiction." In *Wanted Dead or Alive: The American West in Popular Culture*, ed. Richard Aquila, 21–42. Urbana: University of Illinois Press.

Bonnier, Lukas. 2010. "Rolf, jag och Fantomen" ["Rolf, Me and The Phantom"]. In *Fantomen–Från Lila Våland Till Blågul Hjälte* [*The Phantom: From Purple Ghost to Blue and Yellow Hero*], 76–77. Stockholm: GML Förlag.

Bono, Gianni. 1999. "Amok (Italy)." In *The World Encyclopedia of Comics*, ed. Maurice Horn, 91. 2nd ed. [1976]. Broomall, PA: Chelsea House.

Botzakis, Stergios. 2009. "Adult Fans of Comic Books: What They Get Out of Reading." *Journal of Adolescent & Adult Literacy* 53, no. 1 (September): 50–59.

Box Office Mojo. 2013. "Man of Steel." Box Office Mojo. June 23. http://www
.boxofficemojo.com/movies/?id=superman2012.htm.

Brancatelli, Joe. 1999. "The Phantom [2]." In *The World Encyclopedia of Comics*,
ed. Maurice Horn, 612. 2nd ed. [1976]. Broomall, PA: Chelsea House.

Brandweek. 1995. "Hearst, King, Viacom Tied to Phantom 2040 Promos." *Brandweek* 36, no. 33 (September 4): 14.

Brendon, Piers. 1982. *The Life and Death of the Press Barons*. London: Secker &
Warburg.

Broadcasting & Cable. 1994. "Phantom 2040 Goes Online." *Broadcasting & Cable*
124, no. 42 (October 17): 50.

Brown, Curt. 2013. "Remodeler Finds Comic Book Worth $100K in Wall at Elbow
Lake House." *StarTribune.com*. May 28. http://www.startribune.com/local
/208427831.html.

Brown, Jeffrey A. 1997. "Comic Book Fandom and Cultural Capital." *Journal of
Popular Culture* 30, no. 4 (Spring): 13–31.

———. 2001. *Black Superheroes, Milestone Comics and Their Fans*. Jackson:
University Press of Mississippi.

Bulls Press. 1994. © *Bulls Magazine, 1929–1994*. Stockholm: Bulls Press.

———. 2004. *Bulls Press 75: 1929–2004*. Stockholm: Bulls Presstjänst AB.

———. 2014. "Who Is Mr. Walker?" Bulls Press. September 8. http://www
.bullspress.com/news/who-mr-walker/.

Burke, Liam, ed. 2013. *Fan Phenomena: Batman*. Bristol, UK: Intellect Books.

Butlin, S. J. 1955. *War Economy, 1939–1942*. Canberra: Australian War Memorial.

Campbell, Joseph. 1975. *The Hero with a Thousand Faces*. [1949]. London: Sphere.

Campbell, W. J., and Rosemary Keogh. 1962. *Television and the Australian Adolescent: A Sydney Survey*. Sydney: Angus & Robertson.

Cavanagh, John R. 1949. "The Comics War." *Journal of Criminal Law and Crimi-
nology* 40, no. 1 (May-June): 28–35.

Chambliss, Julian C., and William L. Svitavsky. 2008. "From Pulp Hero to Superhero: Culture, Race and Identity in American Popular Culture, 1900–1940."
Studies in American Culture 30, no. 1 (October): 1–33.

Cheng, John. 2012. *Astounding Wonder: Imagining Science and Science Fiction in
Interwar America*. Philadelphia: University of Pennsylvania Press.

"Chitrak." 1964. "A Letter to Our Readers." *Indrajal Comics*, no. 1 (India): n.p.

ChronicleChamber. 2017a. "New Series from FREW–'The Phantom by Gaslight'". ChronicleChamber. January 1. http://www.chroniclechamber.com
/single-post/2017/01/02/New-Series-from-FREW—The-Phantom-By-
Gaslight.

————. 2017b. "New 'Kid Phantom' Series Leaked by Frew". ChronicleChamber. January 18. http://www.chroniclechamber.com/single-post/2017/01/19/New-% E2%80%9CKid-Phantom%E2%80%9D-Series-Leaked-by-Frew.

ChronicleChamber Forums. 2012. "What 'Makes' a Phan?" ChronicleChamber Forums (defunct link). April 3–8. http://chroniclechamber.com/forum/view topic.php?f=5&t=94.

Comicology. 2009. "Rani Comics—Rise and Fall, 1984–2005." Comicology. May 16. http://www.comicology.in/2009/05/rani-comics-1984-2005-rise-and-fall .html.

Connell, W. F., E. P. Francis, and Elizabeth E. Skilbeck. 1957. *Growing Up in an Australian City: A Study of Adolescents in Sydney*. Melbourne: Australian Council for Educational Research.

Connell, W. F., R. E. Stroobant, K. E. Sinclair, R. W. Connell, and K. W. Rogers. 1975. *12 to 20: Studies of City Youth*. Sydney: Hicks Smith & Sons.

Coogan, Peter. 2006. *Superhero: The Secret Origin of a Genre*. Austin, TX: MonkeyBrain Books.

Coppa, Francesca. 2006. "A Brief History of Media Fandom." In *Fan Fictions and Fan Communities in the Age of the Internet: New Essays*, ed. Karen Hellekson and Kristina Busse, 41–59. Jefferson, NC: McFarland.

Couperie, Pierre, and Maurice C. Horn. 1968. *A History of the Comic Strip*. Trans. Eileen B. Hennessey. New York: Crown.

The Courier-Mail. 1940. "American Magazines Import Ban." *The Courier-Mail* (Brisbane), April 12: 2.

Culhane, John. 1974. "Leapin' Lizards! What's Happening to the Comics?" *New York Times*, May 5: 17, 38–39, 42.

Cultural Defence Committee. 1935. *Mental Rubbish from Overseas: A Public Pro- test*. Sydney: Fellowship of Australian Writers.

Current Affairs Bulletin. 1949. "Comics." *Current Affairs Bulletin* 5, no. 5 (Novem- ber 21): 71–73.

————. 1953. "Australian Reading Habits." *Current Affairs Bulletin* 12, no. 3 (May 25): 35–48.

Daily Sun. 1982. "Phantom Man." (Weekend Magazine.) *Daily Sun* (Brisbane), December 4: 3.

Daniels, Les. 2003. *DC Comics: A Celebration of the World's Favorite Comic Book Heroes*. 2nd ed. [1995]. New York: Billboard Books.

Davidson, Steef. 1982. *The Penguin Book of Political Comics*. Middlesex, UK: Penguin Books.

Davies, A. F., and S. Encel, 1965. "The Mass Media." In *Australian Society: A*

Sociological Introduction, ed. A. F. Davies and S. Encel, 205–29. Melbourne: F.W. Cheshire.

Davis, Victoria. 1996. "Phantom Forum." (Letter to the editor.) *The Phantom*, no. 1126 (Australia): 33.

De Paul, Tony, Romano Felmang, and Germano Ferri. 1993. "Fiery Revenge." [*Fantomen*, no. 2, 1993]. *The Phantom*, no. 1044 (Australia).

De Paul, Tony, and Paul Ryan. 2011. "The Python Strikes Back!" [August 24, 2009–May 7, 2011]. *The Phantom*, no. 1602 (Australia).

———. 2015–16. "The Twins' Future." [September 14, 2015–January 30, 2016]. PhantomWiki. June 2016. http://www.phantomwiki.org/The_Twins%27 _Futures.

Dhawan, B. D. 1973. "Economics of Television for India." *Economic and Political Weekly* 8, no. 10 (March 10): 524–28.

Dittmer, Jason, and Soren Larsen. 2007. "Captain Canuck, Audience Response and the Project of Canadian Nationalism." *Social and Cultural Geography* 8, no. 5 (October): 735–53.

Dorph-Petersen, Jes, and Søren Kaster. 2003. *Egmont, 1878–2003: 125 Years*. Copenhagen: Aschehoug Dansk Forlag A/S.

DSN Retailing Today. 2004. "Vintage Properties Get a New Look." *DSN Retailing Today* 43, no. 11 (June 7): 48.

Early, Gerald. 2006. "The 1960s, African Americans and the American Comic Book." In *Strips, Toons and Bluesies: Essays in Comics and Culture*, ed. D. B. Dowd and Todd Hignite, 60–81. New York: Princeton Architectural.

Egan, Kate. 2003. "The Amateur Historian and the Electronic Archive: Identity, Power and the Function of Lists, Facts and Memories on 'Video Nasty'–Themed Websites." *Intensities: The Journal of Cult Media*, no. 3. http://intensitiescult media.files.wordpress.com/2012/12/egan-the-amateur-historian-and-the -electronic-archive.pdf.

Elliot, Hugh. 1960. "The Three-Way Struggle of Press, Radio and TV in Australia." *Journalism Quarterly*, vol. 37 (Spring): 267–74.

Elman, Raymond. 2011. "Conversation with Lee Falk" (*Princetown Arts*, 1989). In *Lee Falk, Storyteller*, 228–39. Stockholm: Scandinavian Chapter of the Lee Falk Memorial Bengali Explorers Club/GML Förlag.

Engblom, Lars-Åke. 2002. "Tidningar Dör Men Pressen Lever, 1945–1958." In *Den Svenska Pressens Historia*, vol. 4: *Bland Andra Massmedier (efter 1945)*, ed. Karl Erik Gustafsson and Per Rydén, 20–133. Stockholm: Ekerlids Förlag.

Ennart, Sigfrid. 2011. "Mandrake—The Phantom's Dad" [1984]. In *Lee Falk*,

Storyteller, 175–77. Stockholm: Scandinavian Chapter of the Lee Falk Memorial Bengali Explorers Club/GML Förlag.

Eriksson, Andreas. 2010. "Dragos—Den Mystiske Mannen." In *Fantomen: Från lila vålnad till blågul hjälte* [*The Phantom: From Purple Ghost to Blue and Yellow Hero*], 210–12. Stockholm: GML Förlag.

Eriksson, Lars. 2016. "Nörden tar över—nu blir Fantomen Skelleftebo." Norran affärsliv. July 30. http://norran.se/livsstil/fantomen-blir-skelleftebo-nu-flyttar -han-in-pa-solbacken-523507.

Erwin, Ray. 1962. "Comics Need Better Position, Promotion." *Editor & Publisher* (March 17): 10, 61.

Falk, Lee, and Sy Barry. 1986a. "The Engagement" ["The Proposal," February 21, 1977–April 2, 1977]. *The Phantom*, no. 848A (Australia): 31–42.

———. 1986b. "The First Born" ["The Heirs," December 18, 1978–May 19, 1979]. *The Phantom*, no. 848A (Australia): 72–99.

———. 1987. "The Witchmen" [January 10, 1972–April 8, 1972]. *The Phantom*, no. 875 (Australia).

———. 1988. "The Giant of Kaluga" [October 16, 1972–January 27, 1973]. *The Phantom*, no. 914 (Australia).

———. 1992a. "The Tyrant of Tarakimo" [August 15, 1977–October 29, 1977]. *The Phantom*, no. 1000 (Australia): 196–213.

———. 1992b. "Walker's Table" [January 5, 1969–April 20, 1969]. *The Phantom*, no. 1030 (Australia): 4–20.

———. 1993a. "The First Phantom" [May 18, 1975–August 10, 1975]. *The Phantom*, no. 1032 (Australia): 56–69.

———. 1993b. "The Epidemic" [February 12, 1962–June 16, 1962]. *The Phantom*, no. 1032 (Australia): 92–128.

———. 1993c. "The Wedding of The Phantom" [October 31, 1977–February 4, 1978]. *The Phantom*, no. 1032 (Australia): 70–91.

———. 1995. "The Mysterious Ambassador" [October 15, 1962–June 1, 1963]. *The Phantom*, no. 1101 (Australia): 6–56.

———. 1998. "Luaga's Undercover Tour" [April 20, 1970–July 25, 1970]. *The Phantom*, no. 1187 (Australia): 169–90.

Falk, Lee, Bill Lignante, and Sy Barry. 1988. "Queen Samaris XII" [November 5, 1961–May 13, 1962]. *The Phantom*, no. 904 (Australia).

———. 1992. "Treasure of the Skull Cave" [May 20, 1962–October 28, 1962]. *The Phantom*, no. 1000 (Australia): 170–94.

Falk, Lee, and Wilson McCoy. 1991. "The Masked Marvel" [January 11, 1948–February 19, 1949]. *The Phantom*, no. 972 (Australia): 149–80.

———. 1992a. "Mister Hog" [October 28, 1946–March 29, 1947]. *The Phantom,* no. 1000 (Australia): 109–52.

———. 1992b. "Diana and the Bank Robbers" [October 19, 1952–February 1, 1953]. *The Phantom,* no. 1030 (Australia): 38–50.

———. 1994a. "The Childhood of the Phantom" [July 2, 1944–January 7, 1945]. *The Phantom,* no. 1063 (Australia): 50–78.

———. 1994b. "The Professor" [December 3, 1951–March 15, 1952]. *The Phantom,* no. 1063 (Australia): 244–74.

———. 1994c. "Carlyle's Good Mark" [May 5, 1958–August 23, 1958]. *The Phantom,* no. 1075 (Australia): 3–34.

———. 1997. "The Toad Men" [October 13, 1952–February 28, 1953]. *The Phantom,* no. 1156 (Australia): 106–46.

———. 1998a. "The Maharajah's Daughter" [August 28, 1944–March 24, 1945]. *The Phantom,* no. 1203 (Australia): 33–93.

———. 1998b. "The Rope People" [June 17, 1951–November 04, 1951]. *The Phantom,* no. 1209 (Australia): 128–49.

———. 1999a. "The Female Phantom" [July 20, 1952–December 10, 1952]. *The Phantom,* no. 1219 (Australia): 6–19.

———. 1999b. "The Belt" [February 7, 1954–June 6, 1954]. *The Phantom,* no. 1219 (Australia): 54–71.

———. 2008. "Bent Beak Broder" [January 11, 1943–May 22, 1943]. *The Phantom,* no. 1498 (Australia): 210–47.

Falk, Lee, and Ray Moore. 1938. "The Phantom." *The Phantom,* no. 1: 3–58. Sydney: Bulletin Newspaper.

———. 1989a. "Adventure in Algiers" [June 20, 1938–July 23, 1938]. *The Phantom,* no. 931A (Australia): 89–98.

———. 1989b. "The Slave Traders" [January 30, 1939–May 6, 1939]. *The Phantom,* no. 933 (Australia).

———. 1989c. "The Golden Circle" [September 4, 1939–January 20, 1940]. *The Phantom,* no. 934: 6–46. Sydney: Frew Publications.

———. 1992. "The Diamond Hunters" [April 12, 1937–September 18, 1937]. *The Phantom,* no. 1000 (Australia): 6–54.

———. 1996. "The Sky Band" [November 9, 1936–April 10, 1937]. *The Phantom,* no. 1147 (Australia).

———. 2000. "The Prisoner of the Himalayas" [February 7, 1938–June 18, 1938]. *The Phantom,* no. 1249 (Australia): 48–86.

———. 2010. "The Singh Brotherhood" [February 17, 1936–November 7, 1936]. *The Phantom: The Complete Newspaper Dailies* (Volume 1, 1936–1937), 15–128. Neshannock, PA: Hermes.

Falk, Lee, Ray Moore, and Wilson McCoy. 1988. "The Phantom Goes to War" [February 2, 1942–January 9, 1943]. *The Phantom*, no. 910A (Australia).

———. 1993. "The Inexorables" [February 2, 1942–January 9, 1943]. *The Phantom*, no. 1041 (Australia).

Fantomen. 1990. "Fantomen Talar" ["The Phantom Speaks"]. *Fantomen*, no. 20 (Sweden): 100.

Feiffer, Jules. 1965. *The Great Comic Book Heroes*. New York: Dial.

Filipson, Leni. 1976. *The Role of Radio and TV in the Lives of Pre-School Children: Summary*, Report no. 52–75/76). Stockholm: Swedish Broadcasting Corporation [Sveriges Radio]/Washington, DC: ERIC Clearinghouse.

Finnane, Mark. 1989. "Censorship and the Child: Explaining the Comics Campaign." *Australian Historical Studies* 23, no. 92 (April): 220–40.

Fishlock, Trevor. 1987. *India File*. 2nd ed. [1983]. Calcutta: Rupa.

Fiske, John. 1992. "The Cultural Economy of Fandom." In *The Adoring Audience: Fan Culture and Popular Media*, ed. Lisa A. Lewis, 30–49. London: Routledge.

Fitzgerald, Ross, and Rick Murphy. 2011. *Austen Tayshus: Merchant of Menace*. McMahon's Point, NSW: Hale & Iremonger.

Fleming, Dan. 1996. *Powerplay: Toys as Popular Culture*. Manchester: Manchester University Press.

Ford, Glenn. 2016. "Glenn Ford (Announcement)." *Frew Publications—Facebook*. February 15. https://www.facebook.com/frewpublications/posts/1550899228 570738.

Forsyth, Ron. 1990. "Introduction: Rumble in the Jungle." *The Phantom*, no. 951A (Australia): 2.

Frank, Josette. 1944. "What's in the Comics?" *Journal of Educational Sociology* 18, no. 4 (December): 214–22.

Freeman, Gillian. 1967. *The Undergrowth of Literature*. London: Thomas Nelson.

Frew Publications. 1995. "The Frew Publishing Chronology—1994." *The Phantom*, no. 1094 (Australia): 314.

———. 2016. "The Phantom—Issue 1761." Frew Publications. http://www .phantomcomic.com.au/collections/this-years-comics/products/issue-1761 -fortnightly-2016.

Friedman, Andrea. 2003. "Sadists and Sissies: Anti-Pornography Campaigns in Cold War America." *Gender & History* 15, no. 2 (August): 201–27.

Friedman, Joshua Lou. 1993. "Phantom 2040." *Toon Magazine* 1, no. 1 (Spring): 8–9.

Friedson, Eliot. 1954. "Consumption of Mass Media by Polish-American Children." *The Quarterly of Film, Radio and Television* 9, no. 1 (Autumn): 92–101.

Furlong, Rob. 1996. "Phantom Forum." (Letter to the editor.) *The Phantom*, no. 1151 (Australia): 34.

Gabilliet, Jean-Paul. 2010. *Of Comics and Men: A Cultural History of American Comic Books.* Trans. Bart Beaty and Nick Nguyen. Jackson: University Press of Mississippi.

Gadre, A. V. ca. 2000. "The Phantom Morristown Post." (Letter to the editor.) *The Phantom*, no. 11 (India): 31.

Gaines, M. C. 1942. "Good Triumphs over Evil—More about the Comics." *Print: A Quarterly Journal of the Graphic Arts* 3, no. 3 (Autumn): 1–24.

Gallup, George. 1932. "What Do Newspaper Readers Read? A Gallup Survey of 40,000 Readers of 14 Metropolitan Newspapers." *Advertising and Selling* (March 31): 22–23, 51.

Gedin, Per. 1977. *Literature in the Marketplace.* Trans. George Bisset. Woodstock, NY: Overlook.

Gerosa, Guido. 2011. "Master of Comics." [1972]. In *Lee Falk, Storyteller*, 114–22. Stockholm: Scandinavian Chapter of the Lee Falk Memorial Bengali Explorers Club/GML Förlag.

Ghorai, Jayeeta. 2010. "Comment." Reprint Indrajal Campaign. September 2. http://indrajal.reprintcampaign.com.

Ghosh, Akash. 2014. "Sepia-Tinged Superheroes." *The Times of India.* April 7. http://timesofindia.indiatimes.com/life-style/books/features/Sepia-tinged -superheroes/articleshow/32479369.cms.

Gibson, Walter B. 1979. *The Shadow Scrapbook.* New York: Harcourt Brace Jovanovich.

Gifford, Denis. 1984. *The International Book of Comics.* New York: Crescent Books.

Gilbert, Douglas. 2002. "No Laughing Matter." [*New York World-Telegram*, ca. 1942]. *Comic Book Marketplace* 3, no. 5 (Summer): 60–73.

Global License. 2015. "King Features Eyes Digital Expansions." Global License (October 28). http://www.licensemag.com/license-global/king-features-eyes -digital-expansions.

Gomm, Eileen. 1997. "Phantom Forum." (Letter to the editor.) *The Phantom*, no. 1167 (Australia): 97.

Gordon, Ian. 1995. "Mass Market Modernism: Comic Strips and the Culture of Consumption." *Australasian Journal of American Studies* 14, no. 2 (December): 49–66.

———. 1998a. *Comic Strips and Consumer Culture, 1890–1945.* Washington, DC: Smithsonian Institution.

————. 1998b. "From *The Bulletin* to Comics: Comic Art in Australia 1890–1950." In *Bonzer: Australian Comics, 1900s–1990s*, ed. Annette Shiell, 1–13. Redhill South, Vic.: Elgua Media.

————. 2012. "Writing to Superman: Towards an Understanding of the Social Networks of Comic-Book Fans." *Participations: Journal of Audience & Reception Studies* 9, no. 2 (November): 120–32.

Gordon, John Steele. 2004. *An Empire of Wealth: The Epic History of American Economic Power.* New York: HarperCollins.

Goulart, Ron. 1986. *Ron Goulart's Great History of Comic Books.* Chicago: Contemporary Books.

————. 2005. "The Ghost Who Walks." *Comic Book Marketplace* 3, no. 121 (May): 70–81.

Granberg, Ulf (attrib.). 1975. "1492–1975: Glimtar ur en ätts historia" ["1492–1975: Glimpses from History"]. In *Fantomen Stora Jubileumsboken* [*Phantom's Big Jubilee Storybook*], 5–16. Sundbyberg, Sweden: Semic Press.

Gray, Jonathan, Cornel Sandvoss, and C. Lee Harrington. 2007. "Introduction: Why Study Fans?" In *Fandom: Identities and Communities in a Mediated World*, ed. Jonathan Gray, Cornel Sandvoss, and C. Lee Harrington, 1–16. New York: New York University Press.

Greenop, Frank S. 1947. *History of Magazine Publishing in Australia.* Sydney: K.G. Murray.

Griffen-Foley, Bridget. 1999. *The House of Packer: The Making of a Media Empire.* St. Leonards, NSW: Allen & Unwin.

————. 2000. *Sir Frank Packer: The Young Master.* Sydney: HarperCollins.

Griffin, Bob, and John Griffin. ca. 1999. "Big Little Books/Better Little Books." The Deep Woods. http://www.deepwoods.org/blb.html.

————. ca. 2002. "The Phantom (1962–1977): Gold Key/King/Charlton." The Deep Woods. http://www.deepwoods.org/phantom.html.

Guaraz, Layla, and Georges Bess. 1985. "Black Ivory" ["Svart elfenben" (1983)] and "The Moment of Freedom" ["Frihetens ögonblick" (1983)]. *The Phantom*, no. 825A (Australia).

Gudmundsson, David. 2015. "The Ghost Who Walks Goes North: Early Modern Sweden in *The Phantom*, 1987–2008." *Scandinavian Journal of Comic Art* 2, no. 1 (Fall): 7–24.

Gustafsson, Karl Erik, and Per Rydén. 2010. *A History of the Press in Sweden.* Gothenburg, Sweden: NORDICOM/University of Gothenburg.

Hadenius, Stig, and Lennart Weibull. 1999. "The Swedish Newspaper System in the Late 1990s: Tradition and Transition." *Nordicom Review* 20, no. 1: 129–52.

Hagedorn, Roger. 1995. "Doubtless to Be Continued: A Brief History of Serial Narrative." In *To Be Continued: Soap Operas Around the World*, ed. Robert C. Allen, 27–48. London: Routledge.

Hagen, Ingunn, and Wasko, Janet. 2000. "Introduction." In *Consuming Audiences?: Production and Reception in Media Research*, ed. Ingunn Hagen and Janet Wasko, 3–28. Cresskill, NJ: Hampton.

Hajdu, David. 2008. *The Ten-Cent Plague: The Great Comic-Book Scare and How It Changed America*. New York: Farrar, Straus and Giroux.

Hake, Ted. 1993. *Hake's Guide to Comic Character Collectibles: An Illustrated Price Guide to 100 Years of Comic Strip Characters*. Radnor, PA: Wallace-Homestead.

Hall, Lee-Anne. ca. 1988. "Garage Graphix." *CAPER*, no. 27: 12–13.

Hall, Phil. 2006. "The Bootleg Files: 'Popeye Meets the Man Who Hated Laughter.'" Film Threat (defunct link). February 24. http://www.filmthreat.com /features/1700/.

Hall, Stuart, and Whannel, Paddy. 1964. *The Popular Arts*. London: Hutchinson.

Handlin, Oscar. 1966. *The American People: The History of a Society*. Middlesex, UK: Penguin Books.

Harmon, Jim, and Donald F. Glut. 1973. *The Great Movie Serials: Their Sound and Fury*. London: Woburn.

Harty, J. L. 1959. "Australia's Secret Censorship." *Nation*, no. 11 (February 14): 12.

Harvey, Adam. 1995. "The Ghost Used to Walk—Now He Drives a Porsche." *Sydney Morning Herald*, January 7: 7.

Harvey, R. C. 1945. "Those Penny Dreadfuls." (Letter to the editor.) *Ideas–For Stationers, Booksellers, Newsagents, Libraries, Fancy Goods*, vol. 25 (November 12): 568, 570.

Harvey, Robert C. 1994. *The Art of the Funnies: An Aesthetic History*. Jackson: University Press of Mississippi.

———. 1996. *The Art of the Comic Book: An Aesthetic History*. Jackson: University Press of Mississippi.

———. 1998. *Children of the Yellow Kid: The Evolution of the American Comic Strip*. Seattle, WA: Frye Art Museum/University of Washington Press.

Hatfield, Charles. 2006. "Comic Art, Children's Literature and the New Comics Studies." *The Lion and the Unicorn* 30, no. 3 (September): 360–82.

Healey, Karen. 2009. "When Fangirls Perform: The Gendered Fan Identity in Superhero Comics Fandom." In *The Contemporary Comic Book Superhero*, ed. Angela Ndalianis, 144–63. London: Routledge.

Hearst Entertainment. 1994. "Phantom 2040: The Franchise of the Future" (advertisement). *Variety* 353, no. 12 (February 24–30): 82.

Henderson, John (attrib.). ca. 1981. "Story Review." *Jungle Beat: The Official Newsletter of The Phantom Club*, no. 1: 6.

———. 1985. "New Products Report." *Jungle Beat: The Official Newsletter of The Phantom Club*, vol. 7 (December): 22–23.

———. 1986a. "What the Swedes Are Doing to the Phantom." *Jungle Beat: The Official Newsletter of The Phantom Club*, vol. 9 (June): 10–12.

———. (attrib.) 1986b. "State of the Club Address—A Report by the President." *Jungle Beat: The Official Newsletter of The Phantom Club*, vol. 9 (June): 14–15.

———. (attrib.) ca. 1989. "President's Welcome." *Jungle Beat: The Official Newsletter of the Independent Phantom Club of Australia*, vol. 22: 2–3.

Hills, Matt. 2002. *Fan Cultures*. London: Routledge.

Hindes, Andrew. 1996. "B.O. Boom: More May Be Less." *Variety* 363, no. 10 (June 15–21): 7, 10.

The Hindu. 2000. "The Ghost Who Walks Is Back." *The Hindu* (online edition), June 18. http://www.hindu.com/2000/06/18/stories/1418218b.htm.

Hockney, Peter. 1984. "Has the Phantom Turned to Feminist Thought?" *On Dit* 52, no. 9 (June 18): 11.

Hogarth, Dudley. 2016. "Phantom Forum." *The Phantom*, no. 1749 (Australia): 33.

Hoggart, Richard. 1998. *The Uses of Literacy*. [1957]. New Brunswick, NJ: Transaction.

Holden, W. Sprague. 1962. *Australia Goes to Press*. Parkville, Vic.: Melbourne University Press.

Hollick, Julian Crandall. 1992. "The American West in the European Imagination." *Montana: The Magazine of Western History* 42, no. 2 (Spring): 17–21.

Holt Public Relations. ca. 1990. *So—Who Is the Phantom?* (Media information kit). Sydney: Holt Public Relations.

Holtz, Allan. 2012. "The Phantom." In *American Newspaper Comics: An Encyclopedic Reference Guide*, 309–12. Ann Arbor: University of Michigan Press.

Hooker, Lee. 1986. "Letter to the Editor." *Jungle Beat: The Official Newsletter of The Phantom Club*, vol. 10 (September): 10–11.

Hunt, Frances. 1986. "Year 7 Reading Preferences in Three Sydney Schools." *Orana: Journal of School and Children's Librarianship* 22, no. 1 (February): 39–46.

Hutchison, Don. 2007. *The Great Pulp Heroes*. 2nd ed. [1996]. New York: Book Republic.

Ideas. 1946. "Tariff Board Inquiry into the Publishing Industry in Australia."

Ideas—For Stationers, Booksellers, Newsagents, Libraries and Fancy Goods
vol. 26 (January 16): 22, 24, 26–28, 30–32, 34–36, 38–40, 42–44, 46–48, 50–86.
————. 1948. "Mickey Mouse, Merchandising Marvel." *Ideas—For Stationers, Booksellers, Newsagents, Libraries and Fancy Goods*, vol. 28 (February 14): 180, 190.
————. 1952. "The D . . . Comics!" *Ideas—For Stationers, Booksellers, Newsagents, Libraries and Fancy Goods*, vol. 32 (March 13): 237.
Iliffe, J. A. 1956. "The Australian 'Obscene Publications' Legislation of 1953–1955." *Sydney Law Review* 2, no. 2 (January): 134–39.
Inge, M. Thomas. 1990. *Comics as Culture*. Jackson: University Press of Mississippi.
Inglis, K. S. 1962. "The Daily Papers." In *Australian Civilization: A Symposium*, ed. Peter Coleman, 145–75. Melbourne: F.W. Cheshire.
Intellectual Property Reports. 1991. "Hearst Corp. v. Pacific Dunlop Ltd." *Intellectual Property Reports*, no. 21 (April 3): 587–94.
Ioannidou, Elisavet. 2013. "Adapting Superhero Comics for the Big Screen: Subculture for the Masses." *Adaptation* 6, no. 2 (August): 230–38.
Irving, Christopher. 2000. "A Piece of the Action: Charlton's Action Hero Line and the Folks Responsible." *Comic Book Artist*, no. 9 (August): 25–28.
Jain, Kajri. 2007. *Gods in the Bazaar: The Economies of Indian Calendar Art*. Durham, NC: Duke University Press.
Jeffrey, Robin. 2000. *India's Newspaper Revolution: Capitalism, Politics and the Indian-Language Press, 1977–1999*. London: Hunt.
Jenkins, Bob. 2007. "On Top Down Under" (Fred Gaffney interview). Licensemag .com. June 15. http://www.licensemag.com/license-global/top-down-under.
Jenkins, Henry. 1992. *Textual Poachers: Television Fans and Participatory Culture*. New York: Routledge.
————. 2013. *Textual Poachers: Television Fans and Participatory Culture*. [1992]. New York: Routledge.
Jensen, Brian. 2010. "Scandinavian Chapter—en kurt historik" ["The Scandinavian Chapter—A Brief History"]. In *Fantomen: Från lila vålnad till blågul hjälle*, 252–57. Stockholm: GML Förlag.
Jensen, Helle Strandgaard. 2010. "Why Batman Was Bad: A Scandinavian Debate about Children's Consumption of Comics and Literature in the 1950s." *Barn* [*Children*], no. 3: 47–70.
————. 2012. "'Nobody Panicked!': The Fifties' Debate on Children's Comic Consumption." In *Situating Child Consumption: Rethinking Values and Notions of Children, Childhood and Consumption*, ed. Abba Sparrman, Bengt Sandin, and Johanna Sjöberg, 253–72. Lund, Sweden: Nordik Academic Press.

Jensen, Joli. 2001. "Fandom as Pathology: The Consequences of Characterization." [1992]. In *Popular Culture: Production and Consumption*, ed. C. Lee Harrington and Denise D. Brelby. Oxford: Blackwell.

Johnson, Derek. 2007. "Fan-tagonism: Factions, Institutions and Constitutive Hegemonies of Fandom." In *Fandom: Mediated Identities and Communities in a Mediated World*, ed. Jonathan Gray, Cornel Sandvoss, and C. Lee Harrington, 285–300. New York: New York University Press.

Johnson, N. R. 2006. *Johnson's Official Phantom Price Guide*. 3rd ed. [1993]. Loganholme DC, QLD: N.R. Johnson.

Johnson-Woods, Toni. 2006. "Pulp Friction: Governmental Control of Cheap Fiction, 1939–1959." *Script & Print* 30, no. 2: 103–19.

Jones, Bertram. 1951. "Australia Goes West: Our Cowboy Cavalcade." *Sunday Herald* (Sydney), January 14: 3.

Jones, Garrett. 1986. "The Ghost Who Walks Is Stepping Out." *Sunday Telegraph* (Sydney), March 2: 130–31.

Jones, Gerard. 2004. *Men of Tomorrow: Geeks, Gangsters and the Birth of the Comic Book*. New York: Basic Books.

Joshee, O. K. 1962. "Craze among Children." *The Times of India*, September 2: 6.

Joshi, O. P. 1986. "Comics, Consumers and Creators of Comics in India." In *Comics and Visual Culture: Research Studies from Ten Countries*, ed. Alphons Silbermann and H. D. Dyroff, 213–23. New York: K.G. Saur.

Journal of Educational Sociology. 1944. "Bibliography." *Journal of Educational Sociology* 18, no. 4 (December): 250–55.

Jungle Beat. 1987. "Recent Phantom Club Publicity." *Jungle Beat: The Official Newsletter of The Phantom Club*, vol. 12 (March): 8.

———. ca. 1989. "Phact 'n' Fiction." *Jungle Beat: The Official Newsletter of The Phantom Club*, vol. 17: 5.

———. ca. 1990. "Update—The Population and Distribution of Club Members Around the World." *Jungle Beat: The Official Newsletter of The Independent Phantom Club of Australia*, vol. 23: 3.

Kane, Bob, and Tom Andrae. 1989. *Batman & Me*. Forestville, CA: Eclipse Books.

Kasbekar, Asha. 2006. *Pop Culture India! Media, Arts and Lifestyle*. Santa Barbara, CA: ABC-CLIO.

Kelsey, Eric. 2013. "Rare 1938 Superman Comic Book Found in U.S. Wall Fetches $175,000." Reuters.com. June 12. http://www.reuters.com/article/2013/06/12/entertainment-us-books-superman-idUSBRE95B10X20130612.

Kent, Neil. 2008. *A Concise History of Sweden*. Cambridge: Cambridge University Press.

Kershler, Ray. 1987. "Ghost Who Walks Not Himself." *Daily Telegraph* (Sydney), March 20: 3.

Kessel, Lawrence. 1943. "Some Assumptions in Newspaper Comics." *Childhood Education*, vol. 19 (April): 349–53.

Khanduri, Ritu G. 2010. "Comicology: Comic Books as Culture in India." *Journal of Graphic Novels and Comics* 1, no. 2 (December): 171–91.

Kiefer, David. 1989. "Phantom Followers in Split." *The Sun* (Queensland), December 13: n.p.

King Features Syndicate. 1967. *KFS Blue Book*. New York: King Features Syndicate.

———. 1975. "King Features Syndicate" (advertisement). *Cartoonist Profiles*, no. 27 (September).

———. 2012. "Vintage Comics." King Features. February 17. http://kingfeatures.com/comics/vintage-comics/.

———. 2016. "The Phantom Turns 80." King Features. http://kingfeatures.com/2016/02/the-phantom-turns-80/.

King Features Syndicate Inc. vs. Sunil Agnihotri & Ors., on 11 April 1997. Indian Kanoon–Search Engine for Indian Law. http://indiankanoon.org/doc/1440160/.

Kinnane, Garry. 2012. *Fare Thee Well, Hoddle Grid*. Melbourne: Clouds of Magellan.

Knutsson, Magnus, and Jaime Vallvé. 1972. "Slavarbetarna" ["The Slaves"]. *Fantomen*, no. 14 (Sweden): 3–24.

———. 1973. "Diana i Djungelpatrullen" ["Diana in the Jungle Patrol"]. *Fantomen*, no. 5 (Sweden): 3–27.

Koenigsberg, M. 1941. *King News: An Autobiography*. Philadelphia: F.A. Stokes.

Lacassin, Francis. 1975. "With the Phantom, Everything Is Possible—Except Boredom." In *The Island of Dogs* (*The Story of The Phantom*, no. 13), vii–ix. New York: Avon Books.

Larson, Lorentz. 1958. "Sverige" ["Sweden"]. In *Report No. 217*, 21–25. Copenhagen, Denmark: Nordic Committee for the Children and Young People's Reading.

Larson, Matts, Håkan Lindgren, and Daniel Nyberg. 2008. "Entrepreneurship and Ownership: The Long-Term Viability of the Swedish Bonnier and Wallenberg Family Business Groups." In *Creating Nordic Capitalism: A Business History of a Competitive Periphery*, ed. Susanna Fellman, Martin Jeslversen, Hans Sjörgen, and Lars Thue, 75–103. Hampshire, UK: Palgrave Macmillan.

Lawrence, John Shelton, and Robert Jewett. 2002. *The Myth of the American Superhero*. Grand Rapids, MI: William B. Eerdmans.

Lee, Alfred McClung. 1937. *The Daily Newspaper in America: The Evolution of a Social Instrument.* New York: Macmillan.

Lee Falk Memorial Bengali Explorers' Club (LFMBEC). 2005. "Our Origins: The First Dinner." *The Lee Falk Memorial Bengali Explorers' Club* (defunct link). http://lfmbec.com/node/1.

Legge, Alistair (attrib.), and Garage Graphix. 1988. *The Phantom Enrols & Votes.* Queen Victoria Terrace, ACT: Australian Electoral Commission.

Legge, Alistair, and Garage Graphix. 1990. *Vote 1 Phantom.* Queen Victoria Terrace, ACT: Australian Electoral Commission.

Lehman, Harvey C., and Paul A. Witty. 1927. "The Compensatory Function of the Sunday 'Funny Paper.'" *Journal of Applied Psychology* 11, no. 3 (June): 202–11.

Leppänen, Kari (artist). 1984. "Ett liv i hemlighet" ["A Secret Life"]. *Fantomen*, no. 17 (Sweden).

Levine, Lawrence W. 1992. "The Folklore of Industrial Society: Popular Culture and Its Audiences." *The American Historical Review* 97, no. 5 (December): 1369–99.

Lewis, Julian. 2016. "The Phantom Celebrates 80 Years Fighting Injustice." *The Sydney Morning Herald.* February 14. http://www.smh.com.au/entertainment/the-phantom-celebrates-80-years-fighting-injustice-20160210-gmhati.html.

Liang, Lawrence, and Ravi Sundaram. 2011. "India." In *Media Piracy in Emerging Economies*, 339–97. New York: Social Science Research Council/The American Assembly, Columbia University.

Lindesay, Vane. 1983. *The Way We Were: Australian Popular Magazines, 1856–1969.* Melbourne: Oxford University Press.

Lovisi, Gary. 2008. *Antique Trader Collectible Paperback Price Guide.* Iola, WI: Krause.

Lundström, Janne, and Jaime Vallvé. 1972. "Gengångaren" ["The Return of the Ghost"]. *Fantomen*, no. 24 (Sweden): 3–30.

———. 1973. "I Piraternas Våld" ["The Pirates' Prisoner"]. *Fantomen*, no. 18 (Sweden): 3–33.

———. 1974. "Mjölkdrickaren" ["The Milk Drinker"]. *Fantomen*, no. 14 (Sweden): 3–26.

Lundström, Janne, and Bertil Wilhelmsson. 1971. "Plantagens hemlighet" ["The Secret of the Plantation"]. *Fantomen*, no. 16 (Sweden): 3–26.

———. 1973. "Handelskriget" ["Trade War"]. *Fantomen*, no. 3 (Sweden): 3–27.

MacDonald, Andrea. 1998. "Uncertain Utopia: Science Fiction Media Fandom & Computer-Mediated Communication." In *Theorizing Fandom: Fans, Subculture and Identity*, ed. Cheryl Harris and Alison Alexander, 131–52. Cresskill, NJ: Hampton.

MacDougall, Curtis D. 1942. "Newspaper Syndication and Its Social Significance." *The Annals of the American Academy of Political and Social Science* 219, no. 1 (January): 76–81.

Madison, Bob. 1996. "Master Magicians & Phantoms: Lee Falk." *Scarlet Street: The Magazine of Mystery and Horror*, no. 22: 47–50.

The Mail. 1947. "Man of Vision" (Obituary—David Yaffa.) *The Mail* (Adelaide), August 16: 4.

Majumdar, Anushree. 2009. "The Ghost Walks Again." *The Indian Express*. June 2. http://www.indianexpress.com/news/the-ghost-walks-again/469667/.

Malhan, P. N. 1980. "Periodical Journalism." In *Mass Media in India, 1979–80*, 11–21. New Delhi: Research and Reference Division, Ministry of Information and Broadcasting.

Malter, Morton S. 1952. "The Content of Current Comic Magazines." *Elementary School Journal* 52, no. 9 (May): 505–10.

Manchanda, Usha. 1998. "Invasion from the Skies: The Impact of Foreign Television on India." *Australian Studies in Journalism*, no. 7 (January): 136–63.

Markstein, Don. ca. 2008. "Phantom 2040." Don Markstein's Toonpedia. http://www.toonopedia.com/phan2040.htm.

Marschall, Richard E. 1999. "A History of *Puck*, *Judge* and *Life*." In *The World Encyclopedia of Cartoons*, 859–945, ed. Maurice Horn. 2nd ed. [1981]. Broomall, PA: Chelsea House.

Marx, Barry, ed. 1985. "Carroll Rheinstrom: DC Travels the World." In *Fifty Who Made DC Great*, ed. Barry Marx, 19. New York: DC Comics.

Mayer, Henry, Pauline Garde, and Sandra Gibbons. 1983. *The Media: Questions and Answers—Australian Surveys, 1942–1980*. Sydney: George Allen & Unwin.

McCoy, Donald R. 1973. *Coming of Age: The United States during the 1920s and 1930s*. Pelican History of the United States, vol. 6. Baltimore, MD: Penguin Books.

McDonald, Daniel G. 2004. "Twentieth-Century Media Effects Research." In *The Sage Handbook of Media Studies*, ed. John D. H. Dowling, Denis McQuail, Philip Schlesinger, and Ellen Wartella, 183–200. Thousand Oaks, CA: Sage.

McGee, Graham. 1981. "U.S. Reprints in Australia—The Early Days." In *Comicon III: Panel Power* (convention program), 20–22. Concord, NSW: Limitless Visions.

McGuinness, Robert M. 1965. *Satires*. Sydney: Horwitz.

McKee, Alan. 2002. "Fandom." In *Television Studies*, ed. Toby Miller, 66–69. London: British Film Institute.

McLain, Karline. 2009a. "Gods, Kings and Local Telugu Guys: Competing Visions of the Heroic in Indian Comic Books." In *Popular Culture in a Globalised India*, ed. K. Moti Gokulsing and Wimal Dissanayake, 157–73. London: Routledge.

———. 2009b. *India's Immortal Comic Books: Gods, Kings and Other Heroes.* Bloomington: Indiana University Press.

McManus, George, and Henry La Cossitt. 1952. "Jiggs and I" (Part 1). *Colliers* 129, no. 3 (January 19): 9–11, 66–67.

McQuail, Denis. 2005. *McQuail's Mass Communication Theory.* 5th ed. [1983]. Los Angeles: Sage.

Meehan, Eileen R. 2000. "Leisure or Labor? Fan Ethnography and Political Economy." In *Consuming Audiences? Production and Reception in Media Research*, ed. Ingunn Hagen and Janet Wasko, 71–92. Cresskill, NJ: Hampton.

Miller, John Jackson. 2008. "Comic Market Shares, 1959, according to Ayer." *The Comichron: The Blog of the Comics Chronicles.* August 5. http://blog.comichron.com/2008/08/comics-market-shares-1959-according-to.html.

Ministry of Home Affairs. n.d. *Young Persons (Harmful Publications) Act, 1956.* Ministry of Home Affairs, Government of India. http://www.mha.nic.in/hindi/sites/upload_files/mhahindi/files/pdf/YoungPersonsHarmfulPublicationAct_1956.pdf.

Molson, Francis J. 1984. "Films, Funnies and Fighting the War: Whitman's Children's Books in the 1940s." *Journal of Popular Culture* 17, no. 4 (Spring): 147–54.

Moorthy, Swathi. 2016. "'Idiyappam Westerns' and the Incredible World of Tamil Comics." The Hindu BusinessLine. June 12. http://www.thehindubusinessline.com/news/national/idiyappam-westerns-and-the-incredible-world-of-tamil-comics/article8721324.ece.

Mosco, Vincent, and Lewis Kaye. 2000. "Questioning the Concept of the Audience." In *Consuming Audiences? Production and Reception in Media Research*, ed. Ingunn Hagen and Janet Wasko, 31–46. Cresskill, NJ: Hampton.

Mosey, Chris. 1981. "Double Trouble for The Phantom." *Sweden Now* 15, no. 2: 54.

Mott, Frank Luther. 2000. *American Journalism: A History of Newspapers in the United States through 250 Years, 1690–1940.* [1941]. London: Routledge/Thommes.

Mukherjee, Ritwik. 2011. "Book Piracy Reaches Alarming Levels in India." *Financial Chronicle* (defunct link). February 3. http://www.mydigitalfc.com/knowledge/book-piracy-reaches-alarming-levels-india-739.

Mullaney, Dean, ed. 2015. *King of the Comics: 100 Years of King Features.* San Diego, CA: Library of American Comics/IDW Publishing.

Murray, Will. 1997. "The First Phantom: The Pulp Connection, Part 1." *Comic Book Marketplace* 2, no. 47 (May): 46–53.

———. 2005. "Lee Falk: Father of Superheroes." *Comic Book Marketplace* 3, no. 121 (May): 34–49.

Murthy, Bharath. 2009. "An Art without Tradition: A Survey of Indian Comics." *MARG: A Magazine of the Arts* 61, no. 2 (December).

"Muthufan." 2007. "During My Recent India Trip." *Muthufan Blog.* October 23. http://muthufanblog.blogspot.com.au/2007/10/during-my-recent-india-trip -one-of-my.html.

Nasaw, David. 2002. *The Chief: The Life of William Randolph Hearst.* London: Gibson Square Books.

Natarajan, J. 1997. *History of Indian Journalism.* Part II of the Report of the Press Commission (1955). New Delhi: Publications Division, Ministry of Information and Broadcasting.

Natarajan, S. 1962. *A History of the Press in India.* London: Asia Publishing House.

The National. 2011. "Home-Grown Superheroes Grace India's First Comic Book Convention." *The National.* February 18. http://www.thenational.ae/news /world/south-asia/home-grown-superheroes-grace-indias-first-comic-book -convention.

National Archives of Australia (Adelaide). 1959. Department of Customs and Excise. D596/1959/6965/Industries Preservation Act–Backdate Magazines and Comics from USA–A59/13942.

Nederman, Ulf, and Jakob Hallin, eds. 2011. *Seriesam's Guide All Serier I Sverige 1907–2011.* 8th ed. [1981]. Sweden: Seriesamlarna.

Newcastle Region Art Gallery. 1977. *Ghost Who Walks Can Never Die: An Exhibition of Comic Strip and Other Superheroes in Australian Art.* Newcastle, NSW: Newcastle Region Art Gallery.

Newspaper News. 1946a. "Australia as Dump for Old Magazines." *Newspaper News* (Australia) 18, no. 9 (April 1): 1.

———. 1946b. "America Feels Magazine Slump." *Newspaper News* (Australia) 18, no. 2 (July 1): 2.

———. 1955. "World's Largest Communications Empire." *Newspaper News* (Australia) 27, no. 8 (June 1): 19.

Newsweek. 1934. "Comics: American Funnies at Home throughout the World." *Newsweek,* May 26: 23.

Ninan, Sevanti. 1995. *Through the Magic Window: Television and Change in India.* New Delhi: Penguin Books India.

Nyberg, Amy Kiste. 1995. "Comic Books and Women Readers: Trespassers in Masculine Territory?" In *Gender in Popular Culture: Images of Men and Women in Literature, Visual Media and Material Culture*, ed. Peter C. Rollins and Susan W. Rollins, 205–26. Cleveland, OK: Ridgemont.

————. 1998. *Seal of Approval: The History of the Comics Code.* Jackson: University Press of Mississippi.

O'Brien, Denis. 1982. *The Weekly.* Ringwood, VIC: Penguin Books Australia.

O'Brien, Philip. 2011. "John Dixon's Air Hawk." *The National Library Magazine* 3, no. 4 (December): 28–30.

The Observer. 1960. "The Comics Business." *The Observer* (Australia) 3, no. 25 (December 10): 5–6.

Pande, Shamni. 2011. "Bennett, Coleman & Co.: Just in Times." *Business Today* (India), July 10.

Paramount Pictures. 1996. *The Phantom: Handbook of Production Information.*

Paranjape, Makarand. 2008. "Cultural Flows in Asia: Australian Locations, Asian Identities and Bombay Dreams." *Situations*, vol. 2 (Autumn): 1–28.

Patrick, Kevin. 2006. "Jeff Wilkinson: Phantoms and Shadows." *Comics Down Under.* December 22. http://comicsdownunder.blogspot.com.au/2006/12/jeff -wilkinson-phantoms-and-shadows.html.

————. 2007a. "Page Publications: The Forgotten Comic Book Company." *Comics Down Under.* November 23. http://comicsdownunder.blogspot.com.au/2007/11 /page-publications-forgotten-comic-book.html.

————. 2007b. "Jim Shepherd: The Man behind the Phantom." Chronicle Chamber.com (defunct link). December 21. http://www.chroniclechamber .com/2007/12/jim-shepherd-the-man-behind-the-phantom/.

————. 2007c. "Peter Chapman: The 'Phantom Artist' of Frew." Chronicle Chamber.com. December 26. http://www.chroniclechamber.com/single-post /2016/08/14/Peter-Chapman-The-%E2%80%9CPhantom-Artist%E2%80%9 D-of-Frew.

————. 2008. "Interview: Kevan Hardacre." *Comics Down Under.* May 26. http://comicsdownunder.blogspot.com.au/2008/05/interview-kevan-hardacre .html.

————. 2011. "A Design for Depravity: Horror Comics and the Challenge of Censorship in Australia, 1950–1986." *Script & Print* 35, no. 3: 133–56.

————. 2012a. "The Cultural Economy of the Australian Comic Book Industry, 1950–1985." In *Sold by the Millions: Australia's Bestsellers*, ed. Toni Johnson-

Woods and Amit Sarwal, 162–81. Newcastle upon Tyne, UK: Cambridge Scholars.

———. 2012b. "'Phans,' Not Fans: The Phantom and Australian Comic-Book Fandom." *Participations: Journal of Audience & Reception Studies* 9, no. 2 (November): 133–58.

———. 2015. "The Transplanted Superhero: *The Phantom* Franchise and Australian Popular Culture." In *Superheroes on World Screens*, ed. Rayna Denison and Rachel Mizsei-Ward, 19–35. Jackson: University Press of Mississippi.

Patteson, Richard F. 1978. "King Solomon's Mines: Imperialism and Narrative Structure." *Journal of Narrative Technique* 8, no. 2 (Spring): 112–23.

Pearson, Noel. 2009. "Radical Hope: Education and Equality in Australia." *Quarterly Essay*, no. 35: 1–105.

Pearson, Roberta, William Uricchio, and Will Brooker, eds. 2015. *Many More Lives of The Batman*. London: British Film Institute/Palgrave.

Perry, George, and Alan Aldridge. 1971. *The Penguin Book of Comics*. 2nd ed. [1967]. Middlesex, UK: Penguin Books.

Pers, Anders Yngve. 1966. *The Swedish Press*. Stockholm: Swedish Newspaper Publishers Association/Swedish Institute.

Peterson, Lars. 1976. *Seriernas värld* [*World of Comics*]. Stockholm: Gidlund.

Phantom Official Fan Club—Australia (POFCA). 1991a. "The Phantom Official Fan Club—Australia" (advertisement). *The Phantom*, no. 974 (Australia): 35.

———. 1991b. "Become a Phantom Correspondent." *Phantom Official Fan Club of Australia—Member Newsletter*, no. 1: 4.

Phantom Phorum. 2012. "Phantom Comic Book Survey—Recruiting 'Phans' from India?" Phantom Phorum (defunct link). June 5–13. http://phantom phorum.com/viewtopic.php?f=1&t=4111.

Pilcher, Tim, and Brad Brooks. 2005. *The Essential Guide to World Comics*. London: Collins & Brown.

Pinto, Jerry. 1996. "Phantom of the Soap Opera." *The Times of India*, June 30: A7.

Playthings. 1994. "King Features Sign 'Phantom' Licensees." *Playthings* 92, no. 9 (September): 40.

Porter, Liz. 1981. "TV Takes Over from Comics." *Sunday Telegraph* (Sydney), January 4: 30.

Possamai, Adam. 2003. "The Social Construction of Comic Books as a (Non) Recognised Form of Art in Australia." *Form/Work*, no. 6: 109–21.

Power, Paul, and Tad Pietrzykowski. 1995. "Jim Shepherd" (interview). *David Anthony Kraft's Comics Interview*, no. 146: 18–40.

Prasad, B. K., ed. 2005. "Multilingualism and Indian Media." In *Media and Social Life in India*, ed. B. K. Prasad, 69–75. Lucknow, India: Institute for Sustainable Development/New Delhi: ANMOL Publications.

Pritchett, Frances W. 1997. "The World of *Amar Chitra Katha*." In *Media and the Transformation of Religion in South Asia*, ed. Lawrence A. Babb and Susan S. Wadley, 76–106. Delhi: Motilal Banarsidass.

Pustz, Matthew J. 1999. *Comic Book Culture: Fanboys and True Believers*. Jackson: University Press of Mississippi.

———. 2007. "'Let's Rap with Cap': Fan Interaction in Comic Book Letters Pages." In *Inside the World of Comic Books*, ed. Jeffrey Klaehn, 163–84. Montreal: Black Rose Books.

Raab, Ben, and Paul Ryan. 2001. "The Invisible Phantom" [*Fantomen*, no. 25, 2001]. *The Phantom*, no. 1308 (Australia).

Radway, Janice A. 1991. *Reading the Romance: Women, Patriarchy and Popular Literature*. 2nd ed. [1984]. Chapel Hill: University of North Carolina Press.

Rao, Aruna. 1996. "Nymphs, Nawabs and Nationalism: Myth and History in Indian Comics." *Journal of Asian Pacific Communication* 7, no. 1–2: 31–44.

———. 2001. "From Self-Knowledge to Super Heroes: The Story of Indian Comics." In *Illustrating Asia: Comics, Humor Magazines and Picture Books*, ed. John A. Lent, 37–63. Honolulu: University of Hawaii Press.

Read, William H. 1976. *America's Mass Media Merchants*. Baltimore, MD: Johns Hopkins University Press.

Reading Eagle. 1974. "J.A. Brogan, Retired King Syndicate Aide" (obituary). *Reading Eagle* (Reading, PA), July 10: 44.

Reed, David. 1997. *The Popular Magazine in Britain and the United States, 1880–1960*. Toronto: University of Toronto Press.

Reimerthi, Claes, and Hans Lindahl. 1994a. "Election in Bengali, Part 1: The Challenger" [*Fantomen*, no. 4, 1994]. *The Phantom*, no. 1079 (Australia).

———. 1994b. "Election in Bengali, Part 2: The Loser" [*Fantomen*, no. 5, 1994]. *The Phantom*, no. 1080 (Australia).

Resnais, Alain. 2011. "Do Comics Disturb You?" [1964]. In *Lee Falk, Storyteller*, 72–79. Stockholm: Scandinavian Chapter of the Lee Falk Memorial Bengali Explorers Club/GML Förlag.

Rhoades, Ed. 2011. "Interview with Falk: 1994." (*Friends of The Phantom* [fanzine], 2:3 [1994]). In *Lee Falk, Storyteller*, 259–67. Stockholm: Scandinavian Chapter of the Lee Falk Memorial Bengali Explorers Club/GML Förlag.

Rhoades, Ed, and Chris Smith. 1997. "Collecting The Phantom." *Today's Collector* (April): 111–14.

Robbins, Trina. 1999. *From Girls to Grrrlz: A History of Women's Comics from Teens to Zines*. San Francisco: Chronicle Books.

Robertson, Dale. 1944. *The Son of The Phantom*. Racine, WI: Whitman.

Robinson, Edward J., and David Manning White. 1962. *Comic Strip Reading in the United States*. Report no. 5. Boston, MA: Communications Research Centre, Boston University School of Public Relations and Communications.

Robson, Frank. 1982. "Phantom Phreaks." *Australasian Post*, February 11: n.p.

———. 1985. "Phantom Phreaks." *Australian Penthouse* (February): 78–83.

Roe, Keith, and Ulla Johnsson-Smaragdi. 1987. "The Swedish 'Mediascape' in the 1980s." *European Journal of Communication* 2, no. 3 (September): 357–70.

Rolfe, Patricia. 1979. *The Journalistic Javelin: An Illustrated History of "The Bulletin."* Sydney: Wildcat.

Rosengren, Karl Erik. 1994a. "Sweden and Its Media Scene, 1945–90: A Bird's-Eye View." In *Media Effects and Beyond: Culture, Socialization and Lifestyles*, ed. Karl Erik Rosengren, 25–33. London: Routledge.

———. 1994b. "Media Use under Structural Change." In *Media Effects and Beyond: Culture, Socialization and Lifestyles*, ed. Karl Erik Rosengren, 43–66. London: Routledge.

Royer, George, Beth Nettels, and William Aspray. 2011. "Active Readership: The Case of the American Comics Reader." In *Everyday Information: The Evolution of Information-Seeking in America*, ed. William Aspray and Barbara M. Hayes, 277–303. Cambridge, MA: MIT Press.

Ryan, John. 1979. *Panel by Panel: A History of Australian Comics*. Stanmore, NSW: Cassell Australia.

S. Ramajayam vs. The Management of Varanthara Rani, on 4 February, 2008. Indian Kanoon–Search Engine for Indian Law. https://indiankanoon.org /doc/192235/.

Sabin, Roger. 1993. *Adult Comics: An Introduction*. London: Routledge.

Sahni, J. N. 1974. *Truth about the Indian Press*. Bombay (Mumbai): Allied Publishers.

Salinkumar. 2010. "The History of This Blog, Indrajal Comics and Phantom." The History of Indrajal Comics and Phantom. April 27. http://comicsoftheworld .wordpress.com/2010/04/27/the-histroy-of-this-blogindrajalcomics-and -phantom/.

Sandlund, Elisabeth. 2001. "Beredshap och repression (1936–1945)." In *Den Svenska Pressens Historia*, vol. 3: *Det moderna Sveriges spegel (1897–1945)*, ed. Karl Erik Gustafsson and Per Rydén, 266–381. Stockholm: Ekerlids Förlag.

Sanghvi, Vir. 1999. "Mr Walker's Last Mile." Rediff on the Net. March 29. http://www.rediff.com/news/1999/mar/29vir.htm.

Sanouillet, Michel, and Elmer Peterson, eds. 1989. *The Writings of Marcel Du-champ*, ed. Michel Sanouillet and Elmer Peterson. 2nd ed. [1973]. New York: Da Capo.

Scandinavian Chapter. 2011. *Lee Falk, Storyteller*. Stockholm: Scandinavian Chapter of the Lee Falk Memorial Bengali Explorers Club/GML Förlag.

Scapperotti, Dan. 1995. "The Phantom." *Cinefantastique* 27, no. 10 (June): 8–9, 60.

Schiller, Herbert I. 1976. *Communication and Cultural Domination*. White Plains, NY: M.E. Sharpe.

Schmidt, Lucinda. 2007. "Profile: Fred Gaffney." *Sydney Morning Herald*. April 25. http://www.smh.com.au/news/investment/profile-fred-gaffney/2007/04/23 /1177180564015.html.

Schwed, Mark. 1986. "Defenders of the Earth: A New Era Begins." *The Daily Defender* (King Features Entertainment promotional publication) (June): 6.

Screen Australia. 2012. "Audio Visual Markets—Cinema: Top 50 Films in Australia Each Year since 1992." Screen Australia (January). http://www.screen australia.gov.au/fact-finders/cinema/industry-trends/films-screened/top-50 -each-year.

Seldes, Gilbert. 1957. *The Seven Lively Arts*. 2nd ed. [1927]. New York: Sagamore.

Server, Lee. 1993. *Danger Is My Business: An Illustrated History of the Fabulous Pulp Magazines, 1896–1953*. San Francisco: Chronicle Books.

Shaikh, Farukh. ca. 2000. "The Phantom Morristown Post." (Letter to the editor.) *The Phantom*, no. 11 (India): 31.

Sharma, Alok (director). 2011. "Chitrakatha 10 Minutes Cut." (*Chitrakatha: Indian Comics Beyond Balloons and Panels*, documentary). YouTube (September 21). http://www.youtube.com/watch?v=U1UgYDkTVpE.

Sharma, Murli. 1997. "Is It a Phantom of Just a Phantom?" *Indian Express* (defunct link). June 16. http://expressindia.indianexpress.com/news/ie/daily/19970616 /16750663.html.

Shedden, Bryan. 1996. "Phantom Forum." (Letter to the editor.) *The Phantom*, no. 1147 (Australia): 96.

———. 2001. "Frew's Unnumbered and 'A' Series Phantom Comics." The Deep Woods. July 23. http://www.deepwoods.org/aseries.html.

———. ca. 2002. "Gold Key/King/Charlton—The Phantom Comics." The Deep Woods. http://www.deepwoods.org/usa/distribution.gif.

———. 2003. "Egmont Imagination India Ltd. Comic Series (2000–2002)." The Deep Woods. September 21. http://www.deepwoods.org/indian_express .html.

———. 2004. "Rani Comics (1990–Present)." The Deep Woods. April 4. http://www.deepwoods.org/rani.html.

———. 2007a. "Phantom Fan Clubs & Fanzines—Australia." The Deep Woods. January 28. http://www.deepwoods.org/fanclubs_australia.html.

———. 2007b. "Moonstone Books (2002–Present)." The Deep Woods. March 19. http://www.deepwoods.org/moonstone.html.

———. 2007c. "What's New in the Deep Woods." The Deep Woods. October 1. http://www.deepwoods.org/additions.html.

Shepherd, Jim. 1989. "Phantom Forum." The Phantom, no. 925 (Australia): 3.

———. 1996. "Phantom Forum." The Phantom, no. 1147 (Australia): 96.

———. 1998. "50 Years of Frew and the Phantom." The Phantom, no. 1209 (Australia): 3–18.

———. 2006. "Phantom Forum." The Phantom, no. 1445 (Australia): 93.

Shepherd, Jim, and Keith Chatto. 1990a. "Rumble in the Jungle." The Phantom, no. 951A (Australia).

———. 1990b. "Return of the Singh Brotherhood." The Phantom, no. 962 (Australia).

———. 1992. "The Kings Cross Connection." The Phantom, no. 1000 (Australia): 275–302.

Singh, Chander Uday. 1982. "Fortune from Fantasy." India Today (September 30): 84–85.

Singhal, Arvind, J. K. Doshi, Everett M. Rogers, and S. Adnan Rahman. 1988. "The Diffusion of Television in India." Media Asia 15, no. 4: 222–29.

Slezak, Mary. 1980. "The History of Charlton Press, Inc. and Its Song Lyric Periodicals." Journal of American Culture 3, no. 1 (Spring): 184–94.

Snowden, John. 1973. "Frew Publications Checklist: Part One." Cooee (fanzine), no. 7: 2–19.

Sol, Mikael. 2008. Till alla jag legat med [To Everyone I Slept With]. Stockholm: Kartago Förlag.

Spear, Percival. 1970. A History of India, vol. 2. Middlesex, UK: Penguin Books.

Spears, Jack. 1956. "Comic Strips on the Screen." Films in Review 7, no. 7 (September): 317–25, 333.

Spiegel, Lynn, and Henry Jenkins. 1991. "Same Bat Channel, Different Bat Times: Mass Culture and Popular Memory." In The Many Lives of the Batman: Critical Approaches to a Superhero and His Media, ed. Roberta E. Pearson and William Uricchio, 117–48. London: BFI Publishing/New York: Routledge.

Spiegelman, Marvin, Carl Terwilliger, and Franklin Fearing. 1952. "The Content of Comic Strips: A Study of a Mass Medium of Communication." Journal of Social Psychology 35, no. 1 (February): 37–57.

Stedman, Raymond W. 1977. The Serials: Suspense and Drama by Installment. 2nd ed. [1971]. Norman: University of Oklahoma Press.

Steen, Kjell. 2011. "The Phantom in Norway during the Occupation, 1940–45." In *Lee Falk, Storyteller*, 336–37. Stockholm: Scandinavian Chapter of the Lee Falk Memorial Bengali Explorers Club/GML Förlag.

Stewart, Bhob. 2010. "Puck the Comic Weekly." Potrzebie. September 11. http:// potrzebie.blogspot.com.au/2010/09/1881-emoticons.html.

Strell, Jeff. 1981. "Me and My Phantom." *Comics Scene* 1, no. 1 (January): 58–61.

Strömberg, Fredrik. 2003. *Black Images in the Comics: A Visual History*. Seattle, WA: Fantagraphics Books.

———. 2010. *Swedish Comics History*. Marietta, GA: Top Shelf Productions.

Stroud, Bryan D. 2015. "Classic Interview: Sy Barry." Comics Bulletin. September 4. http://comicsbulletin.com/classic-interview-sy-barry-changes-are-what -keep-art-and-comics-going/.

Stubbersfield, Barry. 1986. "Publishing History of 'The Phantom' in Australia: Part 1." *Jungle Beat: The Official Newsletter of The Phantom Club*, vol. 11 (December): 14–16.

———. 1987a. "History of 'The Phantom' in Australia: Part 2." *Jungle Beat: The Official Newsletter of The Phantom Club*, vol. 12 (March): 5–7.

———. 1987b. "History of 'The Phantom': Part 3." *Jungle Beat: The Official Newsletter of The Phantom Club*, vol. 13 (June): 9–11.

———. ca. 1989. "Censorship and 'The Phantom.'" *Jungle Beat: The Official Newsletter of The Phantom Club*, vol. 21: 4–7.

———. n.d. [a]. "Censorship and 'The Phantom.'" *Jungle Beat: The Official Newsletter of The Independent Phantom Club of Australia* 22: 4–6.

———. n.d. [b]. "Censorship and 'The Phantom.'" *Jungle Beat: The Official Newsletter of The Independent Phantom Club of Australia*, vol. 23: 4–6.

Subber, Richard C., and John C. Schweitzer. 1980. "What to Drop and What to Keep: A Do-It-Yourself Approach." *Newspaper Research Journal* 1, no. 4 (Summer): 38–45.

Sundaram, Ravi. 2010. *Pirate Modernity: Delhi's Media Urbanism*. Oxon, UK: Routledge.

Swärd, Monica. 2011. "Father Visiting His Son" [1986]. In *Lee Falk, Storyteller*, 206–11. Stockholm: Scandinavian Chapter of the Lee Falk Memorial Bengali Explorers Club/GML Förlag.

Symons, Sandra. 1973. "Phanta the Living Ghost." *Sunday Telegraph* (Sydney), February 11: 90.

Tankel, Jonathan David, and Keith Murphy. 1998. "Collecting Comic Books: A Study of the Fan and Curatorial Consumption." In *Theorizing Fandom: Fans, Subculture and Identity*, ed. Cheryl Harris and Alison Alexander, 55–68. Cresskill, NJ: Hampton.

Taussig, H. J. 1947. "Review of Indian Press." *Newspaper News* (Australia) 20, no. 4 (December 10): 31.

Tebbel, John, and Mary Ellen Zuckerman. 1991. *The Magazine in America, 1741–1990*. New York: Oxford University Press.

Thakkar, Dipali B. 2000. "The Phantom Mailbag." (Letter to the editor.) *The Phantom*, no. 4 (India): 31.

The Times of India. 1955. "Undue Interference in Arts Opposed." *The Times of India*, February 28: 7.

———. 1956. "Prohibiting Production of 'Horror Comics' in India." *The Times of India*, November 23: 9.

———. 1964a. "Indrajal Comics" (advertisement). *The Times of India*, March 30: 13–14.

———. 1964b. "Indrajal Comics—Ninth Issue" (advertisement). The *Times of India*, October 31: 6.

———. 2008. "The Ghost Still Walks." *The Times of India*. June 1. http://timeso findia.indiatimes.com/home/sunday-times/The-Ghost-Still-Walks/articleshow /3089506.cms.

Tollin, Anthony. 1988. "A Visit with Lee Falk." *Comics Revue* 1, no. 27: 2, 44, 48, 65.

Tomasson, Richard F. 1970. *Sweden: Prototype of Modern Society*. New York: Random House.

Tornoe, Rob. 2011. "Funnies Business." *Editor & Publisher* 144, no. 7 (July): 36–37, 40–42, 62.

Tucker, Michael C. 2004. "The Dragon Lady's Well Favored Children: The Transition from Corporatist to Individualist in Comic Strips of the 1930s." *Belphégor* 4, no. 1 (November). http://dalspace.library.dal.ca/handle/10222/47701.

Tulloch, John. 1995. "'We're Only a Speck in the Ocean': The Fans as Powerless Elites." In *Science Fiction Audiences: Watching Doctor Who and Star Trek*, ed. John Tulloch and Henry Jenkins, 144–72. London: Routledge.

Turner, Kathleen J. 1977. "Comic Strips: A Rhetorical Perspective." *Central States Speech Journal* 28, no. 1 (Spring): 24–35.

Twomey, John E. 1955. "The Citizens' Committee and Comic-Book Control: A Study of Extragovernmental Restraint." *Law and Contemporary Problems* 20, no. 4 (Autumn): 621–29.

Van Gelder, Lawrence. 1975. "'Terry' of the Comics Is Facing Taps at 38." [*New York Times*, February 15, 1973]. In *Popular Culture*, ed. David Manning White, 402–3. The Great Contemporary Issues, vol. 9. New York: New York Times/ Hudson Group.

Vecko-Revyn. 2012. *Vecko-Revyn Media Kit.* Stockholm: Bonnier Tidskrifter (defunct link). September 20. http://www.bonniermagazines.se/ftpFiles/Mediekit /VEC_2012_eng.pdf.

———. 2015. *Vecko-Revyn Media Kit.* Stockholm: Bonnier Tidskrifter. April 4. http://www.bonniertidskrifter.se/BT/mediekit/VeckoRevyn_ENG.pdf.

Vigus, Robert. 1942. "The Art of the Comic Magazine." *Elementary English Review,* no. 19 (May): 168–70.

Vineyard, David L. 2009. "Frank L. Packard's Jimmie Dale—An Overview." Mystery File. December 14. http://mysteryfile.com/blog/?p=1715.

Vollmer, Michael. 2002. "Torture, Death and Disrobing: 'Snuff' Comics in the Golden Age, 1945–1955." *The Rocket's Blast and the Comic Collector,* no. 3 (Summer): 70–85.

Wagner, Geoffrey. 1955. *Parade of Pleasure: A Study of Popular Iconography in the USA.* New York: Library Publishers.

Walker, Max. 1986. "The Ghost Who Walks." *Australasian Post,* April 3: 20.

Walsh, Anthony. 1984. "The Ghost Who Walks . . . in Australia." *People* (Australia), October 29: 4–5.

Wangka Maya Pilbara Aboriginal Language Centre. 2007. *Wangka Maya Catalogue.* South Hedland, WA: Wangka Maya Pilbara Aboriginal Language Centre.

Warner Bros. 2013. "Warner Bros. Consumer Products Launches Out of This World Licensing Program for Man of Steel" (media release). Warner Bros. June 11. https://www.warnerbros.com/studio/news/warner-bros-consumer -products-launches-out-world-licensing-program-%E2%80%9Cman-steel %E2%80%9D.

Watson, Elmo Scott. 1936. *A History of Newspaper Syndicates in the United States, 1865–1935.* Chicago: Elmo Scott Watson.

Waugh, Coulton. 1974. *The Comics.* 2nd ed. [1947]. New York: Luna.

Weatherperson, M. J. "Blowmeup" [Dean Latimer]. 1972. 'The Monster Times People's Justice Dept. Presents the Case against The Phantom." *The Monster Times* 1, no. 14 (July 31): 6–7, 9.

Wertham, Fredric. 1954. *Seduction of the Innocent.* New York: Rinehart.

The West Australian. 1952. "Sixty Comics a Week: A Shock in Perth." *The West Australian,* August 30: 6.

White, Ted. 1997. "The Spawn of M.C. Gaines." In *All in Color for a Dime,* ed. Dick Lupoff and Don Thompson, 19–39. 2nd ed. [1970]. Iola, WI: Krause.

Wilhelmsson, Bertil (artist). 1963. "Skatten i Dödskallegrottan" ["The Treasure in the Skull Cave"]. *Fantomen,* no. 8 (July) (Sweden): 3–26.

Wilson, Gavin. 2004. *Harbourlights: The Art and Times of Peter Kingston.* Fisherman's Bend, VIC: Craftsman House/Thames and Hudson.

Witty, Paul. 1941. "Children's Interest in Reading the Comics." *Journal of Experimental Education* 10, no. 2 (December): 100–104.

Witty, Paul, and Dorothy Moore. 1945. "Interest in Reading the Comics amongst Negro Children." *Journal of Educational Psychology* 26, no. 5 (May): 303–8.

Witty, Paul A., and Robert A. Sizemore. 1954. "Reading the Comics: A Summary of Studies and an Evaluation I." *Elementary English* 31, no. 8 (December): 501–6.

———. 1955a. "Reading the Comics: A Summary of Studies and an Evaluation II." *Elementary English* 32, no. 1 (January): 43–49.

———. 1955b. "Reading the Comics: A Summary of Studies and an Evaluation III." *Elementary English* 32, no. 2 (February): 109–14.

Wolf, Katherine M., and Marjorie Fiske. 1949. "The Children Talk about Comics." In *Communications Research, 1948–1949*, ed. Paul F. Lazarsfeld and Frank N. Stanton, 3–21. New York: Harper & Brothers.

Wolseley, Roland E. 1969. *Understanding Magazines.* 2nd ed. [1965]. Ames: Iowa State University Press.

Woman. 1954. "Comics Are No Longer Comic." *Woman* (Australia), December 20: 12.

Wood, Stuart. 1987. "Letter to the editor." *Jungle Beat: The Official Newsletter of the Phantom Club*, vol. 7 (March): 15.

Worker, Norman, and Georges Bess. 1994. "Julie" [*Fantomen*, no. 25, 1985]. *The Phantom*, no. 1068 (Australia).

Worker, Norman, and Kari Leppänen. 2015a. "Duel in Venice, Part 1." *The Phantom*, no. 1741 (Australia).

———. 2015b. "Duel in Venice, Part 2," *The Phantom*, no. 1742 (Australia).

Wright, Bradford W. 2001. *Comic-Book Nation: The Transformation of Youth Culture in America.* Baltimore, MD: Johns Hopkins University Press.

Yale Law Journal. 1952. "Local Monopoly in the Daily Newspaper Industry." *Yale Law Journal* 61, no. 6 (June-July): 948–1009.

Young, William H., Jr. 1969. "The Serious Funnies: Adventure Comics during the Depression, 1929–1938." *Journal of Popular Culture* 3, no. 3 (Winter): 404–27.

Zagala, Anna. 2008. *Redback Graphix.* Canberra: Publications Section, National Gallery of Australia.

INDEX